Date Due	Date Due	Date Due

RECONSIDERATIONS IN SOUTHERN AFRICAN HISTORY

Richard Elphick and Jeffrey Butler, Editors

ART+REVOLUTION

The Life and Death of Thami Mnyele SOUTH AFRICAN ARTIST

Diana Wylie

University of Virginia Press

Charlottesville

For the next generation, Nomathamsanqa Mnyele-Kaunda
and the memory of Sindelo Tebogo Mnyele

First published in 2008 in southern Africa by Jacana Media (Pty) Ltd
10 Orange Street Sunnyside
Auckland Park 2092 South Africa
www.jacana.co.za

and in North America by the University of Virginia Press
P.O. Box 400318
Charlottesville, VA 22904-4318
www.upress.virginia.edu

ISBN 978-0-8139-2764-0

Library of Congress Cataloging-in-Publication Data

Wylie, Diana, 1948–
Art and revolution : the life and death of Thami Mnyele, South African artist / Diana Wylie.
    p.   cm. — (Reconsiderations in southern African history)
    Includes bibliographical references.
    ISBN 978-0-8139-2764-0 (cloth : alk. paper)
    1. Mnyele, Thami, 1948–1985. 2. Artists—South Africa—Biography. 3. Artists, Black—South Africa—Biography. 4. Art—Political aspects—South Africa. 5. Government, Resistance to—South Africa. I. Title.
N7396.M57W95 2008
709.2—dc22
[B]
                                                      2007050137

Design and layout by Jenny Young
Printed in Malaysia.

Contents

Sketching in the bush.
(Courtesy of Sarah
Mamanyena Mnyele)

Preface

It began for me in an art museum in Africa. I was in Gaborone, Botswana, at lunchtime on a summer day in 1980 and the archives where I was researching my first book had just closed. With time on my hands, I wandered into the Botswana National Museum and Art Gallery. A one-man show was hanging on its walls. As I walked through the gallery, I saw images that brought me close to tears. The pictures showed me, better than words, how it felt to have a lid pressing down on your hopes and dreams. The drawings didn't shout. They weren't adorned with sentiment. They made statements that obviously came from deep inside the artist. 'Ah, yes,' I said to myself, 'now I see.'

Weeks later I met the artist, Thami Mnyele, whose story I tell in this book, and we became friends for a while. Five years later, when he died, I wrote down everything I could remember him having said. It seemed the only way to hold on to a remarkably sensitive man who had the talent to change the way people look at things. I was struck by the disparity between our fates. Born the same year as I, he died just weeks before I began my first long-term academic job, teaching African history at Yale University. I couldn't help comparing my trajectory with his: it was upsetting and humbling to come face to face with my relative privilege.

Hard times twisted, distorted, and broke up the story of Thami's life. Documents were lost and destroyed. Much valuable information was never recorded in the first place, and memories are fading. The times did not always permit the sharing of confidences. Fearing that silence could lead to popular ignorance and finally to indifference and alienation, I have written this book.

That this account is fragmented is part of the story. Until I realised this truth, my difficulties in research made me anxious that I wouldn't be able to draw accurately even the major outlines of the man's life. Then I began to understand that the silences and the distortions in fact revealed the extreme insecurity that led Thami to make his political choices.

I never interviewed Thami. We simply talked: I never posed questions for purposes of constructing his life story. A private and reticent person, he did not mean to be the subject of a book. He might well have agreed with critic Janet Malcolm that biography is inescapably trivial because it cannot capture the kernel of a man; it cannot record a person's complexity as well as fiction can.

I have nevertheless soldiered on, partly because Thami's life strikes me as emblematic of his times. His story shows how varied are the causes and consequences of political commitment. We delude ourselves if we imagine we can understand the engine of social movements without investigating the private lives that drive them. Personal goals cannot but be bound up with political ones. Stories that stress one realm to the exclusion of the other fail to capture how decisions are really made and play out.

Paradoxes necessarily emerge when the personal is given its due. We might recognise when apparently political acts had personal roots and when a decent man belied his ideals. An honest and full-bodied biography makes it harder to subscribe to a simple definition of the hero. When a hero is a martyr, mythology is likely to flourish.

Few conventional sources like letters and diaries were available to help me tell the story of Thami Mnyele. The national archives contain only two references to the Mnyeles: the documents pertaining to his parents' divorce in 1950, and an embargoed dossier on his half-brother, David, who was arrested in 1976. The schools Thami attended in Makapanstad and Natal kept no records of his work. In fact, his secondary school moved out of the buildings where he studied; they are now occupied by an entirely different institution. I was reduced to photographing a plaque on the wall and researching the school's history in the state archives. I found the texts Thami was likely to have studied at school by visiting a nearly derelict building owned by the Department of Education in Pretoria; unused and unvisited, the building houses a library of dust-covered books revealing how the world was authoritatively presented to a child in the 1950s. I drove to Rorke's Drift, his art school in rural Natal, only to find the place stripped clean of records.

The written record proved thin right through to the end of Thami's life. In 2003 I applied to the Department of Defence, Centre for Military Intelligence, for permission to read the files produced by military officials planning, executing, and reflecting on the raid that killed him. Nearly two years later, after my request had risen through the queue of documents whose declassification was requested, I paid to receive 889 pages of 'masked' documents. (The names of all participants were concealed.) Very little in those pages bears on the raid itself. The police archive is equally unrevealing. Thami's former comrade, Tim Williams, now deputy national commissioner of police, found that all relevant police files had been destroyed before he began working there in 1994. Former comrades launched a similar effort to find art appropriated by the security police, but came up with nothing.

Partly because the paper trail of Thami's life is so thin, published records relating to him exhibit an astonishing array of errors: one biographical dictionary states, for example, that he 'refused to exhibit in any commercial gallery or to work for advertising agencies' and 'helped establish *Staffrider* magazine'. These statements, and many others, are contradicted by evidence that is both documentary (magazine articles and newspaper photographs) and oral (fellow artists).

Stories about the Gaborone Raid of 1985 are especially full of contradictions and lacunae. Former Rhodesian Peter Stiff wrote a chapter on the raid in his book *The Silent War* that is a flagrant example of efforts to make white soldiers seem in full command. Because the book was published in 1999 when diverse data were easily available, its errors are remarkably revealing of its author's carelessness and callousness. Stiff insists, for example, that the two Botswana domestic servants killed in the raid were ANC agents, a claim contradicted by every single other source. (Some say he also displays Rhodesian chauvinism vis-à-vis the South African Defence Force.) Similarly, evidence given to the Truth and Reconciliation Commission in 2000, necessarily weakened by the passage of 15 years, is filled with what appear to be perpetrators' lies: the raiders made no apparent effort to avoid killing children, as they swore they did, and even their precise targets didn't seem to matter very much.

The cause of these errors lies not only in the sheer flux and destruction rampant in South African life during a time of upheaval. People write myths also because their critical faculties seem to melt away in the face of suffering and the romance of struggle. This apparent fact of human nature struck me forcibly as I sat in the state film archives in Pretoria watching videos presented by the Dutch Anti-Apartheid Movement. In a catalogue dedicated to Thami's memory I found reference to film clips in which he would be glimpsed talking about art in 1982. Eagerly locating the indexed clips, I found myself listening to a young African artist who was not Thami Mnyele. People, I thought, seem to have such an urgent need for heroes that they find them when they are quite literally not there.

Interviews proved more reliable, especially when set side by side so that patterns could be discerned. Between 1989 and 2007 I conducted more than 70 interviews with Thami's family, friends, and associates. One person led to another and, in the process, I gained lifelong friends. Some of the interviews were the outcome of extended conversations, while others were more formal responses to particular questions that were plaguing me. I was unable to answer, for example: When exactly did Thami stop drinking?

When was he picked up and interrogated by the police? Why did his style change in 1974? What were his feelings about underground missions such as the destruction of the Rev. Sam Buti's library? I could never find his lovely diptych of a headless, crucified figure holding a flower in its drooping hand.

Especially since his 2004 exhumation and reburial, oral testimony about Thami's life has increasingly tended towards the heroic. The same inner logic that drives a mother to praise her dead son to the skies leads a movement to adopt and elaborate the stories. These quite understandable urges can wreak havoc on simple veracity. So did the conditions of Thami's adult life. He himself told tales about his past to protect his family and himself, saying, for example, that his father's family came from Lusikisiki in the Transkei (it did not). When he was in the underground he and his comrades deliberately limited their understanding of what each of them was doing. Thami's comrade and fellow artist Dikobe Martins calls this discretion their 'need-to-know' principle: they wanted to know only what was minimally necessary to carry on their underground work. Thami's ten siblings were particularly hard hit by the traumas of township life: only one of the surviving three has a memory on which I was able to rely.

The pictures drawn by Thami helped me tell his story. In conjunction with interviews, they opened the door on a man who was a player in key movements that were not trying simply to change, but actually to transform South African society.

Thami's work, however, is hard to find and it is not always well cared for. The staff at the National Museum and Art Gallery in Gaborone ripped the left side of 'Things fall apart' when removing it from its frame – a sign, perhaps, that the work doesn't have much popular resonance in a country where refugees were often seen as a problem. Insect holes and fungus afflict two other Mnyele drawings stored there. Johannesburg's Standard Bank employees recently discovered and put in storage the 1976 version of 'Things fall apart', after years of not knowing the bank owned the drawing. The security police confiscated some of his work over the years, but they destroyed large sections of their archives. Short of cash, Thami's mother sold to an art dealer the drawing entitled 'There goes a man sad and deep in sorrow, like a river underground'; the only art remaining in her home is a faded reproduction of a seascape.

Thami's art can best be seen in the homes of his friends. Sometimes he gave them work to bring back to South Africa for safekeeping. At other times he sold drawings for low prices as a sign of friendship. The pictures are lovingly, though not publicly, preserved behind glass. They are dispersed around the globe, and can be found as far afield as Birmingham (England), Barcelona, Boston, London, Newry (Northern Ireland), and Stockholm.

How often did I use my imagination to reconstruct the past? I tried to limit severely any flights of fancy. A careful reader will note when I have inserted hedging words like 'probably' to suggest a lack of hard data. (One example of this technique is in chapter 6 when I write that Mnyele was 'probably' of two minds about the fire-bombing of Sam Buti's library.)

I did not use my imagination, but my professional training as a historian, to write the Afterword. I wanted to end the book with a statement of what the story of Thami's life and death might mean, seen from a broad historical and artistic perspective and a vantage point two decades after his death. That summing-up chapter reflects a deep appreciation of Thami's efforts to live honorably in punishing times. Writing it, I gained new appreciation of the dilemmas facing revolutionaries who must make leaps of faith that their actions will bring about a better world. At the same time, I understood better than ever before that, if they are to land anywhere near their goal, those leaps must be tempered with a dispassionate understanding of the strange and terrible workings of history.

Diana Wylie
Johannesburg
January 2007

Thami in Serowe, Botswana,
in February 1981. (Photo by author)

Prologue

In the early hours of 14 June 1985 a man heard footsteps outside his house near the Botswana capital, Gaborone. He flicked on the outside light, so the story goes, and opened his front door. He came face to face with four men who had come to kill him. The shock of the encounter immobilised them all for seconds. Then the marked man slammed the door and ran.

This book tells the story of the victim's life leading up to that moment of recognition when four hunters faced their human prey and Thami Mnyele, South African artist, understood that he would die. Over the course of his 36 years Thami had evolved into a combatant in a field of war, as well as in a war of values. At a time of high risk he faced the most basic questions: what it means to be a citizen, and what it means to be a man.

That Thami died violently in his prime has come to define his life. When people refer to him today, they never fail to state this one big fact. The last curse of martyrdom may be that it reduces a person's life to a footnote to his death.

Expansively told, Thami's story reveals what it means for a sensitive man and talented artist to be enmeshed in a system hell-bent on engineering a closed society, locking out both him and his people. It tells how he became engulfed in the firestorm of that system's last days, opening the door on a new country as well as on his own death. It shows how a revolutionary evolved out of surprising material, a person who liked to draw.

Thami as a student at Nchaupe Secondary School, Makapanstad, in the 1960s. (Courtesy of Lindi Mnyele-Binca)

Chapter 1

Bruising

Thamsanqa Harry Mnyele, known to his friends as Thami and to his family as 'Harry Boy', was born into a square mile of Johannesburg whose tumultuous energy and indiscriminate violence 'bruised his creativity'.[1] At close quarters and on a daily basis he saw the best and the worst of what people can do to one another. Inside Alexandra Township, a black island within the white northern suburbs, gangs 'made meat' of people who crossed their territory at night.[2] Weekend-long parties spewed drunks and intoxicating music onto the unpaved and unlit streets. And yet, despite its literally cut-throat air and the havoc it wrought on intimate relationships – those between husband and wife or between mother and son – Thami grew to love 'Alex' as if it were a woman. Wanton and dangerous, she wounded him so acutely that he developed a sense of doom at an early age. She also inspired him to feel tenderness for what was, in many people's mouths, merely a slogan, 'the people'.

As a child growing up on Sixth Avenue, Thami liked to make little wire models of cars, buses, and trains, a common occupation in that toyless environment. He also drew. One of his early efforts, his mother remembers, depicted a bicycle carrying a coffin with a widow walking behind. This image came from a temperament unusually sensitive to beauty and to hurt. Thami preferred to use his hands rather than words to express what he learned from the streets of Alex. His mother called him 'lazy to talk', and his silences, as well as his gentleness, would baffle the rowdier boys who were busy imitating adult gangs. Perhaps what saved Thami from being overwhelmed by his own sensitivity was his readiness to be bemused by antics. Standing outside a group of boys grimly focused on fixing a broken bicycle, his chin would lift; the corners of his mouth would twitch; his eyes would brighten. And, years later, the boys' adult determination would find its way into a picture reflecting on the phenomenon of ambition with dry and gentle wit.

Alexandra was squalid because people poured into it from the countryside, while its resources failed to grow to meet their needs. When Thami was a child, nearly 100 000 people lived in a space that should have tolerated only 30 000, a fact which led politicians to threaten to 'freeze' or thin out the population. The government gave Alex no money, so its struggling inhabitants had to pay for services like nightsoil collection – that is, the emptying of latrine buckets – through taxes on their meagre wages. The Johannesburg City Council had no incentive to develop the embattled township, partly because its far more affluent white neighbours frequently launched campaigns to have it razed. Legal technicalities – the land was, after all, privately owned – thwarted these efforts, but the fact remained that Alex's survival was uncertain. And so, Thami and his peers grew up playing on dirt roads and breathing air scented with coal fires and raw sewage, even though electric power lines and water mains lay nearby and they could hear the whoosh of traffic on the tarred Pretoria Main Road.

They knew Alex as 'Dark City', not simply because it was lit by candles and kerosene lanterns and shrouded by smoke from coal fires. Alex was also a 'university of crime' where they were taught to fear the players: the Spoiler gang, which dominated the higher ground; the relatively minor and more free-ranging Stonebreakers; and the Msomis, who controlled the lower slope, near the Jukskei River. Peering into that river and the gulleys they called 'dongas', the children might see a dead dog, the rim of a bicycle wheel, broken chamber pots, and corroded frying pans. Since criminals sometimes dumped their victims there, they might even see a person who had been stabbed to death, perhaps with the sharpened spoke from a bicycle wheel. Friday nights were especially dangerous. A gangster with a name like Boston Tar Baby was likely to emerge from the darkness, flick his knife, and lift a week's pay straight from a man's pocket. Even the rats were aggressive.

Children wore cast-off clothes, rode tyreless bicycles, and played with pieces of broken-down machines outside 'railway car' housing where whole families lived in a single room. Space – even on a fence serving as a laundry line – was in such short supply that tempers could flare readily and dangerously, especially when fuelled by home-brewed beer. Some men hunkered down to play dice on the street all day long. New arrivals from the countryside were frequently so terrified by the intensity and danger in Alex's streets that they dared not venture outside their homes.

To describe the Alexandra of the 1940s as merely 'squalid', though, is to slight its vitality. The township buzzed. There was talk of an African 'Selfridges' department store to be built nearby, with models chosen from among the African staff to put on fashion shows. People pressed against one another in the streets and in houses. They used ingenuity to survive. As one long-time resident observed, 'if you were born in Alex into a yard holding 20 families who had one tap and one toilet, politics was part of your life; you were a politician'.[3] People knew the utility of sharing food with neighbours, even when they were too strapped to ride the bus to work. They learned to use humour and bravado to carve a space for themselves in a lifetime of queues. Their street language 'parried and lunged' as if they were prize-fighters: 'Hai, man, bigshot, you must be the reely-reely outlaw in this town' would be a mild English translation from that staccato amalgam of local tongues called *tsotsi taal* (hoodlum speech).[4] Partly due to the uncertain future of the place, and maybe also to the bitter brown beer that dominated social life, people lived in the moment, and that was exhilarating. They knew they were present at the birth of something new, where old constraints no longer worked.

This spirit of adventure took enduring form in the work of musicians like Zakes Nkosi and Ntemi Piliso, both local saxophonists and composers. They were the best-loved people in Alex, rivalling only herbalists and some shopkeepers for popular affection. Sometimes this love had a coercive edge. Thami remembered, 'When I grew up I had heard stories that musicians were made to play one favourite song right throughout the night to the next morning, at knife point.'[5] More commonly, though, the musicians expressed and received the joy and love of their community. They played at weddings and they played at funerals. They could even walk the streets at night and live to pound the wild, jiving beats of marabi music again the next day.

Thami came into the world at Number 9 Sixth Avenue, a three-room home behind the six-room main house which had been owned by his late grandfather, Peter Jobere Thamane, and where his grandmother, Pauline Makgobe, still lived with his aunt and uncles. The Thamane house had a picture window in front, looking onto the verandah, and it was set back from the street. This house was the visible remnant of an idea of urban living to which no one could aspire in the overcrowded and insecure Alex of the 1940s. Developers had built the brick bungalows between 1905 and 1912 for single families, whose members could range through the six rooms, sit on the verandah, enjoy the shade of the willow tree in the front yard, and appreciate the touch of gentility the pedimented pillars gave to what had been intended as a respectable white workingman's neighbourhood. Even though other families lived behind the main house, making the yard crowded, Thami's family was privileged to share three rooms and to be closely related to the people in the big house. Thami knew he excited envy among poorer children when he emerged from that house eating a delicacy they could not afford, like bread with butter and jam. They were urchins; he was not.

Thami's grandfather, Peter Thamane, had made a living as his own boss because he owned a trolley cart and two mules. They allowed him to earn money by carrying old ladies to town, where they picked up the dirty clothes of white families living in flats. Back in Alex they laundered the clothes in the less-than-pure waters of the Jukskei River, before Mr Thamane carted them back to town with their fresh bundles.

Peter Thamane's daughter, Sarah Mamanyena, was so beautiful she could have had any man, or so her son would later say. She was a real township girl: spirited, even sassy; easy. Given to flippant replies to questions, she dared anyone to catch her in a lie or to force her to abide by convention. Inevitably some of her arch remarks had a racial bite, as when she joked that she was more beautiful than her coloured brother. (She did not have one.) Sarah's second name matched her decorative manner; Mamanyena means 'earrings' in her mother's home language of Setswana. Born to respectability, she didn't joke about privilege: she was proud of coming from a good family which, though not rich, at least allowed her mother to possess everything she needed in her house on her 'own property' – that treasured mark of status – specifically, lot number 458 on Sixth Avenue. Her father paid for her to attend a Roman Catholic school on First Avenue but after he died in 1936, she said, she had to stop her schooling at Standard VI; there was no more money to pay the fees.

By that time she was 16 and her beauty had already begun to promise greater excitement than the classroom could ever afford. Sarah danced so well she won a ballroom dancing certificate, which she proudly framed, and, she said with even greater pride, she once sang for the renowned Darktown Strutters at the Bantu Men's Social Centre at the south end of Eloff St.

Thami's parents, Sarah Mamanyena Thamane and David Freddy Harry Mnyele, must have turned heads when they started seeing each other in the 1940s. Their beauty matched, as if each displayed the finest male or female flowering of that particular look: fine-boned, lean, with high cheekbones. David's large eyes were widely spaced and Thami would inherit them. Sarah and David were both flirtatious, as if they were fully aware of their good looks and the impact they made. They both enjoyed dressing fashionably, as when he wore a white suit and she a pencil-slim skirt. Through the 1940s David paid for these clothes with the salary he earned as a clerk translating between English, Xhosa, Afrikaans, and Sesotho, and also doing the paperwork for miners at New Union Goldfields. Sarah took the only job open to black women without specialised nurse's or teacher training: she worked as a maid in white homes.

Thami was born on 10 December 1948, almost nine months to the day after his parents were legally married in community of property by a Johannesburg magistrate. He was the only child born to Sarah and David during their marriage, though his mother bore other children. Thami would later say that his father loved his mother so passionately that he fell in love with her even though she was carrying another man's child. Sarah had given birth to a son she named Desmond in 1944 when David was courting her. Sarah and David's daughter, Julie Mandu, was born in 1946, before their marriage. In 1950, while still married to David, she bore Steve, though David never recognised him as his son, and her last son, Happy, was born in 1955. She says she gave birth to other babies who did not survive. Each had a different father. Thami later complained that he grew up arguing with his brothers about whose father was best. He envied people who had grown up in a 'normal' home.

Thami shared a house with his father for only two years. By November 1950 David had gone, driven out, he would say, by his wife's affairs. Sarah would accuse him of having left her for another woman. Each may have been unfaithful, though the birth of Steve in 1950 made infidelity easier to prove in Sarah's case. Sarah would also blame the divorce and late or absent child-support payments on David's decision to prepare for the ministry. As a 37-year-old studying in 1953, then serving as a minister, he simply didn't earn enough to pay R6 each week to maintain Julie and Thami, as ordered by the magistrate at the time of his divorce. David had earned R14 a week as a clerk at Gummed Tapes in Ophirton, amid the city's oldest mines, but he brought home only R24 to R30 a quarter – that is, about two rands a week – after he became a minister. With that money, after marrying his second wife, Dorothy Moloi, in 1954, David would have to support six more children.[6] The success of his second marriage contrasted starkly with Sarah's enduring bitterness.

As an adult, Thami would criticise the church, in general, and his father in particular, for accommodating white supremacy. Perhaps he never learned the history of his father's family, because he didn't spend enough time around his father to hear it.

The story David could have told – of embattled family privilege, sinking fortunes, and church radicalism – starts in the middle of the 19th century with ambition and hope. David's grandfather, Mnyele, had married a girl from the Dlamini family, landowners in a town called Herschel, just south of Lesotho in the foothills of the Drakensberg mountains. He moved in with them. The family name and the date suggest that Mnyele had the good fortune to marry into a group of modernising Christian converts called Fingos at the time of their greatest prosperity.[7] Enterprising market farmers, they owned ploughs, wore European clothes, and built square, rather than the traditional round, houses, even before the discovery of diamonds in the 1860s brought more cash into the area. As property owners they had the vote. By 1880, though, British colonial laws were shrinking Fingo privileges; they lost, for example, the right to own firearms. Perhaps this sense of decline caused Mnyele's son, Harry, the name his grandson Thami would be honoured to bear, to leave Herschel and move to Heilbron in the Orange Free State where he made choices similar to his father's. Harry also married well. His own bride, Elizabeth Radebe, was the daughter of Methodists who owned their own farm. Harry joined Elizabeth on her family's land.

Elizabeth followed Harry into the African Methodist Episcopal (AME) Church, a Protestant sect founded in America by black people protesting against slavery. African ministers, rejecting control by white Wesleyan Methodist missionaries, founded the AME's local branch in the 1890s. Harry served as a church steward and Elizabeth as a stewardess. From its origins the senior Mnyeles' church had focused on voicing grievances against, for example, the pass laws, which prevented even educated, Christian African men like Harry from moving freely unless they could show identity documents.[8]

In 1932 tragedy struck the family when a bolt of lightning cut Harry down as he worked in his fields. Elizabeth moved with her children to Heilbron's township for a while and then decamped for Sophiatown, the famous black district of western Johannesburg where, as in Alex, Africans could own their own plots. Her son David carried on his parents' devotion to the AME Church.

Because of their strong connection to the mother church in America, AME leaders were even more likely than early African nationalists to speak of Africans as connected to a global diaspora. African-American missionaries had established Wilberforce Institute, where David would train for the ministry, to provide the university education that its namesake, the oldest private African-American university, gave to upwardly aspiring black people in the state of Ohio.

Low levels of funding and hostility from the Transvaal Department of Education prevented the institute from training the attorneys, judges, and bishops hoped for by its founders. Nor did it produce the legions of black tradesmen envisioned by Booker T Washington, the freed American slave who founded and boosted schools for adult vocational education. Nevertheless, during the 1940s, just prior to David's arrival, Wilberforce was disseminating black American music, fashion, cuisine, and business techniques so thoroughly that the principal was moved to say, 'I think we are closer to America here at Evaton than anywhere else in South Africa.' Thami would later scorn his father's affection for American styles and his church-sponsored trip to America. He may not have known that even at Wilberforce pan-African pride swelled in the 1950s, leading one Founders' Day speaker to boast the year before David arrived, 'We can produce Nkrumahs and other notable Africans in schools like this.'[9]

Because Thami was born seven months after the 1948 elections, he grew up in a world conditioned by the victorious National Party's neat vision of races and tribes irrevocably separate from one another. Although five years would pass before the party won the necessary electoral backing to redraw basic institutions – creating 'tribal' governments in the rural reserves, for example, and labour bureaux linking them to town – the behaviour of the police changed the experience of daily life immediately. The South African Police were the shock troops of the new order. From the year of Thami's birth, his family saw the newly zealous and numerous police force sweep through Alexandra more frequently, searching for illegal caches of home-brew. When they found them, buried in tin drums, they broke them open, leaving the women of the household to lament as they watched their potential earnings seep into the ground and vanish. In a given week, Thami's father was more likely than ever before to be stopped several times by the police and asked for a pass signifying his right to be in the city.

Shortly before Thami was born, his family had been alarmed by another kind of invasion: about 7 000 landless people set up tents in one of Alex's dusty squares. The leader of these squatters was one Schreiner Baduza, a mustachioed communist with military bearing who, nevertheless, exerted discipline by building consensus and by explanation. Even so, Thami's family, like all Alex landowners, must have felt fearful that their yards and gardens would be overrun, and relieved when the squatters suddenly decamped for a brand-new township southwest of the city. Any story Thami heard about his ancestors highlighted their privilege relative to squatters like these. As far back as family memory could go, they had subscribed to that trinity of middle-class modernity: they owned land, valued education, and belonged to a church.

The mood of some adults during Thami's infancy was growing increasingly defiant and optimistic. Building on the local tradition of boycotting buses when owners tried to raise the fares in the early 1940s, they launched campaigns and made demands they had never made before.

Shortly before the 1948 election, several hundred delegates of all races met at Gandhi Hall in Fordsburg, an Indian neighbourhood in Johannesburg, and, for the first time, demanded the immediate grant of voting rights to all. On May Day 1950 black workers tested their muscle by not working. The streets of Alex and its bus station were empty at dawn and the township's chimneys spewed no smoke. This stay-at-home tactic would be used two years later as part of a massive campaign to force the repeal of a defined set of unjust laws, including the obligation to carry a pass. While the campaign failed, the strategy succeeded in advertising to black people their strength in numbers, stoking the fires of popular optimism. Perhaps the pinnacle of this hope was reached in 1955 when a mass meeting in Kliptown, Johannesburg, voted en masse to endorse a popularly derived new constitution for the entire country. According to Rusty Bernstein, the drafter of this Freedom Charter, the times were characterised by a sense of 'urgency and pioneering'.[10]

'You are ANC. Why can't I be one, too?' his mother remembers Thami asking one day during this decade of upheaval and hope. The sense of excitement, strong enough for a child to perceive, was newly won. Up to the time of Thami's birth the African National Congress (ANC) had found it so difficult to communicate, let alone to mobilise, that some members of the better-organised Communist Party of South Africa (CPSA) thought the ANC was either a handicap or irrelevant to the struggle. Bernstein, a member of the CPSA, noted regretfully that the ANC was then 'in truth, much more of a mass frame of mind than a centralised modern political body'.[11] On the other hand, some of Alex's notable politicians – like Richard Granville Baloyi, the wealthy owner of a real estate agency and a bus company, and Josias Madzunya, a charismatic former pedlar given to talking politics with unemployed street youth – vehemently criticised the ANC for its communist connections. Madzunya and others also complained that Congress was too friendly with white activists. In the densely packed yards of Alex these debates filled the air, already dense with the sound of music and the odour of beer.

Sarah Mnyele would proudly remember the decade of the 1950s as a time when she added her number to the masses, contrasting her political engagement bitterly with what she called David's escape into the sheltered world of the church. She boycotted sugar when it was too expensive, and she refused to travel on the buses in 1955 when the owners raised the fare by a penny. She says she joined the ANC Women's League and in 1956 became a marshal helping to organise the huge women's march to the Union Buildings in Pretoria against the extension of pass laws to women. She spoke with pride of her association with its leaders, taking care to honour them with their married names: Mrs Ngoyi, Mrs Zodwa, Mrs Florrie Moposho. As a new divorcee raising her children alone, she feared the passes would make her even more vulnerable to the sexual overtures of the officials issuing them, and also to arrest, if she lost her job and the right to stay in town.

Partly for this reason and partly because she was 'scared of the Msomis taking the children', that is, gangs harming or recruiting her boys, she decided in the same year as the pass demonstration to send the children to live with her relative, Salamina Mmusi, in the countryside north of Pretoria. Sarah's Ndebele father's family came from a place called Thabaneng near the village of Makapanstad, where there were schools. Thami and his siblings left for Makapanstad in March 1956. At the end of that year the government arrested 156 activists, broadly representative of the ANC and its allies, and charged them with treason.

The move to Makapanstad shocked Thami. After his mother built a house there and moved back to Johannesburg to work in the suburb of Parkmore as a domestic servant, he saw her only once every month or two between the ages of seven and twelve. He would remember those years as 'hard', speaking of them so compulsively to a few close friends of his young adulthood that they grew tired of his 'moaning'.[12] But it wasn't all mournful. Occasionally he would find pleasure in conversation with an old man or in the singing and dancing at holiday time. Makapanstad, which lies about two hours northwest of Pretoria by bus, was spacious and apparently remote from urban life. Cowbells and birdsong punctuated its quiet. Flat-topped acacia trees dotted the Tswana landscape like sculptures. Cattle grazed freely. There Thami learned to speak 'deep' Setswana without an urban accent and to understand, if not to adopt, values centred more on cattle than on fashionable dress.

And yet, Makapanstad was hardly a haven from politics or from racial conflict. Even its name – an Afrikaans version of Makopane's town – reflected the fact that its Tswana-speaking core clan (the Bakgatla baMosetlha) had been buffeted by conquest. First, in the early 19th century the militarised Ndebele offshoot of the Zulu empire-builders to the southeast had swept through the area on their way north. (Thami's Thamane grandfather was descended from this Zulu refugee army.) Then Dutch-speaking farmers fleeing British overrule moved in, causing the clan to move northwest across the Limpopo River to what is now Botswana. Chief Nchaupe later led some clan members back to the site of their ancient capital, where they started to adopt new values. A society of German Lutherans established a mission in 1867 and helped local people pool their money to buy land communally. Both sides of Thami's family, then, were familiar with owning land. For both families, marrying outside an ethnic group mattered not at all. They did not necessarily give much importance to what the National Party would later call 'tribal' loyalties and values.

Thami's secondary school started as a tribal initiative led by an educated chief, Hendrik Makapan, whose followers seem to have been politicised: they sat on school committees, belonged to land-owning syndicates, protested Makapan's taxes, and were 'vehement' in their opposition to mission schools. They believed they could improve their lives by getting an education and using its lessons to address their complaints, notably about taxes, to native commissioners. In a burst of optimism, then, the solid and spacious secondary school, named Nchaupe II Memorial College in memory of the chief's father (1860s–1911), opened officially on 4 October 1948, two months prior to Thami's birth.[13]

Makapan unveiled a plaque that day whose language and imagery advertised modern achievement in a traditional idiom. The design featured a monkey – the totem of the chief's family – seated in the branches

MAIYANE A KGABO-TONA

BANA BA MMAMAFURA A THEKU

LETLAPA LE LE BEILWE
KE
KGOSI H.R.M. MAKAPAN
MOAGO O O ABETSWE
THUTO YA BANA BA MORAFE
WA BAKGATLA-BA-MOSETLHA
MMAMMUDU.   4 - 10 - 1948.

Plaque at former campus of Nchaupe Secondary School,
Makapanstad. (Photograph by author)

of a tree, reaching toward the lamp of learning. The words below dedicated the building to teaching the children of the chief's 'nation'. It was an appropriate inscription on two counts: the chief's 'children' were, in the local idiom, the people of any age whom he governed; and they needed schools because traditional initiation ceremonies had last instructed local youth more than half a century before. For Thami these prideful references to 'nation' drew attention to his status as an outsider, an unintentional refugee from city life. In time he would have cause to see this idea of 'nation' – one based on 'tribe' or 'clan' – as dangerous.

Through the 1950s, when Thami was too young to have been a student there, the school had enough money to order large numbers of books from Van Schaik's bookstore in Pretoria; and so, by the time he arrived at the school, the library shelves held English-language classics like Kipling and Buchan and Twain (sometimes translated into Afrikaans), Africana like Mzilikazi's *Tales of Zululand* and Mfolo's *Shaka Zulu*, as well as *Jock of the Bushveld*, the classic South African dog story written by a mining magnate. He could even find the odd scholarly book, such as Malinowski's *Crime and Custom in Savage Society*; its title, though, reveals that the school aspired to be a serious place of learning more than it demonstrates serious local interest in the South Pacific, which is where Malinowski's 'savage society' lived.

Thami's school day began at 8 am with assembly and hymns or scripture for half an hour, followed by arithmetic, English or Afrikaans (depending on the day of the week), reading and grammar and dictation in the vernacular, plus hygiene, history, geography, nature studies, singing, and manual work. (The last activity amounted to cleaning the school grounds.) 'The peoples of Africa' (Hottentots, Bantu, Negroes, or so the text said) introduced the study of geography, while history began with 'The foundation of the Cape Colony', thus giving a sense, widely shared at the time, that history did not exist before Europeans arrived in the region. The books in Setswana were written mainly by Europeans. Many of them had missionary connections: the scripture books were all in the vernacular, and mission societies produced some of the English-language readers. There were limits to how much independence from the church a school could achieve, even when founded in a spirit of defiant independence. A number of the history books, including the many in English, were written by people with Dutch names; the titles include *The Voortrekkers of South Africa, Great Men and Great Deeds*, and an Afrikaans history book written specially for Africans, *Geskiedenis vir Naturelle Skole* (History for Native Schools).

These texts suggest that Thami learned history as a tale of progress. The Xhosa Cattle Killing of 1857, for example, was not just a 'national suicide', it also improved people's lives by leading them to convert to Christianity. (Driven by a millenarian hope that they could thereby rid their land of whites, many Xhosa had obeyed a prophet's injunction to destroy their cattle and grain; mass starvation ensued.) European history was to be taught as the inspiration for African progress 'because of its parallel with the stages of civilisation in Africa'. There was, as in most schools of the time, a focus on heroes, African and European: the Africans tended to be chiefs and the Europeans to be missionaries. These men, 'great' because they contributed to the 'development of mankind', included missionary David Livingstone, mine magnate Cecil Rhodes, and prime minister Jan Smuts. The Tswana chief Khama was celebrated for his Christian conversion and his opposition to beer, witchcraft, and war. In a little play about Khama called *The Light*, Khama says, 'Queen Victoria has wrapped us in her *flag* which stands for Christianity, justice and equality.' The civics lesson heartily endorsed this symbol, naming 13 points for schoolchildren to absorb, such as 'how to kill off the evil influences of witchcraft' and 'what we owe to the British Empire'. Number 13 is 'The Brotherhood of Man'.

The emphasis on brotherhood probably faded after 1954, when the National Party introduced Bantu Education, a basic, skill-oriented system strictly for Africans. So, too, stories about different races of men, told to encourage children to sympathise with other races, religions, and colours, would vanish. The new system reacted against a curriculum that stessed British identity (evident in frequent references to the Empire, the freeing of slaves, and the achievements of the British navy) and foreign missionary-inspired rhetoric (as in the 'Brotherhood of Man' and 'equality'). Bantu Education texts stressed, rather, the separateness of peoples and the 'cultural infancy' of Africans.[14]

In June 1954, when Thami was five and not yet in school, Hendrik Verwoerd, then minister of native affairs, gave a speech in the South African Senate responding to questions raised during the budget debate about the new education policy. The philosophy behind the policy, he said, emphasised the progress of the *community* and not the individual. What is interesting here for Thami's life is the meaning given to the word 'community' by people like Verwoerd as opposed to, later on, Thami himself. For Thami the word conveyed affection and respect for those who suffered, whereas Verwoerd thought African communities were 'tribes', whose development was blocked by 'alienation and division'. Mission schools were said to foster this division by serving 'only a section of the Bantu population'. The very pan-South Africanness of Thami's background – his Tswana and Ndebele mother, Xhosa father, Alexandra childhood, Tswana schooling and youth – would have alarmed Verwoerd, and not without reason.

Bantu Education was designed to provide education untainted by politics. Significantly motivated by fear of the organisational successes of educated Africans, it frankly aimed to avoid 'endangering the community life of the European'. As Verwoerd told Parliament with extraordinary condescension and assurance, 'The Bantu teacher … must learn not to feel above his community, with a consequent desire to become integrated into the life of the European community. He becomes frustrated and rebellious when this does not take place, and he tries to make his community dissatisfied because of such misdirected ambitions which are alien to his people.' Thami was too young to have understood these words when they were first spoken, but he would react against the sentiment behind them throughout his adulthood.

Fiscal concerns also drove Verwoerd's desire for a uniform and efficient national policy. In order to allow larger numbers of students to attend school, Bantu Education sent younger pupils to classes for only three hours a day. This short day must have been Thami's regimen at Mmamudu or Thipe, the primary schools he attended prior to starting at Nchaupe. Primary school instruction was the three Rs in Setswana and the rudiments of Afrikaans and English, plus religious education and singing. The justification for the inclusion of the two European languages was that, given 'the economic structure of our country', 'large numbers of Natives [have] to earn their living in the service of Europeans'. Because women were 'by nature' better suited to deal with young children, men, who earned higher salaries, would not be appointed to fill teaching posts in primary schools. (Seventy per cent of all teaching posts were filled by these expensive males, and Verwoerd said the percentage was too high.) So Thami entered school at the time of a decreed shift toward more women teachers. The bias of education was also shifting toward agriculture so that Africans could make a living in rural areas, where 'homeland' policy would require them to live permanently, in contrast to their 'temporary' employment in town. Schooling would be oriented specifically toward taking care of the soil, Verwoerd said, warning that communities would not receive educational support if they resisted the lessons of good farming.[15]

'Other animals' from *Disa Readers Standard I* (1947).

Since Thami's schools received cast-off textbooks from white schools, he would have read stories like one entitled 'Clay oxen', whose first lines are 'Piccanin is our native boy. He can make clay oxen.' The last line reads, 'We get clay and try to make them, but they do not look like the animals that Piccanin makes.' 'Piccanin' is a vocabulary word, as is 'native'. A silhouette illustration shows the black child squatting and holding up to the white boy one of his creations, while the white child leans down toward him holding another clay animal with, the story suggests, admiration.[16]

This interchange took place in a rural area, as texts routinely avoided depicting the city life Thami had left behind in Alexandra. Liza, 'a Native woman', scrubs clothes beside the river with her infant, whom she protects from the water and fire; three little boys squat around a cooking pot on a white farm where they work and don't seem to go to school. Instead they help with the milking, fetch the sheep, lead the oxen during ploughing, water the horses, and weed the garden. 'They are very happy on the farm and do not wish to live in a town.'[17]

Primary school texts depict white children standing upright beside modern transport such as cars and trains. African people are always crouching.

'Nomlinda (a native story)' from A V S Barnes, *Southern Cross Reader IV* (c. 1953).

'Story 9' from A V S Barnes, *Southern Cross Reader II* (n.d.).

Books for slightly older children in the early 1950s depicted rural Africans in postures of astonishment or need, and the vocabulary words included 'cannibal' and 'witch-doctor'. Another text read, 'The Bantu are fond of music. They always sing when they work, and have made a number of primitive musical instruments for themselves. They are very superstitious, and many of them still believe in the power of the witch-doctor.'[18] Reading these words, perhaps thinking back to the weekend jazz appreciation circles he had witnessed in Alex, Thami withdrew into daydreams. He was not, by his own assessment, a good student.

The study of history may have intensified Thami's reveries. One illustrated history described Europeans as civilised 'because we wear attractive clothes, write in books, drive motor-cars, travel by air, use refrigerators and have many other conveniences' as opposed to 'uncivilized people who live close to nature and build huts of mud and grass. They are very scantily clad, they cannot read or write and they are not able to erect fine buildings.' A tree of civilisation depicts the Roman Empire as the trunk, Germany as one of the first two branches, then Holland, and finally South Africa, as offshoots. We learn history, the chapter concludes, 'because it tells us how our nation and civilization originated. It tell us who we are and where we came from'.[19] History, then, is the story of the civilized, and Thami must not have enjoyed it at all. The text never refers, even in photographs, to Africans as individuals but as groups between whom there are boundaries: the reserves are said to be their natural home; urbanisation is said to promote 'detribalization' which amounts to 'increasing lawlessness, degeneration of the youth, instability of the marriage contract'.[20] While Thami knew these three troubling consequences at first hand, he chose not to engage in most subjects emotionally or competitively. He did like English, and he enjoyed classes like biology, where he could draw.

Thami had begun to draw in Makapanstad but in that dusty, flat village, where men were fixated on cattle, he had no one to emulate and no one encouraged him. It was Tswana women, not men, who drew the wavy designs decorating

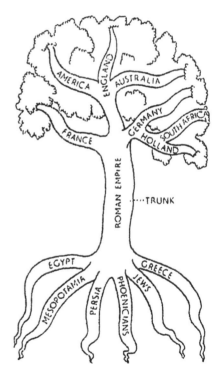

'Our Western Civilisation illustrated by means of a tree' from *Illustrated History Standard VI* (1962).

the floors and sometimes the walls of mud houses; men were the guardians of the cattle wealth in Tswana culture, not artists. Thami longed for people to respond immediately and warmly to what he saw and drew. Family photographs show him standing rigidly in his school blazer, masking with a poker face the ferment of his fears and his longing.

NOTES

1   Molefe Pheto, interview (July 2001).
2   Simon 'Jika' Twala, interview (27 Dec 2001).
3   Ibid.
4   Can Themba, *The Will to Die* (London: Heinemann, 1972), 28.
5   Thami Mnyele, 'Observations on the state of the contemporary visual arts in South Africa' (n.d.), 1. Miriam Makeba tells a similar story in her auto-biography. In about 1953 she was made to sing 'Saduva' for gangsters in an Alex nightclub 20 times, as they sat with their pistols on their tables. Miriam Makeba with James Hall, *Makeba: My Story* (Johannesburg: Skotaville, 1988), 50–1.
6   Native Divorce Court, Central Division, Case #110, 1952, South African Archives (SAA), Pretoria. I have standardised into rands the currency in this file, which extends into the 1960s when Sarah sued David Mnyele for non-support.
7   I am grateful to Poppy Fry for discussing with me her knowledge of Fingo history.
8   There was enough tension in Heilbron for a radical organisation called the Industrial and Commercial Workers Union (ICU) to establish a branch there in the early 1930s, a few years after a white landlord had murdered an African worker. See Helen Bradford, *A Taste of Freedom: The ICU in Rural South Africa, 1924–30* (New Haven: Yale University Press, 1988).
9   Jacob Nhlapo, quoted by James Campbell, 'Our fathers, our children: The African Methodist Episcopal Church in the United States and South Africa' (PhD thesis, Stanford University, 1989), 375; speaker at Wilberforce Founders' Day celebration (1952), 377.
10 Rusty Bernstein, *Memory against Forgetting* (London: Viking, 1999), 150.
11 Ibid, 178.
12 Naniwe Ramatsui, interview (8 Jan 2003).
13 Makapanstad history may be gleaned from P.-L. Breutz, *A History of the Batswana and the Origins of Bophuthatswana.* (Ramsgate: P.L. Breutz, 1989), 333–8; 'Memorandum of tribal schools in the Makapanstat area', KHK 2/2/159 N 12/3/3/(1/1), SAA.
14 A V S Barnes, *The Southern Cross Reader VI* (n.d.), 21–4; *A Practical Guide for Bantu Teachers* (1950); *Bantu Schools of Tomorrow* (1950), 188, 182.
15 Minister of Native Affairs H F Verwoerd, Statement in the Senate of the Union Parliament (7 June 1954), 'Bantu Education policy for the immediate future', 7, 24, 15, 18, 20.
16 'Clay oxen', in B Pullinger and P Hart, *Disa Reader Standard I* (Bloemfontein: Nasionale Pers, 1947), 11–14.
17 Barnes, *Southern Cross Reader II*, 36, 72.
18 A D Dodd, W A Cordingley, W E Trengrove, *Discovering the World, Standard IV* (Cape Town: Juta, n.d.), 42.
19 F A van Jaarsveld, Dorothea Behr, J J van der Walt, *Illustrated History Standard VI* (Johannesburg: Voortrekkerpers, 1958, rev 1962), 13, 14, 16.
20 A J Böeseken, J J Oberholster, M C E van Schoor, N J Olivier, *History for the Senior Certificate* (Cape Town: Nasionale Boekhandel, 1957), 522.

Chapter 2

Into the Vortex

Thami entered adolescence looking out on the flat dry plains of the Western Transvaal bushveld and sensing that the future was being decided elsewhere. During the 1950s the government was transforming African reserves like the one around Makapanstad into 'homelands' or 'bantustans', intended to be the exclusive site of African self-government or, in the words of their planner, Verwoerd, 'Bantu control over Bantu areas'. Black people were being moved out of white areas. The Sophiatown home of Thami's grandmother, Elizabeth, was expropriated in 1955 and she was forcibly removed to Meadowlands in Soweto, along with the 70 000 other residents of that black spot within white Johannesburg. Episodes of mass demonstrations were followed by lulls, but each wave of protest rose higher than the last. A new party, the Pan Africanist Congress (PAC), split off from the ANC in 1959 and, stating that the apartheid regime could be brought down once the masses were mobilised, decreed a national anti-pass campaign. In the townships people tossed their passbooks into bonfires, while people living in Makapanstad spent their energy hunting for stray cattle and engaging in bitter disputes over land.

Newcomers, even those like Thami's mother who had family ties to the area, were eating up the land in Makapanstad. They were flocking to this apparent rural refuge from cities where they had failed to find work or from white farms from which they had been expelled. The headman and chief could do nothing to help, especially since their superior, the new Bantu Affairs commissioner, was failing to enlarge the grazing area, choosing instead to rent neighbouring plots to stock speculators and butchers. Meanwhile, the chieftainship was buckling under the weight of having to defend government policy. When people explained why they opposed the chief, they told stories that went back to before the fractious foundation of the tribal school. Their bitterness reflected the village's 19th-century experience of private land ownership, when syndicates of prosperous Africans had bought land in the names of missionaries. The owners now feared they would lose their land if it were incorporated into a bantustan.[1]

Government officials knew that disgruntled men – the young, the unemployed, the landless, as well as the landed – were holding night meetings in Makapanstad with representatives of the ANC and the Communist Party. Informers sat among them and heard the chief accused of having sold out his people to the whites. Their reports were typed up in Afrikaans, labelled 'Geheim' (secret), and deposited in Native Affairs Department files in Pretoria where the bureaucrats simplified complex grievances by labelling them 'linksgesindes' (left-wingers). Despite its rustic air, Makapanstad was firmly embedded in national politics.

In March 1960, the PAC organised a demonstration 100 miles away from Makapanstad at a police station in a township called Sharpeville. The party hoped to achieve the abolition of the pass system by filling the jails with people who refused to carry those demeaning documents. The police opened fire, killing 69 people. In later years, and in the face of the hundreds who would die in the violence that racked South Africa in the 1970s and 1980s, this toll might seem low, but at the time the shooting of unarmed people, many in the back, was deeply shocking. The resulting furore whipped up 'like a cyclone, drawing people and government into the vortex'.[2] In the cities workers stayed at home, waiting for politicians to tell them what to do next. Military spotter planes flew overhead. The government detained 2 000 activists and declared a State of Emergency, which brought the townships under the control of the police and the army. Because the government had banned both the ANC and the PAC in April 1960, leaders like Nelson Mandela and Oliver Tambo had to go into hiding or exile if they were to continue to organise.

Mass action was again aborted the following year when the government declared South Africa a republic, formally severed from Great Britain. Plans to launch a three-day general strike were met by a more dramatic display of force than ever before. Both the army and the police patrolled the townships in armoured vehicles, while helicopters and fighter planes flew close to rooftops. This time 10 000 activists were detained. These measures may well have succeeded in intimidating protesters. (Their ranks were weakened, in any case, because the PAC, in what activist Helen Joseph called an act of 'political scabbing', issued leaflets from underground, urging people to go to work as usual.)[3] The planned general strike did not succeed. Dispirited, Mandela emerged from hiding for an interview on foreign television, warning, 'If the government reaction is to crush by naked force our non-violent struggle, we will have to seriously reconsider our tactics. In my mind we are closing a chapter on this question of a non-violent policy.'[4] Inspired by liberation armies elsewhere on the continent, especially in Algeria, ANC leaders had been discussing armed struggle even before the failed strike. Some theorists were suggesting that small 'people's armies' could act as 'detonators' of the 'revolutionary spirit of the masses'.[5]

There was no television in South Africa, so Thami saw only newspaper photos of the protests, shootings, and leaders. By word of mouth he would learn that shortly after Mandela's broadcast ANC leaders formed a separate military organisation called Umkhonto weSizwe (Spear of the Nation, known as MK). Some time later a few leaders of the banned ANC and SACP drew up a six-page document, 'Operation Mayibuye', evolving the campaign of sabotage into a strategy for guerrilla war. MK detonated its first, homemade bombs in government offices the week after Thami turned 13.

Rusty Bernstein, drafter of the Freedom Charter and a stalwart communist, thought the emphasis on armed struggle lacked 'political depth'. He believed Operation Mayibuye, in particular, derived from 'a wholly inadequate analysis of the real balance of power in the country' and glossed over the actual strengths and weaknesses of the government and its adversaries. He preferred to focus on a social and political programme which encompassed armed force, rather than rely on 'a fairly simplistic assessment of the logistic problems of guerrilla warfare'. Bernstein felt 'contempt for military thinking and its obsession with numbers and with things' like manpower and firepower; it ignored 'the human factors of consciousness, morale, and ideas'. But, he noted, MK 'comrades' like Joe Slovo and Govan Mbeki tended to regard criticism of Operation Mayibuye as revealing 'lack of courage'.[6] Confrontation between these points of view runs like a leitmotif through the subsequent history of the ANC. Years later Thami would become embroiled in the debate, and its outcome would determine his life's chances.

Occasions for making the state seem less than omnipotent and even foolish grew rare as the decade wore on. In 1963 the MK high command – Nelson Mandela, Walter Sisulu, Govan Mbeki, Rusty Bernstein, Harold Wolpe, Arthur Goldreich, and five others – were arrested, convicted of sabotage and of preparing for guerrilla war, and sentenced to life in prison. The government began hiring an army of informers. Once jailed, their victims suffered increasingly brutal conditions designed not only to ensure that all secrets were divulged, but also to break the spirit. Prisoners began to be kept in solitary confinement. They started to die in detention: between 1963 and 1969, 18 political prisoners died, probably as a result of torture. The following year Parliament passed the Terrorism Act, whose section 6 decreed that any person suspected of being a terrorist, or having information about one, could be detained indefinitely. Defence spending rose so sharply that by 1973 it was 1 200 per cent higher than it had been at the time of Sharpeville. Reflecting on the significance of the years immediately following 1963, South African Communist Party (SACP) leader Joe Slovo lamented the loss of what had been, until 1961, 'gentlemanly terrain' where there was the assurance of a fair trial. The legal structure, he said, 'lulled us' and so 'we underestimated the potential for the growth in viciousness of the enemy security apparatus and the fact that the counter revolution learns from the revolution'.[7]

For the time being, Thami did not become enmeshed in the ratcheting violence. He passed his adolescence simply overhearing dramatic, even romantic, tales of defiance. One bright moment occurred when Goldreich and Wolpe, in jail for their role in planning Operation Mayibuye, escaped from Pretoria Central Prison and fled to Botswana and, eventually, London. Township dwellers were said to have 'gone wild' with delight over the escape, some even imagining they had parachuted into the town of Lobatse across the border in Botswana, 240 km due west of Makapanstad.[8] Years later Thami's mother would date events in her life with reference to their flight.

Thami's childhood had taken place in an atmosphere coloured by free protest and by what Slovo later called 'naïve' confidence that the state would respond constructively. His youth, on the other hand, was coinciding with repression so frightening that it erased public protest. Even Alexandra became, in the words of one of Thami's mentors – lodger, soul musician, and self-taught electrician Simon 'Jika' Twala – 'like Siberia'. People didn't want to discuss politics for fear of being overheard. The young heard only whispers about the 1950s. Slovo would call this mood 'demoralisation'. His remedy for it was 'armed activity ... a demonstration of our capacity to hit at the enemy'.[9] Only then would people be emboldened to rebuild the political underground. These brave words expressed hopes more than realities. MK managed to recruit few, if any, cadres in the late 1960s.

The liberation rhetoric of the newly independent African countries had given momentary hope to African nationalists that they would not fight alone for majority rule. Algeria, for example, having recently fought its way to independence from France, promised 10 000 soldiers to help its 'fighting brothers' in South Africa. But brand-new states found it hard to live up to their defiant words when facing the continent's only industrial giant. Even Julius Nyerere, the socialist president of Tanzania, retracted his offer to the ANC of a home in his capital. In 1965 he told its rank-and-file members to move 230 km west of Dar es Salaam and to set up their MK training camp 200 km further west, at Kongwa. There the leadership, who knew little about guerrilla warfare, attempted to train men who were suffering from a peculiar combination of anxiety and boredom, drinking too much, and festering with grievances five countries away from home.

The sense of futility worsened in 1967 when MK's military action, against Rhodesian and South African forces in Rhodesia's Wankie game reserve, ended in retreat. Cadres belonging to the Luthuli Brigade, including commissar Chris Hani, had intended to build bridges like the Ho Chi Minh Trail for future guerrilla incursions into South Africa. When they were forced to retreat to Botswana, they expected to be treated, in Hani's word, 'amicably' by the Botswana Defence Force (BDF). It was hard for them to imagine that the army of a country belonging to the Organisation of African Unity (OAU) would actually throw them into detention. The BDF – commanded by British and South African officers – did indeed throw its captives into prison for a year and a half, despite 'furious' but futile protests from the OAU.[10] The refugees caught by Rhodesia, on the other hand, stayed in jail for the rest of Rhodesia's days. One guerrilla who reached South Africa joined the South African security police after his capture.

Despite the sorry outcome, many ANC members credit Wankie with inspirational value. It was a 'virgin victory', said Hani, because it was the first time MK had fought against the enemy with modern weapons.[11] And yet, in the aftermath of the defeat, he wrote an internal memorandum blaming ANC leadership for the 'rot' that had resulted in the 'fossilisation' of the revolution's leadership. (An ANC tribunal repri-manded Hani harshly for his critique and came close to ordering 'the most severe punishment'. Hani's life was spared and he went on to open an era of greater rank-and-file participation in the movement.)[12] The following year the heads of 14 Southern African states signed a manifesto in Lusaka, without consulting either the PAC or the ANC, calling for a negotiated settlement. They were effectively repudiating support for the armed struggle given by the OAU when it was founded six years earlier.

This dispiriting news filtered through to Thami as he came of age. His sympathies at the time were probably drawn to the PAC as well as the ANC because both movements aimed to instil black pride and erase all feelings of defeat. The PAC, whose members tended to be younger and less educated than those who joined the ANC, played on popular prejudices against allying with progressive whites and with Indians – like the Asian shopkeepers who lived behind high walls on Alex's First and Second Avenues, taking the money of their African neighbours but never mixing with them – as well as with coloured people who held themselves similarly aloof.

Unlike the Africanists in the PAC, ANC members had to learn to accept such people as comrades. Every white policeman barking for a pass and every white madam issuing shrill orders to her 'maid' or 'garden boy' made it harder for black listeners to accept the leadership of people who looked like them. A granny might caution 'Not all whites are the same', but the PAC reaped support from those who were too offended to distinguish differences. Sarah Mnyele learned to live with her employers, working for only two 'madams' over a couple of decades. While neither she nor Thami joined the PAC, they could not entirely avoid sliding into moments of bitterness towards whites in general.

Thami's appreciation of all these happenings was also attenuated by the preoccupations of a teenager. He had fallen in love with a fellow student at Nchaupe Secondary. Her name was Mantsopo and she was very beautiful. Later some would say she was the most beautiful of all the women in Thami's life. Perhaps what drew him most to her, though, was her love of music. She liked what Thami's cousin Malebo called the 'funny music' of Dollar Brand and Nina Simone, avant-garde jazz that expressed social concerns. Mantsopo bore their daughter, whom they named Mary, but as Thami had no job, he was in no position to assume the role of father.

Thami was entering a dark period. He left Nchaupe in 1965, suffering from 'cronic [sic] feelings of failure' and without taking his matriculation exam.[13] He had not done well enough in school to feel confident that he could pass an examination failed by so many of his peers. He didn't lack ambition or dreams, but at the moment when he should have been emerging into confident manhood, he was nearly paralysed by self-doubt. Sometimes he daydreamed too much to concentrate on playing a game of soccer. He once lost a girlfriend, he said, because he neglected to run after a ball during a match she was watching.

He and his sister Julie returned to Alexandra. They moved into the home rented by his mother's brother, David, two plots away from his birthplace on Sixth Avenue. He lived there for three years without finding steady paid employment or a niche as an artist. The economy was booming, but none of the jobs it provided for black men suited Thami's temperament and emerging talents. Industrial hardware plants in nearby Wynberg and Bergvlei wanted men who could drive and weld and sweep.

Depressed, Thami seems to have moved aimlessly around Johannesburg for a few years. After reuniting with his father and meeting his new brothers and sisters in 1966, when he was turning 18, he lived with them between 1968 and 1970 as his father moved from a church in George Goch to one in Diepkloof, sections of the vast Soweto township. Thami's father provided him with a strict and remote paternal model, a role he in turn played with his younger siblings. His sister Lindi remembers him urging them to study hard, because 'he wanted something big for us'. (She didn't even dare introduce him to her boyfriends.)[14] As Thami shuttled between relatives in Alexandra and Soweto he was at least gaining a strong sense of township life throughout greater Johannesburg.

Julie Mandu, David and Sarah's first-born and Sarah's only daughter, had taken care of Thami during his mother's frequent absences. Only two years older than Thami, she too needed protection, especially in an environment where sex was 'rough' and girls were easy prey.[15] Pretty, though without her mother's sharp beauty, she became a vulnerable teenager. Despite her laughing smile, tilted beret, and well-cut kilt, she was too quiet to garner the kind of attention her mother won effortlessly. While Thami retreated into silence from the turmoil of their home, Julie found herself in the epicentre of the township's glamour when she fell in love with a jazz musician. Moving into his home on Fourth Avenue, she conceived his child, but kept her pregnancy a secret.

The love of a jazz musician draws competitors. The freedom of his music matched the freedom of his ways. Four months pregnant, Julie fell into despair, and then tragedy struck. Late in 1968 Thami received an urgent message to go to Edenvale Hospital. Walking rapidly through a ward of badly damaged bodies, he passed Julie's bed without recognising her. Perhaps he sensed the barely living remains of his sister, brought there from her boyfriend's home, and turned to face Julie's charred body. Her primus stove had exploded and burned her. She died two months later, after her burns grew septic. Weeping, Thami called her death a 'suicide'. The funeral was held in Uncle David's home and Julie was buried on top of her grandmother's coffin in Alexandra cemetery. The sight of her exposed bones as she lay in the hospital bed penetrated Thami's memory and lodged there for the rest of his days. He would draw those bones again and again, but he managed to speak about her 'stupid' death only once to each of a few trusted people.[16]

Musicians, not visual artists or writers, were the people's 'most loved artists' in Alexandra, he would say later. They expressed the full range of their neighbours' feelings – 'joy, pity, love, anger and even violence' – so they were never alone. Even the gangsters feared to touch them. The culture of jazz appreciation was so highly developed that on weekends people would dress up, draw chairs around a battery-driven gramophone in the middle of the yard, and spend hours passing shrewd comments on the sounds of the jazz greats. They competed to see who could build the best record collection, bragging about owning the latest disc by John Coltrane or Charlie Parker. They knew Count Basie's 'Wiggle in the boogie' note by note. The United States may have been the birthplace of many of the cutting-edge sounds, but it could inspire South African versions that were even more popular. In 1968 local saxophonist Winston Mankuku Ngozi recorded his classic 'Yakhal Inkomo' in response to Coltrane. The title, which translates as 'the cry of the cattle at the slaughterhouse', and the sound itself would soon inspire a book of poetry. Thami would yearn for similar inspirational dialogue with other artists but for the time being he could not find it in the 'the loneliness and aloneness of paintings and confinement'.[17]

Even into his early 20s he would have preferred to think of himself as a musician. Music had the power to transport him beyond the bleakness and fear in the township, and beyond his own failures. It generated moments of communal pride and even familial warmth around the gramophone or in song. It connected South Africa to the magical 'Elsewhere'.

NOTES

1   Politieke en ander Organisasies African National Congress, BAO 107/4/29, SAA.
2   Bernstein, *Memory*, 191.
3   Quoted by Vladimir Shubin, *ANC: A View from Moscow* (Bellville: Mayibuye Books, 1999), 16.
4   Nelson Mandela, *Long Walk to Freedom* (Boston: Little, Brown, 1994), 270.
5   Michael Harmel, quoted by Shubin, *ANC*, 20.
6   Bernstein, *Memory*, 251–2.
7   Joe Slovo, writing in 1963, quoted by T Karis and G Gerhart, *From Protest to Challenge: A Documentary History of African Politics in South Africa, 1882–1990*, vol. 5: *Nadir and Resurgence, 1964–79* (Bloomington: Indiana University Press, 1997), 24.
8   Bram Fischer, quoted by Glenn Frankel, *Rivonia's Children: Three Families and the Cost of Conscience in White South Africa* (New York: Farrar, Straus, Giroux, 1999), 144.
9   Quoted by Shubin, ANC, 67.
10 Joe Matthews, one-time ANC representative in London, quoted by Karis and Gerhart, *From Protest*, 30.
11 Chris Hani, 'The Wankie Campaign', Karis and Gerhart, *From Protest*, 376.
12 Hani, quoted by Shubin, *ANC*, 85, 87.
13 Mnyele, 'Observations', 1.
14 Lindi Mnyele Binca, interview (5 Jan 2005).
15 Can Themba, *Will to Die*, 28, 59.
16 Naniwe Ramatsui, interview (8 Jan 2003); Rhona Ogbugo, interview (Dec 2003).
17 Mnyele, 'Observations', 2.

Chapter 3

Tears

In 1970 Thami dreamt of becoming an artist but he had no training. He had no job. He hunted for employment in the factories of Wynberg, the new industrial complex lying on Alexandra Township's western border. He could choose among Barlow, which manufactured refrigerators; Wyns, which produced oil for automobiles; AEG, which made electrical switches; a plastics firm that produced moulds for bottles; and a company that built swimming pools. Eventually he found work at Drake's Outfitters, a clothing store on the corner of Kerk and Sauer streets in Johannesburg's central business district. Thami's natural reticence ill-suited a street tout, whose job was to chat up customers and draw them into the store. The income improved his relationship with his family for a time, then Drake's let him go.

Beer offered solace. One night at his mother's house as he lay in bed with his elder brother, Desmond, the floor began to pitch and heave. Unable to rouse himself, he vomited over his brother. Desmond, enraged, began to smack and beat Thami, yelling curses at the drunken figure who had filled the tiny room with his sour stench. Scared and humiliated, Thami promised never to drink again. He never did. In a world in which socialising relied on liquor, Thami was setting himself apart. One township saying went: the only men who don't drink are either in the church or politics. At this point in his life, Thami was 'in' neither. He had, however, learned that he could assert iron discipline over his appetites.

Though he felt weighted down by the large gap between his aspirations – 'my dream of becoming a good artist' – and his realistic prospects, he was meeting the people who would help him to rise.[1] Music was the midwife. The first fateful encounter occurred one day in 1970 when he crossed a yard on Second Avenue to visit Simon 'Jika' Twala. He was drawn to approach the room next door instead because its tenant, James Bokwe Mafuna, was playing a record by John Coltrane. Bokwe asked the young man who appeared listening at his door what he liked to do. Thami replied softly, 'to draw'.[2]

A news photographer and reporter for the *Rand Daily Mail*'s new 'black' edition, Bokwe knew, and was known by, members of the township's artistic elite. His gregarious and emotional nature drew them to the rooms he shared with his wife Khayo, a quiet Alexandra-born schoolteacher. He used the back room as his darkroom, but the kitchen was a social 'hive'. Perhaps Thami was drawn to Bokwe's door as much by the glamour of his associations as by the sound of Coltrane. He was soon and lastingly rewarded.

Bokwe introduced him to an aspiring young writer named Mongane Wally Serote. Thami immediately brought a drawing to show him. Carefully unrolling a sheet of protective brown paper, Thami revealed a picture of a 'strangely fat and round' pig, which he called 'Prodigal son'. Wally stared at the sketch and found the symbolism inscrutable. Sensing the earnestness of the young artist, who was busily gazing at the ceiling while scratching his cheek and chin, he fought back a smile; then they all burst out laughing.[3]

Trying to express Wally's influence on Thami, friends would later venture the words 'brother', or 'father figure', even 'guru'.[4] At first sight the two young men appeared unlikely comrades. Four years older than Thami, Wally projected a tough mastery of the streets. He could scale walls to reach a shebeen. He knew how to use his fists. The large curved scar above his right eye suggested he would barrel his way, unafraid, out of any quarrel. He would make unreasonable demands on people whose loyalty he wanted to test, calling them in the middle of the night, invading their lives. His intensity led his mother to warn him against slamming doors he might one day want to open.

Wally Serote in 1978, photographed by Tim Williams, on back cover of *Behold Mama, Flowers.*

The two young men shared more than striking good looks, though Thami's almost feminine beauty lay a pole apart from Wally's machismo. They both had highly observant and sensitive natures. They were deeply shy, a trait Wally camouflaged better. They came from relatively well-off, property-owning families in Alex. Their grandparents had proudly led their respective churches after their rural ancestors converted to Christianity in the mid- to late 1800s. Neither had passed his 'matric', though Wally had actually sat for this secondary school-leaving exam, indomitably starting a correspondence course when he failed. Wally remembers being 'half from the streets, very angry about South Africa, not educated, suspecting that I was a writer and, mostly, lost and wondering ... and wandering'.[5] He spent time in the library at 'Wits', the University of the Witwatersrand, and got to know other aspiring writers there. Both young men were hungry to express themselves and to see their lives from a broader perspective.

While Thami, physically smaller as well as younger, might envy Wally's boldness, he was drawn mainly to his flights of fancy. Here was a man who could walk through Alexandra and start simulating a game of catch near the laundry line of a fastidious old lady. She would yell at the mischief-maker until, realising she had become an actor in an improvised piece of theatre, she dissolved in laughter. Here, too, was a man who had fallen in love with books. Wally credited his English literature teacher, a Mr Phefadu, with opening his eyes to the power of poetry and novels. His high school class of 50 young Alexandrans had spent 45 minutes each week examining great works from Europe and America, then applying them, like conspirators, to the South African situation. Napoleon's soldiers retreating from Moscow became living and instructive presences in Mr Phefadu's classroom.[6] Later, when visiting the Wits library, Wally would begin to fit these ideas into a wider frame. He yearned to express the 'disenchantment' that plagued him and Thami and their peers.[7]

Wally's 'disenchantment' deepened at 2 am on 12 May 1969 when he, along with a couple of dozen others, was arrested and thrown into detention for nine months. By the age of 25 he had already seen the inside of many police stations after being picked up in the city without his pass. One of his fellow matric students, who knew at first hand his 'craving' for writing and knowledge, recalls the shock of seeing the young writer seated sullenly on the floor of a police station, handcuffed to other pass offenders.

This arrest, though, was far more demeaning. Perhaps his socialising in mixed, progressive circles had drawn the attention and resentment of the security police. In prison his interrogators demanded that he confess to having relations with white women, an order whose madness caused him to weep with rage. Had that fear led them to force him to stand for days without food or a toilet and to beat and pound him in shifts?[8]

The arrests smacked of harassment, or perhaps they were the fruit of an attempt to harvest a new crop of informers. A *Rand Daily Mail* reporter and its chief African photographer, Peter Magubane, were among the detainees. The newspaper's editor expressed consternation because 'there has certainly been no sign of [ANC] sabotage for a long time'. It was redolent of Stalinist Russia, he wrote, to make people disappear in the middle of the night so that even their families didn't know where they were held or why.[9] On 1 December, 22 of the May detainees would be charged under the Suppression of Communism Act with membership of the banned ANC, but Wally was about to be released. He never learned the charge against him. The police had tried to intimidate him into becoming an informer.[10] Kept in solitary confinement for one month, his diversions amounted to standing on his toilet bucket to watch pass offenders being made to dance naked for their jailers during inspection. Sometimes he just stared at his own foot.

Wally had been picked up in a wave of arrests that were the government's response to stirrings of new life in the ANC. Only 11 days earlier the movement had held a major conference in Morogoro, Tanzania, to discuss how to push forward its revolutionary objectives. Inside South Africa it was trying to resurrect itself after several dormant years. Recently released political prisoner Griffiths Mxenge was beginning to rebuild underground structures in Natal. Winnie Mandela was organising the production and distribution of leaflets in the Transvaal. One member of her circle was Wally's friend, journalist Joyce Sikakane. Another was an informer. Perhaps Wally was too young and too poorly connected to the ANC at the time to actually be charged with any offence. If the impact of his imprisonment was to make him a better poet and to prepare him to be a revolutionary, it had repercussions greater than anyone could have imagined.

Wally's stories seized Thami with fear and wonder. He tried to imagine the deprivation his friend had endured. He moved away from the religious symbols, like the ' Prodigal son', which had preoccupied him, but rather than depict the beating or the naked dance, he focused, like Wally, on the simple and the basic. In an act of empathetic imagination he drew Wally's foot as it must have appeared to him during that solitary month.

At the time of his arrest Wally was avoiding prose that assaulted his readers with extremes. He made no explicitly political references, though he did convey his egalitarian values, his respect for the simple things people do. He wrote, for example, about disappointing fathers and eccentric artists. Perhaps his choice of subject matter and tone reflected his need to avoid provoking the authorities. Perhaps he was influenced by his literary mentors, Barney Simon and Lionel Abrahams, to reach for expressive subtlety rather than the didactic. Abrahams ran a writing workshop where Wally brought his work for critique, and Simon had taken over editorship of a literary magazine called *The Classic*. In it he published three of Wally's poems and three of his stories in 1971. Abrahams thought Wally wrote better after his arrest than before: he used his suffering creatively to reach new levels of expression. Wally himself admitted that his nine months in detention 'opened up [something] in my writing'.[11]

Each story or poem displayed his powers of observation, as when he depicted the empty days of children growing up in Alexandra without much guidance from a self-important father, a 'priest of some unknown church that makes him move about carrying a Bible', 'too busy' to return his children's greetings. Each piece also showed Wally's gift for metaphor: a young man's smile cuts into doubt 'like teeth do the peels of a fruit'. He depicted humour blooming 'now and then' out of an otherwise defeated man; 'Wishing / He'd live, he'd died'. The simplicity of his statements could pack breathtaking power, as in one poem's refrain: 'I want to look at what happened'.[12]

Thami's own attempt to 'look at what happened' in 1971 depicted a man caught between defeat and resignation. A bearded man has raised his right arm, spreading his fingers in a V-sign. The gesture conveys a muted, even tentative, version of the gloved fist raised by black American athletes at the Olympic Games three years earlier. And yet the man's head has lolled onto his shoulder, as if victory were merely a half-hearted dream. In his then reticent manner Thami was expressing the emotional consequences of living on a cusp: the old resistance movement had been driven away, a new one was still young, and the boldest inspiration was coming from overseas, especially from black Americans.

One of Wally's early stories, 'When Rebecca fell', tells of South Africa's premier African artist of the time, his friend Dumile Feni. In this short story Dumile lies inconsolable underneath his bed because his broken sculpture, 'Rebecca', is lying on it.[13]

Thami Mnyele, untitled, 1971, Ike Ramothibe Collection (Photograph by author)

Although Thami never met Dumile, Wally filled him with stories of this beloved figure's eccentricities and irrepressible creativity. Impulsive and dramatic, Dumile ostentatiously threw away his pass when he left the country forever in 1968. Artistically, too, his hallmark was the honest and direct expression of strong feeling.

When Thami saw Dumile's art, though it was reproduced poorly in a 1968 issue of *The Classic*, he finally discovered a visual artist whose way of life and art inspired him. Only one man in Alex, J L Masisi, was known to draw, but people today struggle to remember him. Dumile, on the other hand, flared up and lit the world around him. A nurse in his tuberculosis ward at Baragwanath Hospital had discovered her patient's talent for drawing in 1963 and asked him to paint murals in the sanatorium. Over the next five years he had three one-man shows and represented South Africa in the São Paulo Biennale. Through Wally's stories Thami knew that 'the troubled music' of Coltrane and his young South African disciple, Winston Mankunku Ngozi, played in the background as Dumile drew and sculpted. 'When I listen to jazz, I get ideas,' Dumile explained.[14] Thami later remembered seeing Dumile's images of 'a church made out of a few corrugated iron sheets ... a preacher preaching while holding a mad woman's hand on the one hand and the bible on the other, whereas right on top of the shoulders of the priest himself, a youth is eating oranges from the tree with fork and knife; hungry child-bearing women; men with drooping shoulders; ugly buses without window panes, skeletal dogs and those aggressive township rats in dark avenues'.[15] During his early years as an artist Thami would choose similar themes: agony, fear, mother and child, a shape suggestive of a womb.

Dumile Feni, 'An age', charcoal, from *The Classic* (1968).

Dumile Feni, untitled, from *African Arts* (1970).

Like Wally, Dumile was adept at metaphor. He boldly depicted the emotional realities of his time, entitling one of his most ambitious canvases 'African Guernica'. In it the world has been turned upside down: a baby sucks at the udder of an errant ox, a woman cradles a man in her arms, a three-legged madman and a seated preacher gesticulate to no one in particular. Across another canvas, 'Railway accident' (1966), Dumile splashed the human and material debris of a train wreck, conveying the dynamic horror not only of the accident itself but of any system run out of control.

Dumile's imagery extended beyond the disastrous. His sculptures took on monumental forms, expressing the solidity of the body in a modern African style, one he himself was initiating. He wanted to convey human dignity. He said he wanted to make political statements obliquely, as when he drew a group of manacled prisoners he had seen struggling to salute a passing coffin. Thami would later praise Dumile's art for its 'noble element of communalness ... that touching clinging together of simple people'.[16] Dumile could draw an African trio – a man supporting a woman's shoulders as she pedalled a bicycle, an infant in her arms – as tenderly as if they were holy.

During the last two years that Dumile worked full time as an artist in South Africa he lived in a Parktown home, the site of Rebecca's fall, belonging to a white painter named Bill Ainslie, who painted large, colourful abstract canvases. These paintings reflected the influence of the New York school of abstract expressionists, as well as the wide-open spaces of the Karoo farm where Ainslie had spent his childhood. Ainslie took pride in the fact that he was descended from 1820 Settlers (a group of some 4 000 Britons sent out to settle the district of Albany in the Eastern Cape) who had fought against slavery and for press freedom. He updated their principles by championing multi-racial art education: he believed that South African culture was stultified by people's isolation from one another. Wally would long remember the excitement of that house on Jubilee Road, the jacaranda blossoms popping underfoot as he hurried toward it.

Many of the people who gathered there were artists of one kind or another – writers, poets, actors, and dramatists. Some of the women were models. The house was a refuge from the laws prohibiting social events where black and white mixed. Intuitive and romantic, Dumile was prone to fall in love with people and ideas and experiences, and there was plenty of scope for adventure in the Ainslie house.

From 1970 Wally would include Thami in similar forays among the Johannesburg avant-garde. He would introduce him to the bureau chief for Agence France Presse, Claude Juvenal, whose Italian wife would translate Wally's poems and photograph him. Through his friendship with Nadine Gordimer, forged at about the same time in small local literary circles, Wally would come to know the work of West African writers like Léopold Senghor, Christopher Okigbo, and Wole Soyinka.[17] The beauty of the white suburbs must have generated rueful discomfort in the two young men, as they reflected on the squalor of Alex, while delighting in the widening of their world. Wally would later reflect that during this period he was living 'in the twilight', belonging fully neither to the white suburbs nor to Alex.[18]

And indeed their world needed widening because African literary and visual arts had suffered gravely in the 1960s. By 1966 the government had banned the work of virtually every established African writer. Some people managed to read them, of course, but clandestinely. Their names conjure up the vanished optimism of the high-spirited 1950s: Todd Matshikiza, Dennis Brutus, Ezekiel Mphahlele, Lewis Nkosi, Alex La Guma, Can Themba. Wally and one other poet, Oswald Mtshali, then working as a driver at an advertising agency, were rising to take their place, both advised by Barney Simon and Lionel Abrahams.

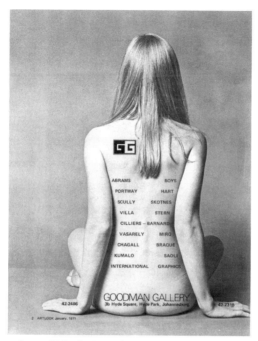
Summer 1970/1 advertisement for Goodman Gallery, Johannesburg.
(Courtesy of the Goodman Gallery)

The government had not bothered to ban painters, but work by black artists was as absent from galleries and museums as if it had. In the mid-1960s Gallery 101 was one of the few Johannesburg galleries to devote exhibitions to African artists. Its French owner, Mme Fernande Haenggi, had contracted with Dumile to sell his sculptures, after giving him his first solo show in 1963. The Goodman Gallery in Hyde Park, a Johannesburg suburb, must have inflamed some humourless bureaucrats in late 1970 when it advertised its artists by placing their names on the back of a naked white woman. And yet even Goodman mounted solo shows for only five African artists – Dumile, Julian Motau, Leonard Matsoso, Winston Saoli, and Cyprian Shilakoe – between 1967 and 1972.

Dumile and his disciple, Motau, the most overtly political of the group, both sketched tortured feelings and scenes in charcoal. Matsoso chose to depict slightly more oblique subject matter, like a bullfight, by drawing massive, sculptural figures. Saoli and Shilakoe drew or etched dreamscapes, mystical renderings of a personal world. These five artists defined the commercially viable range of African art as the sixties turned into the seventies.

That Linda Goodman put on so few shows by black artists – one a year, on average – suggests that the South African art market at that time simply wouldn't support African visions. Colonial attitudes shaped what many white South Africans revered: they either considered Old Masters to be indices of European cultural greatness, or they admired patriotic and curiously unpeopled Southern African landscapes. The nature of South African museum holdings – most bought only European art – and the country's distance from major collections kept South African art provincial. Thami could barely discern international artistic currents from his vantage point at the foot of Africa.

In any case, black South Africans had virtually no institutional apparatus for acquiring painterly lore and skills. There were no books about black artists, so people like Thami had to learn by word of mouth about the pioneering black painters of the 1940s, men like Gerard Sekoto, John Mohl, and Ernest Mancoba. (All three studied art in Europe, but only Mohl resisted the temptation to stay in exile, coming home from Germany to settle in Cape Town.) Shortly after Thami's birth, the Johannesburg City Council had set up the Polly Street Art Centre and, in 1952, staffed it with Cecil Skotnes as a 'cultural recreation officer'. South African-born Skotnes 'discovered' African art one year later through the work, ironically, of two German artists. His newfound respect for African design inspired a highly influential effort, in the words of critic Steven Sack, to 'search for an expressive language informed by Africa'.[19] Though strapped for money, Skotnes and his colleague, sculptor Sydney Khumalo, offered workshops at Polly Street that encouraged artists to develop styles blending Western and African artistic traditions. While apartheid laws and ideology were, at best, extraordinarily unencouraging to black artists, they could not block the urge to forge a modern African aesthetic. Thami's ambitions had a long 20th-century pedigree.

In 1971 these ambitions were stoked when he met a dashing musician, Molefe Pheto, who had just come home after studying classical music for four years at the Guildhall School of Music and Drama in London and was now working as musical and cultural programme director at Dorkay House, the down-town home of the African Music and Drama Association, a node of black creativity. A handsome man radiating lively intelligence, Molefe played the trumpet and was a serious collector of records; he was also writing a novel and poems and directing plays.

Thami and four close friends – Setshedi or 'Squeezy', Montshiwa Moroke, Baba Jordaan, and Wally – had read press reports about the triumphal return of this Alexandra native. Keen not only to meet him but also to join creative forces, they went to his home and asked if they could work together. They said, 'Let's found a theatre group toward a liberatory art form to let our people know they must be free. We should use the theatre not to say "oppress us kindly", but "get off our backs".' Molefe's devoted wife, Deborah, a nurse, intuitively believed the young men were not informers and convinced Molefe to join them.[20]

Molefe and five young black men gathered under a tree in Alex one October morning to discuss how 'to uplift black life and present it through our own eyes'. By afternoon they had founded a black theatre group called Mihloti, a word that means 'tears' in Xitsonga; it is the name given to a child born at a time of mourning. Mihloti members were determined 'to control whatever we produced', which meant, for example, having Wally's book cover designed by a black artist, preferably from within Mihloti itself.

The following year Molefe acted as the main catalyst in founding an arts troupe called, less poetically, MDALI (Music, Drama, Arts and Literature Institute); afterwards they discovered the acronym meant 'creator' in Zulu. Drawing its performers more broadly from the entire city of Johannesburg than had the Alex-based Mihloti, it also sought to seduce audiences with music first, and then give them a dose of prideful black poetry. According to Molefe, they chose 'hard black writers … as opposed to the "house nigger". Malcolm X in Soweto. Fanon in Alexandra Township. Neto at black universities. McCurien in Mamelodi. The Diops in Tembisa …' Only 18 people showed up at the first performance in the YMCA Hall, Orlando East, but the second time they played to a full house. Each year they added one new work. In addition to moving among 'all the major ghettos of our country', they ventured into Botswana and Swaziland. They added African percussion instruments and planned to follow up with a programme of indigenous dance. Never short of energy or dreams, the young men, rarely numbering more than 12, even talked of linking MDALI with theatre troupes throughout the diaspora.[21] Wally's grandmother took one look at their dashikis and announced that they looked like women.

Mihloti and MDALI followed an urban artistic tradition begun in the 1960s when groups like the Malombo Jazz Men included dramatic readings in their performances. The musicians would declaim poetry that some called 'virile' because it boasted so resoundingly of African strength and anger; they liked to talk of spears pivoting in the punctured marrow of the villain. Membership was highly fluid: people moved in and out of a variety of similarly named groups – Dashiki, Malombo Jazz Messengers or Makers – according to their allegiances of the moment. Based in the lively Pretoria township of Mamelodi, or in GaRankuwa, a rural township to the northwest, these groups had benefited from contact with the American Embassy. In the early 1970s the Loveday Street, Pretoria, home of South Africa's first African-American diplomat, James Baker, became 'like an arcade … open to all' where African men dressed up in suits and ties to listen to jazz; Baker was known to loan books readily and not to mind when they weren't returned.[22] Baker and the books linked Mihloti to similar community arts organisations founded in black America in the 1960s. They all frankly aimed to use culture to bind a community that could then struggle to liberate itself.

Thami got the first of his two big breaks in 1972 when Gallery 101 chose to exhibit one of his pieces in a show devoted to 25 black artists, many of whom had almost heroic stature in his eyes. His conté (hard chalk) crayon drawing hung alongside work by Dumile, Azaria Mbatha and Sydney Khumalo, all of whom had already exhibited internationally. The medium of most pieces – watercolour, pencil, charcoal, pen and ink – underscored the limited resources of the artists. Thami's untitled drawing was priced at R75, considerably less than work by better-known artists could fetch; a sandstone sculpture by Lucas Sithole was priced at nearly R1 000, though there is no evidence that either it or Thami's work sold. *Bantu*, a government magazine, ran an illustrated article referring to the recent explosion of 'promising artists'. A few years before, it said, Khumalo, Dumile, and his recently deceased disciple, Julian Motau, were 'virtually the only well-known ones in Bantu art'. The Afrikaans newspaper *Die Vaderland* ran a review under the headline 'Daar is min vordering in Bantoes se kuns (There is little progress in Bantu art)'.[23] Titles like ' Idlers', 'Gamblers', and 'Penny whistler' suggest that much of the work in the 1972 show belonged to the genre of 'township art'. But it was exposure, and a welcome exposure for Thami.

His second break came the same year, as a direct result of Wally's own breakthrough as a writer. Through two Wits students Wally had become the only black member of Lionel Abrahams's writers' workshop. When he had written enough poems to assemble as a manuscript he took them to Abrahams, the pivot of this 'reading circle'. Abrahams, a poet, was then editing a frivolously named but quite serious literary magazine, *The Purple Renoster*. (*Renoster* is Afrikaans for 'rhinoceros'.) Despite their occasional artistic quarrels, when Wally would snatch back his manuscript and leave, he respected the sensitivity and skill of the older man. The title of his collection, though, caused some heated discussion; who would understand that 'Yakhal' inkomo' meant the bellow of a cow or ox; would anyone know it was a volume of poetry? And so, the word *Poems* was placed above the Xhosa words on the cover.

Abrahams had no doubts about the value of Wally's work. He praised its subtlety, complexity and originality, even though he rebelled against the melding of political and artistic expression. He distrusted activism and 'intensified morality'. He preferred to express his own outrage by writing editorials in *Purple Renoster* protesting against the banning of a range of African writers in 1963 and 1966. The silencing clause, he fumed, was 'a direct assault upon the indivisible spirit of man, whose thought, whose essential life, is a life of words'.[24] (The issue of the journal containing these words was also banned.) Along with his own mentor, the South African short-story writer Herman Charles Bosman, Abrahams believed 'Art and

YAKHAL'INKOMO
Mongane Wally Serote

Thami Mnyele, untitled cover of *Yakhal' Inkomo*, 1972 (1983 edition).

life and God are one'. This credo meant that high critical standards had to be maintained in the arts. Abrahams thought that even victims of unjust regimes or those who sought to change the world through politics should not be spared from rigorous criticism. Only when its art was true to life would South African literature rise. Abrahams found his ardent individualism challenged by the collectivist ethic that, Wally argued more and more passionately, lay at the heart of African culture.

Some people believe that *Yakhal* signified 'an irrevocable shift in the centre of gravity of South African literature', presumably from British to African models and experience.[25] Abrahams, whose two partners had raised funds to subsidise the publication, called the book a 'publishing triumph' because 'black poetic voices had been rare and never so appealingly accessible, so rich in the testimony of experience'.[26] Wally's poetry comments on South African society with acute though subtle honesty, salted with a few black Americanisms like 'ofay' and 'manchild' and the word 'black' itself. He reflects on the damage incurred in a place like Alex where children give birth to children, where men carry passes and wear frozen expressions, and women leave in the early hours to serve morning tea to women 'sick with wealth'.[27] Neither Wally nor Mtshali preached revolution in their first volumes. They were interested in recording what was, rather than in declaring what should and should not be.

After discussing the matter in Mihloti, Wally asked Thami to draw the cover of *Yakhal' Inkomo*. Responding to the poems voicing distress and begging for maternal comfort, Thami drew a pregnant figure with a baby still on her back. The creatures themselves were neither comforting nor fully human. Sightless and bowed, they seem nascent beings, not yet defined or active.

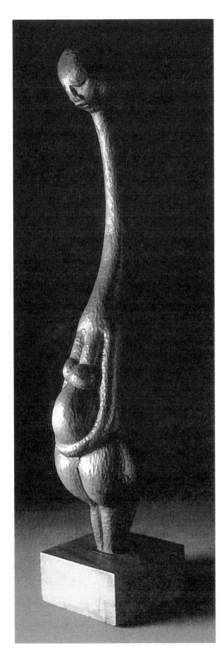

Thami appears to have interpreted one poem, entitled 'Mother and child', in which 'The mother clings her hands / At the back, the child should not fall'.[28] That he portrayed the mother as an embattled protector may reflect his own experience. Perhaps he was referring sorrowfully to Mantsopo, his young girlfriend in Makapanstad who had borne his child. He may even have been inspired by the work of a sculptor named Thomas Masekela, who had lived in Alexandra as a health inspector during his childhood. By transforming a ball and claw leg from an abandoned table, Masekela had carved a maternal figure strikingly similar to, but far more comforting than, Thami's creation.

The newly published poet held an 'African' book launch, complete with home-brewed beer and a roasted sheep, behind his grandmother's solid house on Seventh Avenue in Alexandra. Molefe Pheto remembers that the group believed an African launch, one that offered thanks to the ancestors, was long overdue. Molefe's wife Deborah brewed and strained the beer because no others among the assembled girlfriends and wives knew how. Having thought all the work of slaughtering would, by default, fall on his shoulders, Molefe was 'amazed at Wally's skills from slaughtering to skinning and finally carving and disembowelling the beast; he was expert. All those who were there were learning from him. As soon as I realised his expertise, I stopped bothering and spent most of the evening drinking the beer that had been freshly strained.'[29] While a more conventional launch took place at the Orlando East YWCA, people felt they were witnessing a revolution: 'to get things done the way we wanted was an innovation'; 'we can tell our own story'; 'this is the first book cover by a black South African'.[30]

Thomas Masekela, untitled sculpture, teak, 76 x 14 x 15 cm, Elsie Williams Collection.

In the yard where Wally launched his book there was a detached room. In another neighbourhood it would have been the servant's quarters. Wally and Thami called it 'The Office', and it became Thami's new base in his beloved Alex in 1972 after Mrs Mnyele sold the Sixth Avenue house and moved to Tembisa, a new township northeast of the city. There Wally and Thami normally stayed, bringing their friends to talk at all hours, blasting the surrounding area with the recorded sounds of Miriam Makeba, John Coltrane, Joan Baez, Nina Simone. Often they would follow those sessions with forays into live music, visiting Dorkay House where Sowetans, too, would gather to hear Dollar Brand, Kippie Moeketsi, Abigail Kubeka, Sophie Mgcina, Early Mabuza, Mackay Davashe, and many other local jazz greats. 'Jika' Twala observed, 'We made the [American] music our own. When we played, we drew crowds so dense that people seemed to be hanging on the air. We drowned our whatever in the music.'[31]

Thami and Wally disapproved of imitative music. They agreed with the sentiment expressed by Dollar Brand, one of their musical heroes, who had recently converted to Islam and adopted the name Abdullah Ibrahim: too much South African music was 'commercial crap'. 'In South Africa,' Ibrahim announced to *Drum* magazine before sweeping onto an airplane in 1969, 'there has been no reaction musically to our oppression.' No one, he went on, had created an original art form like the Blues of the American South. The few local artists like Mankuku Ngozi who rejected 'foot-tapping, happy-go-lucky jive' were losing popular favour.[32] Dispirited, the vast majority of the talented others – Chris McGregor, Hugh Masekela (the son of sculptor Thomas), Dudu Pukwana, Jonas Gwangwa, Mongezi Feza, Makaya Ntshoko, Sonny Pillay – had, like Ibrahim, left the country.

South Africa, Thami and Wally believed, needed an artist like John Coltrane; someone who could defy convention, reach deep into himself, and say something new. In Coltrane's case, those sounds were often violent. To paraphrase critic Amiri Baraka, whom the young artists also devoured, Coltrane dared to murder the popular song and do away with weak Western forms.[33] Whether Coltrane's sound was mellow, jaunty, or screaming, they loved his confidence. It helped that Coltrane, who composed pieces entitled 'Liberia' and 'Dahomey', apparently loved Africa, too.

Soft-spoken and humble, Thami lingered on the fringes of the crowds at shebeens or concerts, listening with absorption but never thrusting himself into the fray. While drunks raised their voices, he never displayed anger himself. Instead, he would observe with empathy, 'That drunk is actually crying.'[34] He showed greater interest in children and old people than in the antics of his peers. They would see him leave their company to cross the street and talk, rather, to an old man passing by. Sometimes he would lose interest in beer-sodden arguments altogether and simply walk home alone from a shebeen, even in the middle of the night when the streets belonged to gangsters. Hours might pass before his companions noticed that their silent partner was gone. The next day Wally would berate him for putting his life at risk, but even a friend's words failed to stop his solitary ways. His temperament, like his love of drawing, set him apart.

Thami particularly loved Nina Simone's song 'To be young, gifted, and black'. It could have been the anthem of his milieu. There was, for example, a room on Fifteenth Avenue where people gathered to talk so intensely about ideas – Maoism, Marxism, existentialism – that they called themselves 'the intellectuals'. The room belonged to Masindi ('Sindy') Radley, a classmate of Wally and the only woman included as an equal by a group of half a dozen intense and cerebral young men. Sindy remembers that one cynic, Moji Mokone, treated her dismissively because she felt too shy to hold forth in that company of men. Moji dubbed them all, inaccurately, the 'pseudo-intellectuals'. Hungry for ideas and a wider analytical understanding of their world, they sought out progressive whites – writer and academic Tim Couzens, Lionel Abrahams, playwright Paul Slabolepszy – as well as Africans with interests similar to those of the departed Dumile, with whom they could talk about art and about politics. Thami sometimes came to gatherings of 'the intellectuals' with his drawings under his arm, and when he exhibited with the 24 other African artists at Gallery 101 in 1972 he introduced these young and gifted comrades to the gallery world.[35]

Sindy provided the vital connection between Alexandra and the Indian Ocean city of Durban, which, in a departure from its normally sleepy nature, was starting to generate new ways of looking at South African politics and labour relations. Mamphela Ramphele, a medical student in Durban, had introduced Sindy in 1968 to her boyfriend, a fellow student named Steve Biko.

From his base at the University of Natal's black medical school Biko had been eager, since 1967, to start an alternative organisation to the National Union of South African Students (Nusas), which he believed was dominated by white liberals too prone to obey apartheid laws. And so, Sindy brought back to Johannesburg first-hand news about the desire to establish an all-black South African students' association. Soon after meeting Sindy, Biko visited Johannesburg, where he was introduced to Bokwe. Spotting Wally walking in the street near his house, Bokwe, in turn, introduced the two younger men. Because none of 'the intellectuals' was enrolled at a university, Sindy provided them with the crucial link to a movement of black pride and self-help spreading among students at black universities. This movement, the South African Students' Organisation (Saso), perhaps tempered the pleasure people like Wally had felt in the small, defiantly integrated circles at the Ainslies' house. At the very least, Saso would allow them to articulate their ambivalence about having been granted privileged access.

Saso's manifesto made it clear that it was seeking to change Africans' attitudes towards Africa. The 'basic tenet of Black Consciousness' read: 'the Black man must reject all value systems that seek to make him a foreigner in the country of his birth and reduce his basic human dignity'.[36] This careful, psychological definition of goals reflected lessons learned from the PAC and ANC. At the time, Congress was able to spread its democratic message mainly at funerals and via clandestinely distributed leaflets; and from 1973 people could reliably hear its broadcasts from Tanzania on Radio Freedom. They still censored themselves, though, by referring to the ANC's successful campaigns to mobilise the masses in the 1950s as the 'big thing'. It was safer for the Black Consciousness Movement to launch a quest for 'true African style' and values and to disseminate principles through 'formation schools' than to bid explicitly for freedom. For the moment, pictures – of chains being burst asunder, for example – conveyed what most people did not yet dare to say. The National Party press even lauded the movement's efforts because they fell nicely into line with the ideal of separate development.

Saso invited groups like Mihloti and Dashiki to warm up their rallies by asserting their diasporic pride through song and speech. In July 1972 Dashiki performed at Saso's historic week-long General Students Council meeting at Hammanskraal, helping the organisation achieve its goal of 'conscientisation', which meant elevating communities' critical awareness of their situation. In Biko's words, they all wanted 'to engage people in an emancipatory process, in an attempt to free one from a situation of bondage'.[37] Saso members aimed to break the political silence inherited from the 1960s. They were so exultant over their success at mobilising the youth that leaders Biko and A O Tiro had to calm down the impetuous young revolutionaries among them who spoke of wanting to 'launch our own armed struggle'. The organisation was filling a void because the ANC was then, in Oliver Tambo's words, in a period of 'regrouping and recovery' after the Wankie fiasco and Chris Hani's critique of the movement's leadership.[38]

The prideful energy of the times was exhilarating, but it couldn't seduce everyone. In Durban thugs invaded the Lamontville township hall where Dashiki was due to perform, a mêlée began, and the drummer wielded a vibraphone bar as a weapon. Thami tried to use reason. 'We are brothers. Brothers should never fight brothers,' he beseeched the *tsotsis*. Even today Thami's comrades break into laughter when describing his earnest attempt to use the language of Black Consciousness to win over armed men.[39]

Other township folk preferred to be entertained by stories about unfaithful women, crimes, and bewitching. Some loved shouting their own opinions to the actors on the stage. Thami and his friends tolerated these free-spirited effusions, emphatically rejecting the kinds of theatre that catered to white audiences or that conveyed despair. 'We tell the people to stop moaning and to wake up and start doing something about their valuable and beautiful Black lives,' said one Mihloti comrade in 1973.[40] They embraced Black Consciousness as a way of building confidence without relying on white artists, critics, or donors.

And yet, every one of them had had to rely on white help at one time or another. Wally invaded Claude Juvenal's life, borrowing his car at odd hours; he partied at Bill Ainslie's; and Lionel Abrahams critiqued his writing. Any hint of dependency rankled. Seeking to escape from it, Wally suggested to Abrahams that he hadn't been properly paid for his poems. Similar feelings of resentment plagued Thami, though he expressed them far less aggressively. Aware of his own 'difficulty of articulation' he had tried to improve his technique and knowledge of art by visiting white artists like Ainslie 'who were as sympathetic as to impart their skills'.[41] When these trips to the white suburbs were followed by city-centre exhibitions and a few sales, Thami wondered what audience he was really producing for. Mihloti saved them all from the sense that they were selling out. It allowed them to believe they were waking people up and provoking them to act, though not yet in an overtly revolutionary way.

The young men from Alex had a particularly potent reason to feel angry at that time. The government was steadily implementing the 1954 Bantu Resettlement Act, abolishing the right of Africans to own urban land. Only 800 of the former 2 500 African landowners still lived in Alex. Mrs Mnyele had been one of them, but she relinquished her parents' home and moved to the new township of Tembisa. (Thami showed his young friend Dikobe Martins, also an aspiring artist from Alex, one of the new Tembisa homes; it had a tree stump jutting up into the living room. The builders, he said, had suggested it be used as a table.) In place of Alex's single-family homes, the government was erecting single-sex hostels, each one to house nearly 3 000 workers. The façades of the massive brick barracks were decorated with small coloured designs patterned on Ndebele wall paintings. Thami was pained by these cynical gestures to African 'tribal' style.

Inside, the illusion of homeliness was shattered by electronically controlled 'drop doors'. The authorities would lower them 'in the event of unrest', one administrator calmly explained, in order to isolate the troubled sections of the corridors 'for the protection of the residents themselves'.[42] The sight and sound of this construction fuelled the anger of the young Mihloti men. The removals were also tearing the group apart, as one friend had to leave with his family for Soweto and another was obliged to move in with his brother in the coloured township of Eldorado Park.

Thami designed programmes for Mihloti's performances and helped produce the group's half-dozen newsletters. Performance thrilled him. He enacted lines from Aimé Césaire's poem 'Return to my native

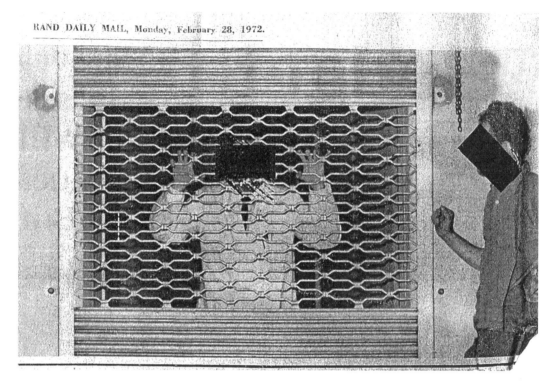

Alexandra Township's 'Hell-hostels: they can cause violence', *Rand Daily Mail* (28 Feb 1972).

land' and from 'When the revolution comes' (1970) by The Last Poets, a New York-based group who took their name from a poem by South African Keorapetse Willie Kgositsile. 'When the moment hatches in time's womb there will be no art talk,' Kgositsile had written, 'we are the last poets of the world.' The group had bought incendiary, and often banned, records like these, as well as the speeches of Martin Luther King and Malcolm X, from Kohinoor Records in Diagonal Street, in the city centre.

Occasionally Thami would strum a guitar on stage, as when he sang Nina Simone's 'Assignment'. For the first time in his life he was able to communicate his deep feelings to an audience. He loved the immediacy of it. His quiet demeanour allowed him to observe others closely, and he had become a splendid mimic. When he became Malcolm X in order to recite long passages from 'Message to the grassroots', self-confidence surged through him as never before. He would pretend to remove a pair of glasses and then deliver his lines with what Wally called 'a chilling slowness and deliberateness'. He loved 'standing there and towering over the little crowd of people of my township, seated, silent but nodding their heads

Mihloti
Black
Theatre

● Members of the Mihloti Black Theatre in action.

Montshiwa Moroke (left) and Molefe Pheto (right) acting in a Mihloti production, from *Weekend World*, 'People's College' (6 March 1977).

occasionally, when I had made another good point ...' Moreover, the stage gave him the opportunity to express the aggression and even venom he had rarely been able to vent.[43] Molefe, who had 'converted' Thami and sculptor Ben Arnold to acting and cast them in the Mihloti plays, thought they were better than 'real' actors because they brought to the stage 'the subtlety of sculpture and painting'.[44]

While some of his comrades had no apparent need for greater self-confidence, they all felt emboldened by the act of publicly declaiming the defiant words of black Americans. The young men of Mihloti read, discussed, and sometimes performed books like George Jackson's *Blood in My Eye*, Eldridge Cleaver's *Soul on Ice*, Angela Davis's *If They Come in the Morning*. They talked about the movements of Marcus Garvey and the Black Panthers. They used a speech W E B Du Bois had given in China. It was as if the wilting man Thami drew in 1971 had raised his head from his shoulder in emulation of the black athletes who thrust their gloved fists in the air at the 1968 Olympics. Thami drank in what he would later call the 'feelings of purpose and practical fulfilment'.[45]

Their context, of course, limited how much venom they could display in public. To avoid giving the security police ammunition to sabotage the group, they shrewdly used props rather than words to express extreme aggression. Silently brandishing mock AK-47s, the actors could send their audience into raptures. Journalists, like Don Mattera of *The Star*, wrote articles praising their performances. Commercial black theatre companies began to mimic their assertiveness, leaving behind politically neutral domestic potboilers. They replaced titles like *Unfaithful Woman* with ones like *Too Late* and grew tired of comics who imitated Bob Hope.

Then the problems began. The caretaker of the Alexandra Clinic, where they were due to perform, would vanish with the keys. Alexandra Secondary School denied them rehearsal space. Parents would send their children to Soweto on the day of a performance. It turned out that Special Branch policemen had warned the clinic and the parents against colluding with the young troublemakers. The size of the audiences began to wane.

Mihloti had 'start[ed] something different'. Its members had fashioned a radical cultural mix of inspirations that were urban and rural, American and African, church and secular. They extended this mix from the realm of music and put it on stage in both music and drama. And they took it on the road. Their shows were forging links across the region – with KwaMashu and Umlazi in Durban, with Grassy Park in Cape Town, with New Brighton in Port Elizabeth. Mandla Langa remembers the group camping out at various township houses when they travelled, with Thami helping the mother prepare breakfast for the 'hung-over hordes scattered in the lounge, [and] retreating, later, to draw'.[46] Ben Arnold's memories are more macabre. He remembers rehearsing so late in a clinic that they had to sleep over, only to find themselves in the morning lying uncomfortably close to corpses.

Molefe went as far afield as Mozambique to bring back art to display at their annual MDALI Festival of Black Arts. He drove with Ben Arnold in 1972 to Lourenço Marques to fetch paintings by Malangatana Valente Ngwenya and sculpture by Oblino Mundau. Displayed at the Donaldson Community Centre in Orlando, Soweto, for seven days in March, the art won an 'out-of-this-world response'. The show was so popular that someone stole its advertising banner on opening night. Malangatana's work was already priced too high for local people to buy, but all Oblino's work sold. One old man paid R203 so he could take the sculpture home immediately.[47]

Thami and Ben Arnold also exhibited but Thami refused to sell his work as he said it was unfinished; it was not yet what he wanted it to be. Soweto saw similar MDALI shows in March 1973 and 1974, timed to coincide with traditional 'first fruits' or harvest ceremonies. The festivals also featured a collection of black American literature to be viewed, not purchased – works like Baldwin's *Blues for Mister Charlie* and *The Fire Next Time*, Fanon's *Black Skin, White Masks*; books by James Ngugi (later known as Ngugi wa Thiong'o) and Ezekiel Mphahlele as well as lesser-known writers from colonised countries like Angola and Rhodesia, many of the works banned in South Africa.

While Thami performed in Mihloti by night, he was employed by day at the South African Committee for Higher Education (Sached). Its offices, in Rissik Street and later in Loveday Street, provided one of the few workplaces in 1970s Johannesburg where people of all races could mingle. They forged friendships despite the laws that forbade black people to drink coffee in the café downstairs, travel in the lift, or use the toilets on their floor. The aims of the organisation and the personalities of its members overcame many, though not all, of the resentments naturally generated by these petty restrictions. Some said the Christian Institute and the South African Institute of Race Relations were the only other places in Johannesburg at that time where whites could work for progressive change alongside black people.

Sached, funded by local and European charities and businesses, had been providing alternatives to state education for more than a decade by the time Thami joined it. That the organisation needed to be created indicates the lack of state support for black education; it also advertised the absence of black community structures and resources capable of launching this sort of innovative programme. In 1959, the year black people were forbidden to attend white universities, Sached was founded to offer London University courses to all South Africans by correspondence. After a decade it was obliged to shift its sights to secondary education and to upgrading black teachers instead; the quality of Bantu education was so poor that it had shrunk the pool of black candidates sufficiently prepared to pass the rigorous London exams. Sached's work was not without its own controversies. The Bophuthatswana (Bop) Teacher Upgrade Project, for instance, provoked intense internal debate in the 1970s, overheard and joined by Thami: would such programmes support apartheid by making bantustans like Bop more viable?[48]

While the debates were undoubtedly educational in their own way, Thami's precise task was technical. He was layout designer for the workbooks sent to students. He also drew the more dramatic biology, mathematics, and social science illustrations. Since there were only half a dozen people in the office during his first couple of years, everyone had to become a jack-of-all-trades. Overseeing these workers was a big-hearted and self-deprecating Johannesburger named David Adler, a man with natural empathy for the excluded. His home became another welcoming point on Thami's map of white Johannesburg. Wally, who had studied for his matriculation examinations with Adler's wife, Josie, introduced Steve Biko as well as Thami to Adler. The threesome sometimes pitched up there to spend the night upon returning late from a trip to the Eastern Cape. Thami came to know the house so well that he felt comfortable walking into its kitchen to make himself a peanut butter sandwich.

Adler's young brother-in-law, Andy Orkin, shared an office with Thami. They worked at adjacent drawing boards, listening all the while to a small record player set on the windowsill. Frequently asked to turn the volume down, they drew while listening to township jazz, Beethoven, Dvořák, Vivaldi, and classic Spanish

Thami at Sached. (Photograph from Mayibuye Archives, UWC)

guitar concertos played by Narcisco Ypes. The two young men, drawn together by their love of music and drawing, occasionally talked politics. Orkin respected Thami's attraction to Black Consciousness and was grateful that Thami implicitly accepted him as a South African, despite his white skin, but Thami never told him about Mihloti and its travels. They did take each other to visit their families. Thami was surprised to see almost as much bustling humanity in Orkin's Parktown flat as there was in an Alexandra home. Orkin remembers Thami's 'huge decency and civility'.[49] He did not engage in abusive and exploitative behaviour like asking for money or pitching up at 3 in the morning.

As always, Thami used music to communicate deep concerns. He once pointed out to co-worker Carohn Cornell an old man riding a bicycle, asking, 'Do you know who that is?' The man was one of South Africa's jazz greats, but he was living the life of a delivery 'boy'. Noting a further example of white ignorance, he said the South African Broadcasting Corporation (SABC) had just destroyed its collection of old township jazz recordings. He was furious at the arrogance of this destructive act. More frequently than it caused fury, though, music bound people together. After Orkin emigrated to Canada, Janet Ewing took his place at the next drawing board; she played a recording of Keith Jarrett's *Köln Concert* endlessly, suffusing Thami with a life-long devotion to the piece.[50]

If Thami ever lamented that his Sached job diverted him from his own art and from Mihloti, he had only to remember what his pay cheque would buy. He bought records – like Coltrane and Jarrett – from Kohinoor Records so often that the owners, the Valli brothers, greeted him like a friend. He built up a collection of jazz recordings from the 1950s onwards, of which he was competitively proud. He also bought books – like the volumes in Heinemann's African Writers Series by Ngugi, Achebe, p'Bitek, Soyinka – and became absorbed in their revelations about the rest of the continent, which he had never visited.

The dramas at Sached were not, of course, always about race. A near tragedy occurred one day when Orkin's long hair – a white man's Afro – got caught in the printing press. Printer Joe Setloboko turned off the machine just in time to prevent his skull being crushed. Another incident also upset Thami greatly, though it was not life-threatening. A bright African mathematician at Sached was so enraptured by Thami's beauty that he embraced him. Thami, ordinarily the gentlest of men, was so upset he threatened to bring a knife to work in order to defend himself. White staff members were told to keep out of the matter because the issue wasn't part of their culture, and it had to be defused by another African man. Thami was prone to fall in love, but always with women, and he kept the details of his personal life private.

In 1972 he gave Joe Setloboko a drawing of a man and a woman, entitled 'Love'. He placed the fashionable pair rather cryptically beneath a length of burst chain. The drawing represented one of the ways in which Thami was searching for an African aesthetic. The man and woman are identifiably African in their hairstyles: her hair is braided and he sports an Afro. Like the 1971 drawing of a man holding his fingers in a V-sign, the inspiration seems to have been African-American, that is, Africa as seen from the diaspora.

In 1972 Thami started to move away from this idealised and illustrative style. He began experimenting with more abstract figures, full-lipped and vacant-eyed. They look like a personalised version of African masks. At first, they expressed sentiments: a man embraces a woman, a cassocked priest holds an embryo-like baby and gestures toward a woman in a suit. He experimented with colour by placing the figures, drawn in black and white, on a red ground. He extended the mask-like forms into more inscrutable situations: a woman's lips and breasts are pierced by a spear (see p. 63); a gaping black diamond shape outlined in white sits on a red ground like a silent scream. Perhaps this last drawing was an attempt to visualise the cry of cattle – 'yakhal' inkomo' – for the cover of Wally's first book.

Thami Mnyele, untitled, 1972, Collection David and Josie Adler. (Photograph by Wayne Oosthuizen)

He also explored his own dream world for inspiration. Some African artists kept secret from whites the fact that they used their dreams in this way, fearing whites wouldn't understand or would regard them as primitive. Others, like Cyprian Shilakoe, celebrated the role their ancestors played in their imaginations. The subject of a one-man show at the Goodman Gallery in 1971, Shilakoe had even achieved considerable success with his representations of the spirit world, drawing tubular humanoid creatures with titles like 'When will they come back?' Thami used his dreams in a less spiritual way. He incorporated the head of a cow in an organic shape that encompasses one of his Africanist heads; the reason, he told Sached's Snoeks Desmond, was that he had found himself dreaming about a lowing beast after it disturbed his sleep. While the mood of this particular image is peaceful, others portray dispiritedness. Sometimes the Africanist figures slouch, like the maternal figure on the cover of *Yakhal' Inkomo*, as if they lack all muscle or sense of direction. One particularly spineless creature bears the title '… there goes a man … sad and deep in sorrow, like the river underground' (see p. 61).

One artist from Mozambique, Malangatana, created art that was both modern and African, and quite unlike Thami's. When Thami first saw Malangatana's paintings in 1972 they reflected the war Mozambicans had been waging against their Portuguese colonial masters for eight years. Large and vibrant, the crowded canvases expressed the anxieties of a man who had seen carnage and the inside of a prison. Creatures bare their teeth; blood flows from gored flesh; furrowed brows sit above staring eyes and downturned mouths. Malangatana situated primal fears in an African setting by painting mask-like faces and parallel zig-zag lines like those his own mother had tattooed on women's bodies. The Mozambican's style also reflected familiarity with the work of European modernists like Picasso, Braque, Klee, and Dubuffet. He had studied at art schools and academies in Lourenço Marques and Lisbon and benefited from the patronage of Portuguese architect Amâncio (Pancho) Guedes. Thami probably felt both inspired and awed by both the older artist's experience and the sheer boldness of his style.

Molefe told Thami and the other Mihloti members about his visit to Malangatana's exuberantly colourful home in a township near Lourenço Marques. Its red outer walls were trimmed in brilliant blue, and the artist had painted a mural on the ceiling of his dining room. There Molefe learned about Malangatana's philosophy of art, one that resonated with both his own and that growing among his young protégés. The Mozambican, also a drummer in a folkloric group, believed music was central to his work, just as it seemed to be to Thami: art, he said, is a 'musical instrument full of messages'. Because it is a 'collective expression' that comes from the lives of the people, it necessarily contributes to their evolution in every conceivable way. There should be no art for art's sake, none that cut itself off from the people or was too

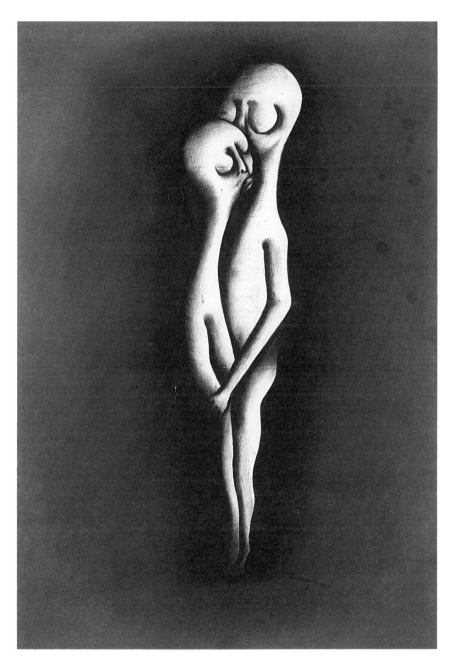

Thami Mnyele, untitled, 1972, Collection David and Josie Adler. (Photograph by Wayne Oosthuizen)

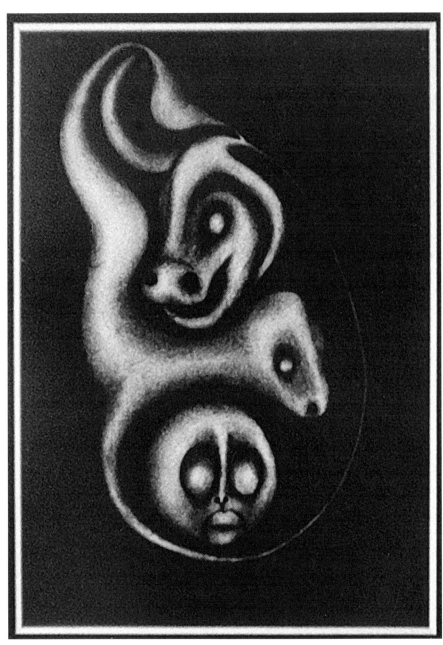

Thami Mnyele, untitled, 1972, 40 x 56 cm, Snoeks Desmond Collection. (Photograph by Snoeks Desmond)

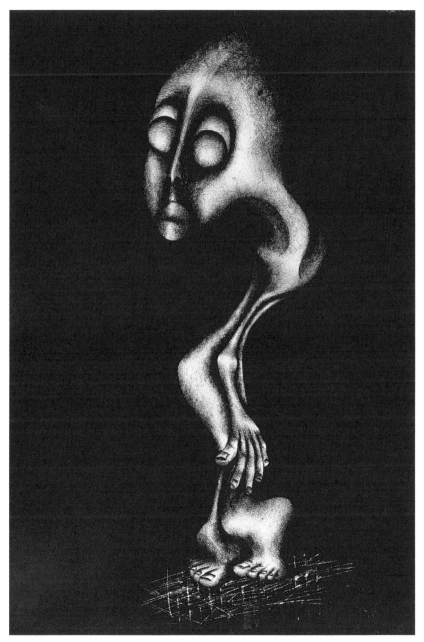

Thami Mnyele, 'There goes a man … Sad and deep in sorrow, like the river underground,' 1972, crayon, charcoal, mixed media, 51 x 34.5 cm, Collection of Iziko Museums, Cape Town. (Photograph by Wayne Oosthuizen)

obscure for them to understand. After all, Malangatana said, the black kings of old had merged religion and art and power. Thami had begun to learn about Frelimo, the Mozambican liberation movement, through discussions with his Mihloti friends. Malangatana's paintings and Molefe's stories were teaching him about the expressive possibilities of art that emphatically did not ignore politics.[51]

Thami knew he needed art instruction. Bokwe suggested he consider an art school run, he thought, by Catholic nuns in Natal. It turned out to be a Lutheran mission, and it had a good reputation. It was also the only place a black person could go to devote himself full-time to the study of art because the government had closed down the Polly Street Art Centre when Thami was 14, and its successor downtown, the Jubilee Art Centre, had folded when apartheid laws decreed that such facilities belonged only in the townships. Anglo American, the mining conglomerate, undertook to pay his fees and the time seemed ripe for him to pursue further training. After all, he was about to lose his muse. Though Wally was still waiting for the visa that would allow him to take up his Fulbright scholarship and study film at Columbia University in New York, he would doubtless be leaving soon.

Thami's journey to the Rorke's Drift school comprised a 320 km train ride from Johannesburg to Dundee and a trip by school bus 32 km further into the Natal countryside. He disembarked at a place whose vistas could have inspired an anthem. The rocky outcropping of hills provided vantage points over sweeping plains dotted with clusters of round Zulu homes. The sculptural acacia trees reminded him of flat Makapanstad, the sole rural area he had previously known.

The Rorke's Drift art school was matter-out-of-place. Established on the white land of Natal in 1962, it did not fit within the apartheid vision of how the races should be divided. In order to avoid arrest as a vagrant, Thami, like all the other students, needed his reference book (the much loathed 'dompas') stamped and signed each month by his 'employer', the school's principal. From its inception the school was staffed by foreigners, mainly Swedes. The government gave them short, two-month visas to deter them from making political protests; sometimes the authorities put them on 24-hour notice to leave, only to grant temporary extensions at the last minute. And so, Thami believed, the art teacher and principal, Otto Lundbohm, 'clearly avoided discussion on content in a work of art and we supposed he was afraid to jeopardize his stay in South Africa'.[52] Outside the school gates, life had been, and probably still was, dangerous. A local farmer had beaten one of his labourers to death in 1966. Peder Gowenius, one of the first art teachers, was beaten by another farmer at about that time. People thought the local postmaster was an informer and that their phone calls were sometimes monitored.

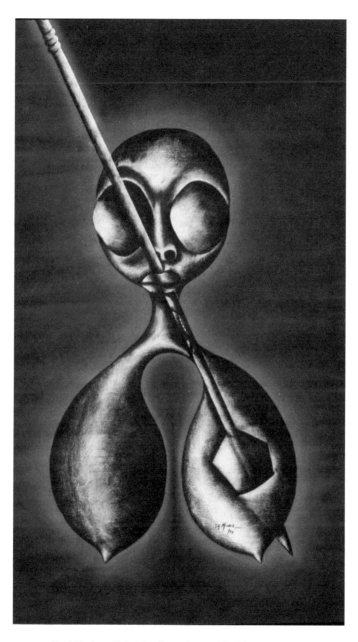

Thami Mnyele, untitled, 1972, Collection Ike Ramothibe. (Photograph by author)

Despite the hostile environment there was much to be learned inside the school. Rorke's Drift's two-year course taught linocutting, etching, sculpture, tapestry, graphic design, and also the history of art. Thami learned to make his first linocut and wood-block prints there. He found thrilling the moment when the paper was removed from the block and the design was revealed for the first time. But he wasn't happy.

Thami later said he appreciated that the school was 'something like a humanitarian institution where the underprivileged people would be encouraged into developing those skills and techniques which would enable them to be self-supportive.' He acknowledged that, by giving small paying jobs to local 'peasants', the school helped members of the 'starving Zululand community' to fight malnutrition. His barbed words, crackling with resentment at the fact and inadequacy of missionary paternalism, convey the politicised perspective of the 1980s, when he wrote them.[53] Cyprian Shilakoe voiced the same anger in the early 1970s. While appreciating what he had learned at Rorke's Drift, he complained, 'Too often the missionaries said: Look at what I have made. They put us, the Africans, on display. I do not always have to be saying thank you.'[54]

Thami resented the fact that he hadn't found himself at a 'top class art academy', a complaint that reflects not only his dissatisfaction but also the extent of his ambition. He wanted to be very good, even great, but found himself at a school that was suffering a bad bout of growing pains. It had taken in no new students in 1972 so there were no 'seniors' around to acculturate the seven newcomers, Thami's class. There was one art teacher, Lundbohm. Training in lettering, poster design, and colour were added to the curriculum only in 1974, after he left. And so, unlike fellow students Paul Sibisi and Charles Nkosi, who stayed on, he never tackled multiple block colour linocuts. Lundbohm and his wife were said to regard painting as elitist and didn't encourage it among their students. The Ellertsons, an American couple who arrived late in 1973, did add a basic design course, classes in drawing, a structured approach to painting, and more art history, but for Thami these innovations came too late.

He also complained that the school placed too much stress on religion, even though no one had actually taught religion there since the early 1960s. 'Much time', he later wrote, 'was spent under a deserted atmosphere of religion where only technique was the core of art discussion and learning.' Chapel was, indeed, compulsory, and the students may have felt obliged to choose biblical themes.

The Bible, of course, needn't inspire conservative imagery. Another graduate, Azaria Mbatha, proved that point when he made a linocut of a black David holding a white Goliath's head while white soldiers fled. Peder and Ulla Gowenius, the school's founders, had taken turns attending church in the 1960s in deference to the Lutheran missionary who paid Peder his salary, but no one proselytised then or later. Thami wasn't, in any case, hostile to religion, except when it diverted people from politics. Indeed, his friend Paul Sibisi saw him go to church; Thami, he explained, was a 'born disciplinarian' who 'emphasised respecting the rules that govern institutions'.[55] So, what precisely was his complaint?

When Thami tried to sum up what he acquired at Rorke's Drift, he noted he had gained 'experience from the principal(?)'. The question mark and the sheer openness of the word 'experience' suggest that he felt ambivalent about the way Lundbohm taught fine art. The tall, bearded, young Swede believed he was holding back from imposing his own style on students. He invited them to debate issues in his living room. He loaned them books – like Helen Gardner's *Art Through the Ages* and Goya's *Complete Etchings* – which mainly concerned European art history, though the school did subscribe to *African Arts*, the University of California-based journal that defined the entire field. Thami nevertheless experienced Lundbohm's reticence as politically sterile. He would later write that the mission art school 'confined itself cautiously' to teaching technique and '"art history" meaning European art history, with subtle avoidance of state confrontation. Maybe they subtley [*sic*] collaborated.'[56]

To learn more about the area and what it had to teach him about life, Thami sought out local people during long, lonely walks. Given his general sympathy for old people, his gentle manner, and his Black Consciousness-stoked curiosity about African artistic traditions, he undoubtedly won them over and absorbed Zulu lore in quiet conversation. His fondness for asking people questions – 'Are you enjoying life? What are you thinking?' – led them to exclaim, 'You are so inquisitive!'[57]

The general poverty of the area was eating into local creativity. Few people bothered any longer to mould black beer pots and carve wooden meat trays, let alone embellish them with bubbly, tattoo-like designs. And yet, some craft, like the geometrical designs on racks for storing sleeping mats, persisted and found its way into new forms, like the woven wool tapestries for which the school became famous. The sale of those weavings – women's work – helped to subsidise the school's programmes, to the distress of the weavers, who felt they were supporting the fine arts students.

Thami's life in Alexandra and Makapanstad had prepared him to feel at home physically, if not spiritually, in the school. There was no hot water or electricity; each student was given four candles a week. People slept two or three to a room on the ground floor of a large hall and official recreation mainly amounted to football games. Unofficially, people relaxed by smoking dagga (marijuana), a drug that had never been to Thami's taste. Thami asked for a room of his own so that he didn't have to put up with anyone's smoke. Occasionally the students visited art centres in Swaziland and Durban.

The times had primed Thami to feel restive. Political rhetoric was ratcheting up faster than political progress, and he took out his frustrations on the school. His disappointment would have saddened founder Gowenius, who set it up to teach *bildsprāk*, a visual language that would promote self-awareness and critical thinking rather than sentimentality and submission to white taste. Especially prior to the 1976 student uprising, the school's ethos could not but be driven more by Swedish than by South African political and educational concepts. Coming to the school straight from the 'conscientising' of Black Consciousness, Thami must have felt, and resented, that the engine driving his art education was foreign.

He was deeply conflicted. He wanted to be an intuitive artist, creating art from the bottom of his heart. He articulated this impulse clearly in words as well as in his images. But he also believed that artists should communicate strength. What if they were feeling feeble? He certainly knew weakness: sometimes his confidence would falter, and even his bodily health gave out from time to time. Should he not express these faltering moments? His linocuts, in fact, express both strength and a form of weakness that could be called foreboding.

Three of his surviving Rorke's Drift prints show children at play. They are grim-faced, whether they are fixing a bicycle, pausing from rolling a hoop, or sitting on the floor of a church. They appear joyless and stunned, overwhelmed by what is happening in the adult world, whether it is a funeral cortège passing by or a church service. They are either in the foreground or larger than the adults, passing silent commentary on them. Even when Thami produced a less explicitly critical image he achieved a similar effect. 'The obstacle', apparently influenced by Dumile's 'Fear', combines a stolid tree and ox with a leaping 'goblin' and a shrouded figure, its head bowed. To underscore the mood of being on a threshold, he entitled an earlier version of this scene 'We are still waiting'.

Being part of a well-known institution widened the exposure of Thami's work to outside viewing. Three of his woodcuts appeared in a Port Elizabeth show devoted entirely to Rorke's Drift students, though his pleasure must have been mitigated by the fact that Kaiser Matanzima, chief minister of the Transkei homeland, was given the honour of opening the exhibit. His work also appeared in Durban in the biennial show, *Art South Africa Today*, supported by the liberal Institute of Race Relations, which had inaugurated non-racial art exhibitions in 1963, and was still unusual in covering all art produced in South Africa without respect to race. A 'British art expert' and former South African, Pauline Vogelpoel, MBE, chose 136 works from a pool of 500 to display on the walls of the Durban Art Gallery. Among them were some of Thami's woodcuts, which a reviewer in the Natal *Daily News* described as 'sincere.'

Dumile Feni, 'Fear', 1966, charcoal and conté on paper, 132 x 75 cm, Pretoria Art Museum.

Perhaps Thami felt he gained little from such slight mention and from the Rorke's Drift connection generally, as his political comrades were continuing to display his work. In March and April it appeared in three shows: Mihloti mounted an exhibit at the Methodist Youth Centre in Central Western Jabavu, Soweto; his Saso contact, Saths Cooper, put up a one-man show in the Revelation Record Bar in Durban; and English professor Gessler Nkondo showed Thami's work during African Art Week at the University of the North. Thami's isolation in rural Natal prevented him from attending any of these events, even the one in Durban. Cooper's show was so glamorous that *Drum* magazine devoted to it a two-page illustrated spread, unfortunately entitled 'Thami and free beer'. Thami's drawings of tortured figures – those big-footed, round-eyed creatures that Black Consciousness artists commonly used to express their disenchantment – can be spotted behind the chatting guests.[58]

Because Thami was not happy at Rorke's Drift, he slept a lot and he didn't connect with most of his fellow students. For the past three years his life had been enlivened by contacts with other politicised artists. Now the excitement and growth and comradeship he had found in Wally's company seemed to have vanished. Living on a remote mission station, he feared he was following his father's retreat, as he imagined it, from politics into religion. The radio was his lifeline to the outside world, reminding him of what he was missing. He learned that workers were striking for higher wages in Durban, and for the first time actually winning them, but there was no sign of that defiance or success in Rorke's Drift. The old feeling of being a failure and marginal crept back.

He decided not to return to Rorke's Drift in September. At the time he gave more personal reasons than the ones he would record nearly a decade later. Writing to his friend Paul Sibisi in 1973, he explained, 'I must inform you of the honest fact that I am not prepared to study art anymore and anywhere academically, for I discovered the terrible fact that it won't do me any better than I was but channel or program me – an academic death.' The lecturer made him feel vulnerable when he scrutinised his work. More generally, he believed sharp academic criticism could discourage creativity. Creative vision – an artist's imperative to go beyond outward appearance and depict the inward mood of things – had to be respected. He told Paul that a secondary reason for leaving was his state of health. He had recently spent some time in a hospital ward with an unspecified ailment. He implied that his health wouldn't allow him to work until all hours of the night.[59]

Thami also left, he told Paul, because of his 'strict principles'. As soon as these are ignored, 'one is doomed'. He told Paul that the most important thing for an aspiring artist was to think deeply about the

Thami Mnyele, 'The obstacle', 1973, linocut, Paul Sibisi Collection. (Photograph by author)

struggle. The artist must read a lot and selectively. Thami himself was able to quote James Baldwin, Frantz Fanon, Stokely Carmichael, Marcus Garvey. An artist must walk tall and speak confidently, never wavering in what he was doing. 'We must show whites', he wrote, 'that we're capable of doing anything they can do.'

Thami used the occasion of a 'gumba' (a party in 1970s slang) at Wentworth, the University of Natal's black medical campus, to cut his ties. He took a long walk to the Durban train station and started on 'a lonely journey back home to Alexandra township, Johannesburg'.[60]

While absent in the Natal countryside, Thami had missed the travails of his friends. He couldn't have helped them, of course, but learning the news of their fate at the hands of the police and the courts must have made his rural retreat seem even further from the cutting edge of South Africa's future. At the beginning of 1973, as he was preparing to leave for Rorke's Drift, Thami learned disturbing news about Bokwe Mafuna, who had bought two of his drawings the preceding year. Bokwe had been banned under the Suppression of Communism Act along with seven other Black Consciousness leaders, including Steve Biko, Barney Pityana, and Harry Nengwekhulu. The banning orders sent them back to their places of birth and strictly limited their contacts with other people for five years.

Sponsored by Saso and Black Community Programmes (BCP), four of the banned men had been running a leadership-training seminar in Port Elizabeth. Rather than preaching communism, they were aiming to raise young people's confidence and skills so they could launch 'creative initiatives' locally; they wanted to spread literacy in the townships and propagate community involvement rather than ivory tower isolationism. Bokwe wanted to help bridge the divide between students and their worker-parents. The South African government still wasn't sure whether to regard these efforts as compatible with segregation or as potentially subversive, so it is not clear why the four men excited so much official attention. Perhaps it was because the Schlebusch Commission, a parliamentary committee investigating groups deemed a threat to national security, had warned only months earlier against the activities of 'liberal' organisations. Thami and his friends did not need to trace their victimisation to a specific report, though; they probably read their fate as part of the irrational 'system' thwarting their manhood.

When Bokwe failed to obey the terms of his banning order and report to the Alex police station one Monday morning in March, he was arrested. He used his trial to speak on behalf of all 'victims of unjust laws' and thrust his fist in the air, shouting 'Power to the people'. He was thrown into prison for three months, an experience that he says radicalised him. In September 1973, shortly after his banning order expired, he fled to Botswana, beginning the first of what would prove to be 20 years of exile, and Thami never saw him again.

Thami Mnyele, 'A church at home, as poor as a churchmouse', 1973, linocut, University of Fort Hare Collection.

A glance at what led Bokwe to choose exile helps to clarify the 'disenchantment' afflicting even the most privileged black South Africans at the time. In his mid-30s Bokwe had worked as a 'cub' reporter for *The World* newspaper, which he accused of engaging in 'yellow journalism'. In 1972, for example, *The World* featured a crime story instead of the Durban dockworkers' strike. (The paper headlined an Orlando township man called Vilakazi as 'public enemy number one', even though, Bokwe observed, Vilakazi had robbed no one in Orlando.) Bokwe also resented that national labour legislation required black reporters to register officially as 'freelancers' rather than employees, so they received no benefits. Whenever he made radical proposals – that white and black journalists, for example, should work under the same conditions – black reporters were fearful. They had to be converted to the idea that the workplace could also be a site of struggle.

When he witnessed the relatively uninhibited radicalism of the Saso youth, his long-simmering frustration came to a boil. For some time he had been angry with the media for not reflecting black life accurately. He and Wally had often said to each other, 'We are not saying our own story. If we don't do it ourselves, no one will.' When the *Rand Daily Mail*, which he joined after his stint at *The World*, removed the word 'black' from one of his articles and inserted 'non-white', he had had enough. He resigned. He then undertook full-time work for Black Community Programmes. Because this work resulted in his banning and imprisonment, he no longer recognised the South African government and its laws, and he said so in court.[61]

Thami and Wally had not yet reached Bokwe's level of radical commitment. Still waiting for his passport, which Nadine Gordimer was helping him to get, Wally was then working at the J Walter Thompson advertising agency. With his gift for words and his own middle-class background, he must have struck the personnel department as an ideal candidate for an ad man. The poet was being trained to cultivate the consumer tastes of the new black middle class. Wally drew Thami in. With his graphics flair he, too, looked like a good bet. His heart in his mouth, Thami took the elevator to the top of the agency's Carlton Centre offices in downtown Johannesburg.

Neither man lasted long at the job. Wally had the habit of arriving at work 'pissed'. Thami left to return to Sached. As usual, he didn't confide to his colleagues and friends the personal details of the experiences he was putting behind him. He preferred to tell funny stories about snakes he had encountered in the bush around Rorke's Drift.

Thami Mnyele, 'Come every day, come down to my home, come down to my home and tast[e]', 1973, linocut, 68.4 x 41.5 cm, Malin Lundbohm Collection.

NOTES

1   Mnyele, 'Observations', 1.
2   Bokwe Mafuna, interview (April 1991).
3   Wally Serote, 'Thami Mnyele: A portrait', *Rixaka*, 3 (1986), 5.
4   Interviews: Paul Sibisi (8 July 1989); Fikile Magadlela (22 May 1989); Piero Cuzzolin (13 July 2001).
5   Wally Serote, *Hyenas* (Florida Hills: Vivlia, 2000), 133.
6   Wally Serote, 'Liberated voices' in *Liberated Voices: Contemporary Art from South Africa* (New York: Museum for African Art, 1999), 15.
7   'My background of Alex made me feel extremely disenchanted, like everybody else. I wanted to use writing as a medium to express this disenchantment.' Quoted by Jaki Seroke in 'Poet in exile: An interview with Mongane Serote', *Staffrider* (April/May 1981), 30.
8   Josie Adler, interview, (22 Jan 2000); Serote, *Hyenas*, 132.
9   Editorial, 'Silent arrests', *Rand Daily Mail* (20 May 1969).
10 Serote, *Hyenas*, 40.
11 Doreen Levin, 'Yakhal'Inkomo', *Sunday Times Township Edition* (22 Oct 1972).
12 *The Classic*, 3, 4 (1971); Wally Serote, 'Oh-fay watcher looks back', *Yakhal' Inkomo* (Johannesburg: Ad Donker 1972), 57.
13 Wally Serote, 'When Rebecca fell', *The Classic*, 3, 4 (1971), 5–7.
14 Lionel Ngakane, 'Dumile: A profile', *African Arts*, 3, 2 (winter 1970), 13.
15 Mnyele, 'Observations', 3–4.
16 Mnyele, 'Excerpts from interviews' (originally in *Medu Newsletter*, 2, 1 and *Staffrider* (Sept/Oct 1980)), *Statements in Spring* exhibition brochure (Gaborone: Botswana National Museum and Art Gallery, 1980).
17 Gordimer co-edited a 1969 issue of *The Classic* in which Serote's first published work – a poem entitled 'Cat and bird' – appeared.
18 Wally Serote, autobiographical essay dated Jan 1995, MCH 115, Mayibuye Centre, University of the Western Cape.
19 Steven Sack, *The Neglected Tradition* (Johannesburg: Johannesburg Art Gallery 1988), 16. The two German artists who led Skotnes to African art were Rudolf Scharpf and Willie Baumeister.
20 Molefe Pheto, interview (2001); Molefe Pheto, 'Mihloti black theatre', *Medu Newsletter*, 1, 2 (June 1979), 41–6.
21 Ibid.
22 *Oto la Dimo*, Catalogue of joint retrospective exhibition of Lefifi Tladi and Motlhabane Mashiangwako (Pretoria: Unisa, 1998), 10.
23 'Artistic announcement', Bantu (July 1972), 16–19; Bonnita Davidtsz, 'Daar is min …', *Die Vaderland* (12 April 1972).
24 Editorial, *The Purple Renoster*, 5 (summer 1963), 5.
25 Michael Gardiner in Graeme Friedman and Roy Blumenthal (eds.), *A Writer in Stone: South African Writers Celebrate the Seventieth Birthday of Lionel Abrahams* (Cape Town: David Philip, 1998), 44.
26 Lionel Abrahams, *The White Life of Felix Greenspan* (Joahnnesburg: M&G Books, 2002), 101–2.
27 Wally Serote, 'What's in this black shit?' in Mbulelo Mzamane (ed.), *Selected Poems* (Johannesburg: Ad Donker, 1982), 42.
28 Serote, 'Mother and child', *Yakhal' Inkomo*, 37.
29 Molefe Pheto, letter to author (26 Aug 2005).
30 Molefe Pheto, interview (2001).
31 Simon Twala, interview (27 Dec 2001).
32 Article on Dollar Brand, *Drum* (June 1969); 'Mankuyku's lament: Jazz has lost its people with the touch', *Drum* (Jan 1970), 28–9.
33 Amiri Baraka quoted by Scott Saul, *Freedom Is, Freedom Ain't: Jazz and the Making of the Sixties* (Cambridge, Mass.: Harvard University Press), 229.
34 Ike Ramothibe, interview (18 July 1989).
35 Masindi Radley, interview (27 Dec 2001).
36 Quoted on the back cover of *SASO Newsletter*, 5, 1 (May/June 1975).
37 Steve Biko in Millard Arnold (ed.), *Black Consciousness in South Africa* (New York: Vintage, 1979), 120, 140–1.
38 Tambo, quoted by Shubin, *ANC*, 132.
39 Interviews: Lefifi Tladi (17 July 2001), Mandla Langa (3 July 2001).
40 Mafika Pascal Gwala quoting a Mihloti spokesperson, *Black Review 1973* (Durban: BCP Publications, April 1974), 113.
41 Mnyele, 'Observations', 3.
42 G J van der Merwe, chairman of the Transvaal Board for the Development of Peri-Urban Areas, quoted in 'Hostels rapped: Van der Merwe hits back', *Rand Daily Mail* (4 March 1972).
43 Serote, 'Thami …', *Rixaka*, 3 (1986), 6; Mnyele, 'Observations', 2.

44 Pheto, letter to author (26 August 2005).
45 Mnyele, 'Observations', 3.
46 Mandla Langa, unpublished obituary of Thami Mnyele, read at his reburial (24 Sept 2004).
47 Molefe Pheto, interview (July 2001).
48 Gareth Coleman, 'A history of the South African Committee for Higher Education (SACHED), 1959–87' (MA dissertation, University of Natal, Durban, 1989).
49 Andrew Orkin, interview (1 June 2002).
50 Carohn Cornell, interview (17 Jan 2000); Janet Ewing Callinicos, e-mail.
51 Betty Schneider, 'Malangatana of Mozambique', African Arts, 5 (winter 1972), 40–5.
52 Mnyele, 'Observations', 4.
53 Ibid.
54 Shilakoe, quoted by Hal Eads in an untitled memorial article, African Arts, 7, 1 (1973), 69.
55 Paul Sibisi, interview with Philippa Hobbs, 1 Feb 2002, quoted in Hobbs, 'Shifting paradigms in printmaking practice at the Evangelical Lutheran Church Art and Craft Centre, Rorke's Drift, 1962–1976' (MA dissertation, University of the Witwatersrand, 2003).
56 Mnyele, 'Thoughts for Bongiwe', Rixaka, 3 (1986), 28.
57 Paul Sibisi, interview (8 July 1989).
58 'Something of everything at art show', Natal Daily News (13 Sept 1973); 'Thami and free beer', Drum (22 May 1973).
59 Mnyele to Paul Sibisi (17 Sept 1973). I am grateful to Paul Sibisi for showing me this letter.
60 Mnyele, 'Observations', 5.
61 Bokwe Mafuna, interview (Dec 2003); Mamphela Ramphele, Across Boundaries: The Journey of a South African Woman Leader (New York: The Feminist Press, 1996); Karis and Gerhart, From Protest, chapter 5; Karis-Gerhart Collection, Sterling Memorial Library, Yale University, microfilm, reel 90.

Chapter 4

Trying to Live an Ordinary Life in Extraordinary Times

Dave Adler strolled down the Sached corridor puzzling over a graphics dilemma that had cropped up in one of the workbooks. Perhaps Thami could sort it out. Rounding the corner into Thami's office he found the young layout artist on the floor, rubbing boot polish into a large piece of paper. 'Look at my new style,' Thami called over his shoulder. He had drawn the back of a retreating figure, its flesh dissolving into pebbles, its head vanishing. Down the centre and right he had rubbed long slashes of red. At the margin he penned, 'remember me, I am going, time calls me'. Adler would later wonder if he had seen Thami rubbing his own blood into the paper.[1]

The style was indeed new. The full-bodied figures he had drawn a few years earlier were gone. So were the Africanist forms, perhaps based on photographs of West African masks. In their place he was using mysterious, open, almost dreamy imagery. The mood could be macabre, the figure disintegrating like a corpse into other natural elements. He seemed to be depicting the very moment of transformation, when a living being was no longer what it had been and not yet what it would become. One might detect, though, some wistfulness in the words 'remember me'.

Thami's new style came partly from the influence of other local artists. One stylistic brother was Cyprian Shilakoe. Thami seems to have drawn his title directly from Shilakoe's 'Remember me', and his style similarly invites viewers into a mysterious, private world. Shilakoe drew his images – like the bubble-headed creatures that surround his portraits of loved ones – from such deep, personal reserves that he has been called a 'mystic'. His pictures are more dreamlike than Thami generally allowed his own images to be; some called them 'sentimental'.[2] The two may never have met as Shilakoe preceded Thami by three years at Rorke's Drift and died in a car accident shortly after graduating. Thami probably saw his work in at least two places: a posthumous exhibition at the Goodman Gallery in Johannesburg in 1973 and a Rorke's Drift exhibit that included Thami's work.

Fikile Magadlela exercised a more direct influence on Thami and the two were often compared, usually to Fikile's detriment. They had met in 1970 through Saso's Cultural Committee, then spent evenings in Tembisa listening to music and discussing their art, especially their appreciation of Dali. Fikile didn't want to be called a surrealist, preferring to call his style 'mysticism'.[3] Painter David Koloane, Ainslie's student and friend, who worked closely with him at the Johannesburg Art Foundation, took one look at Fikile's idealised images of black people and observed that they were so obviously 'planned' and 'prefigured' that there was no surprise in them; Thami, on the other hand, had a much less self-conscious approach to creating a new visual world.[4]

Their temperaments differed, too. Though two years younger, Fikile was a competitive extrovert and didn't mind singing his own praises, as when he crowed that his ideas were 'like the river Nile, never running dry'. Thami's inherent modesty kept him from making such claims, and also from behaving as flamboyantly. Fikile, for example, once walked naked into a women's dormitory at the University of the North. It was the middle of the night during a Saso 'Africa Day' conference and he needed to pee. Thami cautioned him, 'I can see you're wearing a coloured string around your waist and a smile, but that's not enough around here.'[5] What bound these two disparate personalities together for a while was their love of drawing. Fikile was an excellent draughtsman.

Thami had absorbed drawing lessons not only from Rorke's Drift but also from classes he had taken, on Wally's advice, with Bill Ainslie. When he entered the door of Ainslie's home, he encountered an intense man in his late thirties with a rugged build and paint-smeared clothes. Ainslie lamented the 'really desperate' lack of facilities to involve black people seriously in the arts, so he welcomed all South Africans into his classes. They would draw and paint as they wished every day but Friday, the day they gathered without distinction of rank to critique each other's work. When Thami joined his informal classes with a couple of other young men from Alex, Ainslie found their approach to him 'guarded'. Others were more confident: Fikile went regularly, and Dikobe Martins found the classes enriching. Thami, already sensitive to criticism, was probably also daunted by the worldliness and assurance of the older white man.[6]

Ainslie's own credo was highly individualistic: an artist must search bravely for his own creative wellspring. He believed that Dumile had expressed a vision so original it could even be called hallucinatory. Less ambitious work fell into the category of mere illustration. He urged his students not to show man on the outside, but to get inside him. The difficult task of becoming truly creative involved 'getting used to being lost and … working in the dark'. As a teacher, he saw his role as guiding students towards what he called 'the threshold of the unconditional'. He scoffed at the idea that art could be didactic, 'We don't make art to change people, we make it to change ourselves, and if it works it will change others by the appeal it makes.'[7] Thami kept a very low profile in the classes, but he ruminated over these sentiments, while gaining new expressive skills that were apparent for all to see.

Meanwhile, a vice was tightening on Saso and its sympathisers. Thami's new style expressed the mood of heightened hope and fear. No longer finding Black Consciousness reassuringly separatist, the government began cracking down on it in early 1974. Individuals were the first targets. The newly brutal phase began innocently enough in February when a schoolgirl at Kgale Secondary in Botswana delivered the mail to a popular young teacher, A O Tiro, recently arrived from South Africa. The parcel blew up in Tiro's hands, killing him. The attack paid him back for a provocative graduation speech he had given at the University of the North two years earlier, when he told his audience they would become 'the vanguard in the struggle against alien rule'. The 'aliens' in the audience included Afrikaner professors and administrators. They cannot have been pleased to hear Tiro's brave words: 'the day shall come, when all shall be free to breathe the air of freedom which is theirs to breathe and when that day shall have come, no man, no matter how many tanks he has, will reverse the course of events.'[8]

The manner of Tiro's death, the first of its kind, was deeply disturbing, and Thami, who had met Tiro at Saso events, felt the death keenly. He had connected so emphatically with the bold young man that he wrote several letters to him, cautiously asking his cousin, Malebo, to address the envelopes, so his handwriting wouldn't arouse the suspicion of informers in the postal service.

Four months after Tiro's death Clarence Hamilton, an 18-year-old high school student, was detained for 16 days because he advocated boycotting Republic Day celebrations. The magistrate said one of Hamilton's poems literally called for violence. Rather than face a likely banning order under the Suppression of Communism Act and 'spend the best years of my life confined', Hamilton fled across the border to Botswana.[9] The government was apparently now finding even Black Consciousness poetry and graduation speeches subversive, an official stance that had clear implications for Mihloti's freedom to 'conscientise'.

Wally left, but his departure was cause for joy and envy. After a two-year delay the government finally granted him a passport, allowing him to study film in New York. (In the meantime, he had published another book of poetry, *Tsetlo*, whose cover – featuring a contorted seated figure raising its hand toward

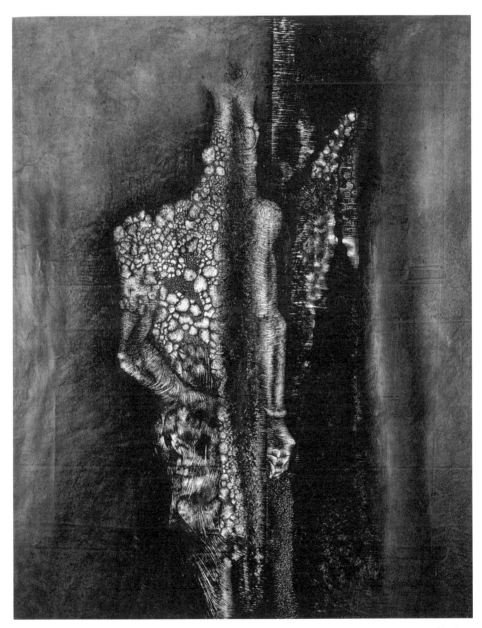

Thami Mnyele, 'Remember me ... I am going ... Time calls me ...', 1974, wax crayon, conté, ink on paper, 127.4 x 99.9 cm (sheet), Collection David and Josie Adler. (Photograph by Wayne Oosthuizen)

TSETLO

Mongane Wally Serote

Thami Mnyele, untitled cover of *Tsetlo*, 1974.

a departing bird – Thami had also designed.) In New York Wally would hear Nina Simone and Abdullah Ibrahim play their music live. He would see Dumile again. He would expand his expressive capacity by learning a new craft. He would escape the daily humiliations, petty and grand, of life in South Africa.

Thami was part of the 'retinue', as Bill Ainslie called it, that went to Jan Smuts Airport to bid Wally goodbye. A big white man and his chauffeur picked a quarrel with the group, challenging their right to be there at all. Thami winced. Ainslie noticed the expression of pain cross his face and realised then how much anger and frustration Thami suppressed on a daily basis. Because he was so 'introverted' he rarely let these feelings show, but the rage was there, bottled up.[10] Leaving the airport, Thami faced life in Johannesburg without the muse who had helped him express his rich emotional life.

Thami made two more pictures in his 'new style' that year. In one, which he called 'Brotherhood on Ninth Avenue', a figure advances toward the viewer, his head tucked under the arm of another man. The dangling arms of the second figure suggest the first is bearing his dead weight. One friend thought Thami was drawing a drunk being carried home, a sight often seen on the streets of Alex, where Ninth Avenue is located, but the picture is more open and mysterious than this interpretation allows. By wetting the paper and getting his pencil marks to blur, Thami managed to capture the act of glimpsing. He had thrown water at the paper to disperse the powder and suggest, rather than delineate, the rib cage of the carried figure. The two men seem to have emerged from the dark streets for only a moment before the darkness swallows them up again. By the time he drew this ambiguous tribute to comradeship in Alex, his mother had been living in Tembisa for two years and Wally's departure had just deprived him of his surrogate link to the place. Instead of conveying nostalgia or a moral lesson, Thami was allowing the imaginations of his viewers to enter freely into the moment.

Thami Mnyele, 'Brotherhood on Ninth Avenue', 1974, 41 x 50 cm, Judy Seidman Collection. (Photograph by Clive Stewart)

When David Koloane called Thami's approach intuitive and unplanned, he was describing the qualities in another drawing from the same year, 'The best of our kind'. In it Thami portrayed two exposed but genderless humans. One body is striated, as if its ribs were also muscles. Armless, its mouth downturned and agape, the person looks stunned. It has a foil: a person at the lower left has raised its right hand in a fist and has opened its mouth as if to express a slogan. The weight of the drawing lies with the passive figure, as if Thami were depicting the emotional consequences of inaction. Its title is more uplifting than its mood. Paradoxically, art produced within Black Consciousness, a movement that prided itself on hope, often expressed such despair.

While Wally prepared to leave, he had been putting finishing touches to his long poem *No Baby Must Weep*, published in 1975, once again with a cover design by Thami. Thami created a number of striking images to express the general mood of the poem, though only a fragment of his large drawing appears on the cover. Wally wrote that 'the moon sheds its silver sweat' above a sleeping town, complete with an insignificant little church, where the narrator has lived, suffered, and caused suffering. A waterfall drops sharply beneath the village, giving the entire landscape a precarious air. Embedded in the nearby rock face, itself buttressed by bricks, are three naked figures, arms outstretched, mouths open. They emit 'muted screams suffocating in the depths of the river'. The screams may have been evoked by the death of Tiro, whose name appears in Wally's poem only once, almost hidden at the end of a line beginning 'rest in 'pieces you beastly corpse'. Though Wally candidly admits fear and damage, he concludes the poem with a vision of the African child 'one day' coming home. Thami's imagery lacks this optimism. He has drawn an eerie vision of a place on the verge.[11]

Despite turmoil and loss Thami's world was expanding in surprising ways. In January 1974 the Johannesburg municipality opened public libraries and museums to all races. To supplement the used books that his Sached income allowed him to buy on the steps of City Hall, he could now borrow Jeno Barcsay's *Anatomy for the Artist* or books on his beloved Van Gogh. Perversely thumbing his nose at the law which had kept him out of the Michaelis Art Library, Thami kept the Barcsay volume and paid the penalty for losing it. He justified this appropriation to his friend Mpe by saying that the book wasn't available in bookstores anymore, and he needed it.

He refused to feel grateful that the law now allowed him to visit museums and see shows like the solo exhibit mounted at the Pretoria Art Museum by Judith Mason in 1975 (he seems to have been inspired by her use of bone motifs drawn in shades of brown).

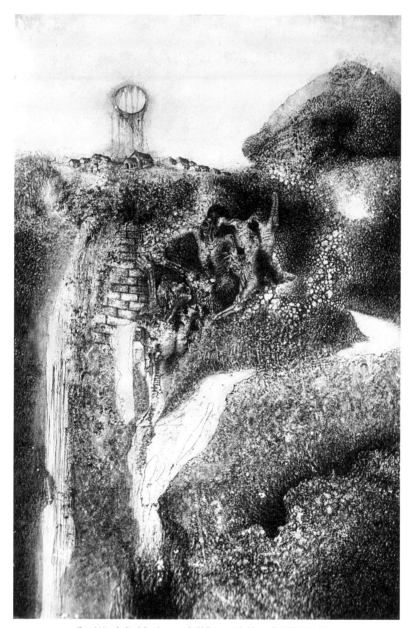

Thami Mnyele, 'And the river was dark' (later entitled 'Home'), 1975, 96 x 62 cm,
Botswana National Museum and Art Gallery. (Photograph by Mark Henningsen)

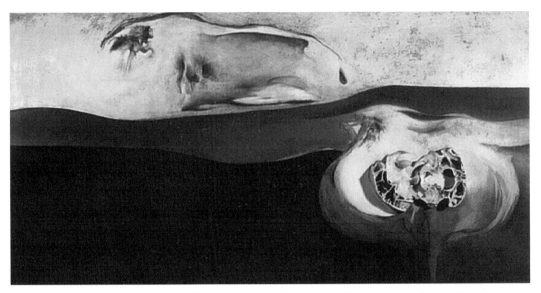

Judy Mason, 'Movement of a lion', 1968, oil and bone on masonite, 90 x 180 cm, Pretoria Art Museum on loan from the Haenggi Foundation.

The Pretoria museum was more liberal than most museums at that time; since its creation in the early sixties, its director had believed the work of black artists was integral to its collection and the museum should be open to all races. While the Johannesburg Art Gallery had long before admitted all visitors, it continued to acquire art belonging only to 'the last one hundred years of the English, French and Dutch nations from which South Africa derives its cultural roots'.[12] In 1940 it had bought Gerard Sekoto's painting 'Yellow houses, a street in Sophiatown', but not until the 1970s did it purchase other works by African artists, like Sydney Khumalo's bronze sculpture of a naked woman combing her hair, or Ezrom Legae's pencil and oil wash 'Chicken series', his oblique tribute to Steve Biko. The gatekeepers of high art mainly regarded African art as craft.

Thami accused most Johannesburg art galleries of impressing upon African artists that they should paint pleasing or pathetic township scenes. Unlike Dumile, whose work was 'an anguished outpouring of revolt' against the system, these 'township artists' made 'sentimental caricatures' of primitive people who were satisfied with their way of life. They would paint urchins playing penny whistles or eating watermelon, and the galleries would make 'thousands' of prints to sell. He believed the gallery world not only made artists compete to the point of speaking of one another with contempt but also deliberately

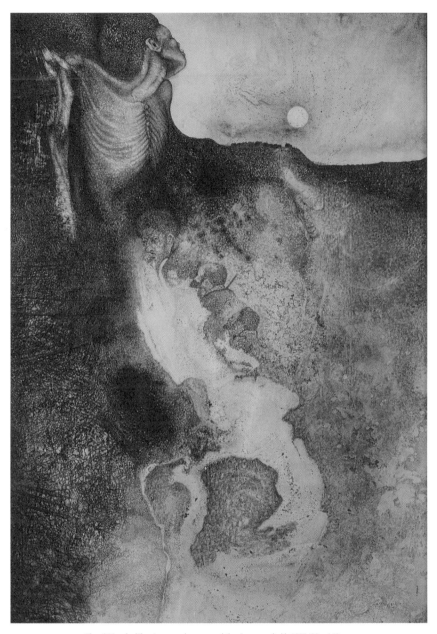

Thami Mnyele, 'The river was deep … and the river was dark', 1975, 98 x 140 cm,
Albio Gonzalez and Teresa Devant Collection. (Photograph by Lorenzo Fuentes)

blunted any political message. He swore that one director of a popular Johannesburg gallery warned him not to associate with politicians or they would ruin his art, just as they had ruined Dumile's.[13]

Thami was torn, though: attracted to as well as repelled by the recognition and money the galleries offered. Along with several other African artists he was invited to display his art in Pretoria's Arcadia Centre for two weeks in July 1975. The public space, on the lower ground level of a white shopping mall, surrounded by a hair salon, a liquor store, and Africa's Best Dry Cleaners, fell short of being a gallery, but it gave him exposure. The sale of a work would lead to 'a month's improvement of relations in my mother's house'. Of greater personal importance to him were MDALI's First Fruit shows, at which he both performed as an actor and exhibited.

The times, as David Koloane was later to observe, were 'exciting'.[14] They were not simply oppressive. Events in far-away Portugal were reverberating throughout Southern Africa. In Lisbon in April 1974 reformers in the Portuguese military had toppled a military regime determined to hold on to its African colonies. On 25 September that year, in the wake of the new Portuguese government's willingness to give up the colonies, Saso and the Black People's Convention (BPC), its non-student wing, tried to hold a rally at Currie's Fountain in Durban in support of a transfer of power to Frelimo in Mozambique. Two thousand people managed to sing the anthem 'Nkosi Sikelel' iAfrika' before the police attacked. Not only were the organisers of the rally arrested, the entire Black Consciousness Movement (BCM) leadership found itself in jail pending a trial that began in January 1975 and ran for two full years. During this time Mozambique became independent under a Frelimo government. The South African army invaded Angola to prevent a similar, left-leaning government from coming to power there. These events – coup, independence, invasion – not only led to a leadership vacuum in the BPC and Saso, but also unleashed various forms of havoc on almost every person and every organisation Thami knew.

Mihloti members had debated among themselves about the wars of national liberation going on in the Portuguese colonies of Angola, Mozambique, and Guinea-Bissau. Some members thought these wars were peripheral to Mihloti's concerns, but 'one scholarly friend among us, quite a sharp boy in terms of political theories', Thami thought, used the occasion to educate them about global imperialism. They listened to the radio all day long when Mozambique got its independence. 'All we thought about', Montshiwa remembers, 'was fighting, fighting, fighting.' By raising the issue of black collaboration with colonialists, the debates among these friends sharpened Thami's confusion over the anti-white bias of some Black Consciousness thought. 'Most of us,' he wrote, '... [tried] to convince ... ourselves that every single white-man is fundamentally a murderer. I developed a conflict deep within …'[15]

Thami later wondered 'why had MDALI never concretely come off the ground after so many years of militant articles in the newspapers?' One answer was clear: words of protest had limited use when the state used its power like a sledgehammer. On 4 March 1975 his revered mentor and the mastermind behind MDALI, Molefe Pheto, was roused from his sleep at 3.30 am by rude young policemen, whom Molefe silently called 'scum'. They brought him to John Vorster Square police headquarters where he was made to stand for days of interrogation and beaten. A Van Gogh print on the wall of his interrogator's office 'watched' while he was assaulted, making him hate the artist at the time because he 'was White, too'.[16]

The police repeatedly asked Molefe about his alleged ANC activities. Since he didn't support the ANC's multiracialism, he wondered how they could have imagined that he was a member. They believed Molefe had recruited Clarence Hamilton for military training and had helped him escape into exile in Botswana.[17] They focused obsessively on MDALI, some demanding to know whether the organisation was actually a person named Madali. The confusion suggests that their rage against a well-spoken black man who had studied in England and given occasional lifts to a white Canadian woman was visceral rather than calculated.

Molefe spent 281 days in jail, 271 of them in solitary confinement. The police shunted him around Johannesburg prisons until he landed at the Fort, in the middle of the city. He entered this turn-of-the-century fortress through a slit in a bland hillside that revealed nothing of what went on within. Sadism was the order of the day from the moment new prisoners passed under the emblem of the old Boer republic decreeing 'Eendracht Maakt Magt' (unity is strength): naked, they were made to perform an action known as the *tauza*, leaping with legs spread so warders could inspect their private parts; they used toilet buckets while the warders watched, leading Molefe to wonder at the jailers' 'nonchalance at their own debasement'; they ate rotten fish and curdled pig-skins; they were made to run madly through their chores, giving the place the air of an asylum. When Molefe and three comrades protested against the systematic humiliation, he found himself exiled to a 2 x 1.2 m cage covered with wire gauze. Earlier he had gained solace from singing freedom songs with neighbouring prisoners or from glimpsing the sun through the high window in his cell. Now, alone and in the dark, he wept.

On 10 December, Thami's 27th birthday, Molefe was acquitted after a summary review of a baseless case. MDALI artists, actors, poets, and singers sat in the courtroom, and Molefe saluted them with a clenched fist as he went to hug his daughter for the first time in ten months.

The police had not only ripped Molefe out of the Johannesburg arts community for most of a year, but a month after arresting him they took Mihloti's books and records, confiscating *The Last Poets* record and Montshiwa's banned literature. These losses spelled the end of Mihloti's first phase.

Thami tried to imagine the prison world he had learned about most recently from Molefe. His only prison drawing shows a man sitting on the floor staring into space. Far above his head a small window is crossed by four bars. Before him floats an amorphous black shape. Thami has rubbed red into the black cloud, but he has not been able to articulate its form in any meaningful way. An art critic called the drawing 'trite' accusing Thami of not having 'explored his subject matter with sufficient imaginative vigour'. It is true that the passive man betrays no thought or emotion; the black shape seems intended, but unable, to bear this expressive burden. Perhaps Thami's emotions were too challenged by the stories Molefe told. Despite his best intentions he had not yet dared to enter imaginatively into that world of lonely, dark tears.

Thami's reticence makes it hard to date his own detention but we know he was swept up in the repression at around that time. The police picked him up and interrogated him, making him stand on two bricks for hours while they pumped him with questions so he would tell everything he knew about Mihloti and its members. His future bride would later comment that the experience 'scared the hell out of him'.[19] While the detention was brief, it brought him closer than ever before to official brutality. He didn't want to talk about the experience, though he felt compelled to mention it to a few close friends.

He was not the only one among his close friends to be threatened by the security police. Montshiwa, then reporting for the *Rand Daily Mail*, went into hiding in April 1975, after the security police raided his Diepkloof home. Baba Jordaan, another of Mihloti's founders, was arrested at the Durban office of the BPC and sent all the way to John Vorster Square in Johannesburg for questioning. Brigitte Mabandla, youth organiser for the Institute of Race Relations and active in Saso, had been held for 171 days after the pro-Frelimo rally, and was then exiled to Tsolo in the Transkei. She and her husband, Lindelwe, fled to Botswana, where he began to work publicly as a headmaster and secretly for the ANC.[20] Khayo Mafuna was detained in November. By December 1975, 71 people had been jailed under the Terrorism Act, suspected of recruiting black people for military training in Botswana and elsewhere.

Meanwhile, homeland leaders seemed to be making their separate peace with the apartheid government. In March 1974 Kaiser Matanzima began to negotiate for the independence of the Transkei, an act emulated by Lucas Mangope in Bophuthatswana the following year. Mangosuthu 'Gatsha' Buthelezi launched the Inkatha National Cultural Liberation Movement (Inkatha) in June 1975, and the Zulu organisation soon began to look like a counterfoil to the ANC. The ANC hadn't been able to launch an attack on South African soil since 1968 and few young people knew its history. The movement would later partially explain its hard times by noting that the black population, burdened with state censorship compounded by self-censorship, had become demoralised.

One form that demoralisation had taken in Thami's own family was silence. Thami knew nothing about his father's political views and actions. He was used to hearing older people refer to 'politics' as if it were a disease or something forbidden. Nor did he know that his sister Lindi had the potential to protest.

Demoralisation was more than silence. It was a real psychological state, what 19th-century Europe had called 'melancholy' and the 20th would call depression, states of being Thami knew only too well. Steve Biko, like the ANC, spoke (while giving testimony in court) of the alienation of the black man: 'He rejects himself.'[21] 'Black people', Biko said, were 'steeped in fear' of the 'System', so they hid their true feelings. Demoralisation meant that the revolution had not begun. Thami's art succeeded in conveying what it was like to live on the cusp, looking into an unknowable future.

Were the times, in fact, so lacking in energy? The activities of Mihloti and MDALI seem to belie this view, and Molefe sensed people were crackling with new political life. A few months after his release from prison he would be offered a fellowship to tour the United States, but he turned it down because he could sense that 'something was in the air', and he wanted to be part of it. This 'something in the air' was not lethargy and hopelessness. The word 'demoralised' may have expressed middle-class underestimation of the uneducated. After all, labourers in Durban had been organising to demand higher wages and more workplace rights since 1973, and they were succeeding. So, when Black Consciousness adherents and ANC leaders in exile called people at home 'demoralised', they may simply have been expressing frustration that the revolution had not yet begun. They expected it to be violent, and the young men in Mihloti, who had absorbed the teachings of Frantz Fanon with enthusiasm, yearned for the chance to express their manhood through rage.

Events both domestic and foreign heightened the tensions in the Sached offices where black and white worked together ideally as equals, though their educational differences inevitably affected their status. Many of the organisation's white employees could be classified as liberals, a category of person Black Consciousness had gained energy from attacking.

Luli Callinicos, a radical historian specialising in the working class and later a biographer of Oliver Tambo, felt intimidated by black staff who radiated the belief that she shouldn't be writing about black people. When she published a story about an exhausted rural wife encouraging her husband to find a fresh, young co-wife, some black co-workers told her she shouldn't write about what she didn't know. Carohn Cornell felt the black staff treated her like a foreign aid worker, putting her on trial as a human being; their test of how well people did their job was whether they trained black people to replace them. Some whites provoked resentment among the less educated black staff when they dominated meetings by expressing 'lofty' and abstract ideas.

From time to time, the outer world literally invaded Sached's space. When the police unexpectedly dropped into the office to interview Janet Ewing about her stolen car, Thami receded into the background and said not a word.[22] The place was a limited haven.

Secretly the white employees sympathised with the multiracialism of the ANC, but no one dared to broach the topic in the workplace. There was a tacit agreement not to discuss politics. When Dave Adler tried to engage Thami in debate he would respond, only half jocularly, 'Why are you asking me these questions? Are you trying to colonise me?' 'If Dave Adler had his way,' Thami and Wally had said, 'we'd both be at Oxford and failed revolutionaries.' In any case, the movement the black employees adhered to in the 1970s was Black Consciousness and not the ANC. Receptionist Vesta Smith, for example, joined the staff in 1975, the same year she became a member of the Black Women's Federation, which rejected affiliation with white organisations. In her fifties, she was older than the majority of people drawn to Black Consciousness organisations, yet she used classic BCM terms to praise the clinic Steve Biko and Mamphela Ramphele had founded in 1975 at Zanempilo, near King William's Town: the clinic proved 'we could educate our people, and make them realise that they were human' rather than rely on 'the kindness of heart of the white man'.[23]

In early 1974 Thami had already begun forming a new network that would replace Mihloti, and its composition revealed his self-confessed 'conflict deep within' about race. The new group had a glamorous, almost international air. Fikile introduced him to Piero Cuzzolin, an Italian architect. Piero, passionately devoted to the arts, became a father figure and loved Fikile like a son. Thami might stop at Piero's for breakfast on his way to work, and sometimes illegally slept over. Unabashedly sensitive to beauty in music and art, Piero was happy to talk about and to store the artists' work. He bought them art books on ancient Egypt and Greece and one on Michelangelo. Because he came from a 'humble' background – his father had been a boatman in a small village near Venice, and he himself had been a 'socialist or a communist' growing up – he readily empathised with the young men.

Piero's young artists habitually drank too much vermouth, brandy, and whiskey as they sat around his Troye Street apartment on Saturday afternoons listening to classical music and jazz, but Thami was familiar

Ben Arnold, 'Family', terracotta, 43.5 x 26 x 25 cm.
(Courtesy of Ben Arnold)

with the bombast and lethargy of drunks and didn't succumb. At Piero's, Thami encountered sculptor Ben Arnold, a minister's son who was intrigued by Islam. (Religion and theatre provided good defences, Ben said, against liquor.) Together they went to the studio Ben shared with Ezrom Legae in the Jubilee Art Centre and to jazz concerts at Dorkay House, both in Eloff Street. Ben taught drawing and sculpture there, challenging students to draw a stone by holding it behind their backs and simply feeling it. These artists were exhilarated to share in the African renaissance springing up all around them, though no one had labelled it so then. As Ben explained, 'We were just doing what was necessary.'[24]

The romance of his working life was soon joined by another kind. A smart young radiographer named Naniwe had caught his eye. Their work was oddly complementary; both were fascinated by the deep structure of the human body, though their purposes were radically different. Her perspective was literal and scientific, while his was figurative and exploratory, but they could delight in sharing an obscure language when they referred, for example, to the upper neck as 'medulla oblongata'.

Straightforward in manner, radiating competence and confidence, Naniwe worked at Tembisa Hospital, not far from the four-room home to which Thami's mother had moved three years earlier. She fell deeply in love with him, fascinated by his 'spiritual', if not conventionally religious, nature and his profound feelings about oppression and insights into suffering. She recognised that it was in his nature to look at things not as others saw them, but to want to know more. 'Why not draw a sunset in full colour?' she would ask him in frustration. 'Why not draw a rose in full bloom?'[25] Her strong-willed mother and compliant father had given her a stable upbringing quite unlike his own, in a rural area of the Transkei called Nqamakwe. Thami appreciated Naniwe's practical strength. She was intelligent and down to earth.

He acknowledged that happy families were rare in the townships. Politics could fray marital bonds as easily as liquor and infidelity did. When a politically active acquaintance vanished without telling his wife

Thami with his first wife, Naniwe Mputa, in Tembisa township, 1976. (Courtesy of Naniwe Ramatsui)

about his underground assignment, he watched the loving and trusting wife dissolve into madness. A different fate befell Bokwe Mafuna's wife, Khayo. Two years after he fled to Botswana, Khayo was arrested at her school and held without charge for over a year, leaving their two daughters in the care of her parents. Thami and Naniwe's own steady and skilled jobs seemed to promise a more reliable family life, one that struck Thami with greater allure than ever before.

Things around him were falling apart. His mother objected to Naniwe, allegedly on ethnic grounds, preferring his previous, but now rejected, girlfriend, a Tswana girl from Sarah's mother's Kgatla clan. (Given her own mixed background, marriage, and liaisons, Sarah's reasons undoubtedly lay deeper than the simple realm of 'tribe'.) While courting Naniwe, Thami had to pack his trunk and move to live elsewhere in Tembisa, with his new friend, Nape Motana. Wally was in America and Mihloti was on the brink of dissolution. Even Alexandra looked impermanent, as the government continued to remove families to Tembisa and build its single-sex hostels with the goal of making Alexandra child-free, peaceful, and forever transient. Sam Buti, a Dutch Reformed Church (NGK) minister, who was leading a campaign to save Alex from this fate, helped people replace their doors and windows and move their furniture back into their homes after officials prepared to demolish them. (The Rev. Mnyele's children remember their father helping Buti to save Alex; one of his tactics was to perform marriage ceremonies so common-law spouses could gain the legal right to stay in the township.) People proved harder to control than a steel grate. When some removals succeeded, newcomers simply moved into the vacant spaces.

Thami took off from work the first week in May and travelled to Pretoria to listen to Steve Biko defend Black Consciousness. The movement's leadership had been on trial for a year and a half, accused of trying to bring about revolutionary change by violent means. As he sat in the back of the courtroom, Thami was awestruck by Biko's aplomb in responding to those charges. With candour, a shrewd understanding of history, and even some humour, Biko took care to explain to the court what was really happening in the country. He spoke of the 'misery' of the poor, confessing that he 'could not take it' when he visited a resettlement camp barren of all services and beauty.[26] He noted the extreme vulnerability of township folk to rape and murder. When he had visited artist Lefifi Tladi in Mabopane, for example, he had witnessed two unprovoked assaults on strangers.

Biko warned that black people commonly condemned white society 'in very, very tough language', thus deflecting the charge that his movement was creating inter-racial hostility. The BCM was simply expressing what most black people felt. And he often succeeded in making those in the court laugh, as when he 'doubt[ed]' that the Transkei would work as an independent state, or when he joked about the racial identity of the short-haired, white prosecuting attorney. ('Maybe people will take you for a coloured,' he implied, in a sly critique of the spurious ethnic category.) Exemplifying the hope and dignity he said Black Consciousness stood for, he asserted simply, 'I have a right to be consulted by my government on any issue.' Change was 'inevitable', he stressed.[27]

Biko commanded the moral high ground in the face of the prosecutor's insinuation that 'you people' were not 'developed' enough to deserve those rights. He asserted that the goal of one-person one-vote did not imply that white people would have to leave South Africa. As this goal was also part of the ANC's platform, he was implicitly endorsing that organisation. He could not reveal that for three years he had been trying to reconcile the two banned liberation movements with Black Consciousness.[28] He refused to disavow either the PAC or the ANC. What he himself may not have known is that Oliver Tambo now believed they should meet. (Tambo hoped to recruit the BCM to mobilise the masses, while the ANC led the actual revolution.) For the time being, though, it was too risky to arrange a meeting. Biko's base may have been among students, but his voice was carrying far wider. The courtroom provided him with a splendid forum for disseminating and clarifying his vision even among those who were, like Thami, already converted.

Less than a month after Biko's testimony, Soweto exploded. Thami experienced the uprising of Soweto's youth on 16 June 1976, with anguish, but at some remove. When the police fired on uniformed schoolchildren protesting against the imposition of Afrikaans as a medium of instruction, he was pained by the enormity of the response: the government tallied nearly 600 'unrest deaths' over the next nine months. Thami did not throw stones or set fires as his half-brother, David Sipho Mnyele, did. (At least this is what the police said he did. David argued, even in private to his family, that he had simply been picked up at football team practice in Alexandra stadium.) Thami did not, like David, have to face another round of interrogation at John Vorster Square, nor was he incarcerated, like David, for months in the Fort. Having left school behind, he had no formal means of joining the revolt. He was unaware that his sister Lindi was involved until he saw her picture on the front page of a newspaper. Elated, he put his arm around her and, waving the news clipping in his free hand, excitedly introduced her to the white staff at Sached.[29]

As a 27-year-old employed man with a fiancée, he had too much at stake to rush immediately to the border and offer himself to the armed struggle. His immediately pressing concern was that his father pay *lobola* (bridewealth) to Naniwe's parents, the Mputas, so the couple could marry. David Mnyele initially balked, arguing that the Transkei was too far away. His wife Dorothy had to intervene. Soon he relented and sent money to Nqamakwe. Cattle, the traditional form of bridewealth, were out of the question for an urban man. He wrote a letter to the Mputas, asking for Naniwe's hand in marriage to his son, and sent money instead. After that Thami was free to travel with Naniwe to the Transkei to meet her parents.

Thousands of young men and women did go into exile, swelling the ranks of the ANC so that by the beginning of 1978 there were more than a thousand trained MK cadres outside South Africa. 'Don't mourn! Mobilize!' had been the ANC's response to the massacre of protesting students. Before 1976 the movement's underground structures inside South Africa had been limited. Only a couple of acts of 'armed propaganda', designed to announce 'once again' the presence of MK, had disturbed the peace of the preceding year. After 16 June the exodus, in the words of one of the strongest Soviet boosters of the ANC, 'both stimulated and severely taxed the ANC'. The movement had to charter planes to airlift young militants to Luanda, Angola, before placing them either in the ranks of MK or in schools abroad. It also had to deal with undisciplined youth – even ones dreaming about robbing banks – who were not necessarily committed to the ANC.[30]

One full year after the uprising, the National Executive Council of the ANC dedicated ten days to discussing its impact. It wanted to take advantage of the economic slump the riots had provoked, as foreign capital fled and foreigners talked of imposing sanctions on a regime that shot at schoolchildren. The 1977 meeting led to the structural reorganisation of the movement; it had become abundantly clear that its political wing was seriously underdeveloped both inside and outside the country. The good news, as deputy chief of ANC operations Joe Slovo told the Soviets in the spring of 1977, was that the people inside South Africa were no longer demoralised. The youth had ended a terrible period of apathy and bitterness. The bad news is that they were alone. No other segment of South African society had risen with them.

There was no escaping the spill-over from the violence and Thami witnessed it, even at Sached. A few weeks after the townships exploded, two men came to the front desk and announced they were taking away Vesta Smith, the receptionist. Director Theo Derkx rushed out of his office, asking 'why?' and whether she would be put in solitary confinement. The men replied she was being arrested 'for security reasons'. Mrs Smith spent six weeks of her six-month imprisonment in solitary. Upon returning to Sached in December, she told Thami and the other staff members that she was never charged or told why she had been detained. She was never even interrogated. Disparaging comments about whites proliferated in Sached's hallways.

Rather than become involved in rock-throwing and arson, Thami entered a Standard Bank competition designed to create links between the 'living African community' and modern banking. The five winners would paint murals. Thami won only a high commendation but the bank kept his submission, putting it into storage. Thami chose to interpret lines from W B Yeats's poem 'The Second Coming', in four segments. The four parts make up a 'widening gyre'. A man sits beside an upended pot at the lower left, presenting his back to the viewer. Above him a bird takes flight. It flies to the right towards a panel of carnage where a naked body twists, its arms outflung and its head dissolving. The fourth panel, at the lower right, could be the 'mere anarchy … loosed upon the world' as it displays an arm, a knee, perhaps a rib cage and the mangled bird. They are shoved together in a mass of inchoate energy as if by a gigantic and mysterious force.

Compared with other work inspired by the youth revolt, Thami's piece is strangely detached, as if he thought the events were an engulfing storm that had to be weathered. For him, 1976 was a year of reflection and quiescence. His Rorke's Drift acquaintance Vuminkosi Zulu, on the other hand, depicted in a less distilled fashion a group of prisoners awaiting trial, their heads poking through and trapped under an all-encompassing grid.

The month after Thami drew this version of things falling apart, he and a three-months pregnant Naniwe married in a magistrate's court. They moved in with Pauline Malebo, a Thamane cousin, because Sarah was still hostile to Naniwe. Then they bought a four-room house in Tembisa, their double bed nearly filling one room. Thami continued to work at Sached and in his free time exhibited at Diakonia House in Braamfontein and at the Nedbank near the Cresta shopping centre in suburban Johannesburg. He entitled one of his new pieces 'Meditation', as if he were signalling his reaction to the year's turmoil. A man closes his eyes in thought, his chin resting on his fist. A leafy plant bows toward him, and on the horizon there are two trees. Dark shapes, originating in Thami's scattered water technique, swirl above the landscape and the head. The Soweto uprising seemed to have banished from his lexicon the melting moon and writhing, rock-embedded forms of the previous year. The eerie affect now comes from a depiction of calm.

In both his art and his conversation Thami preferred to observe and to inquire rather than to strike furious attitudes. He loved to talk about books and ideas with his friend Nape, an elegant man who resembled him in stature and, like him, dressed fastidiously. They had met because Nape, a social worker in Tembisa, made it his business to involve artists in entertainments he was planning in the township and he had taken note of Thami's cover illustration for *Yakhal' Inkomo*. He invited Thami to display his art and give a paper assessing African art at African arts festivals. When Thami lived in Nape's home for four months in 1976 they had stayed up late discussing books like Khalil Gibran's *The Prophet*, whose rejection of materialism they appreciated. They talked about Ali Mazrui's *The Trial of Christopher Okigbo*.[31] Mazrui intrigued them by posing questions that were highly relevant to their predicament, though he avoided easy moral judgments: the Kenyan writer asked, but did not answer, whether it was worthwhile for the poet Okigbo to die for the idea of a Biafran nation.

Thami and Nape played off each other's art, as when Nape wrote poems like 'Village from the portion of my mind', based on Thami's drawings 'Words' and 'Village'. They also listened to Radio Freedom,

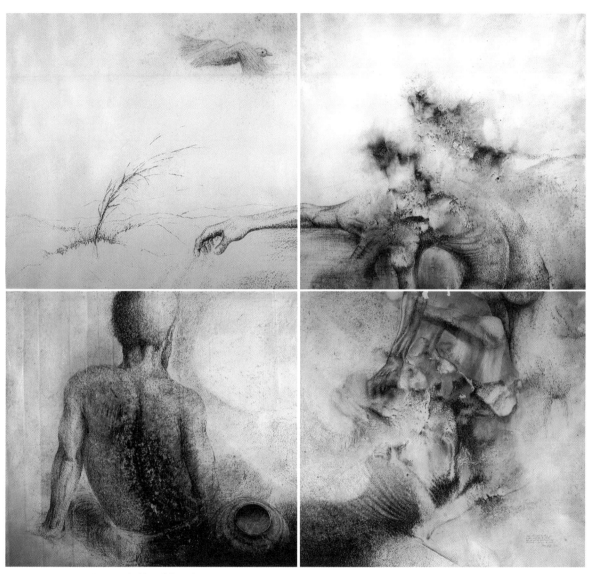

Thami Mnyele, 'Things fall apart', 1976, 61 x 64.5 cm per quadrant, Standard Bank Collection. (Photograph by Wayne Oosthuizen)

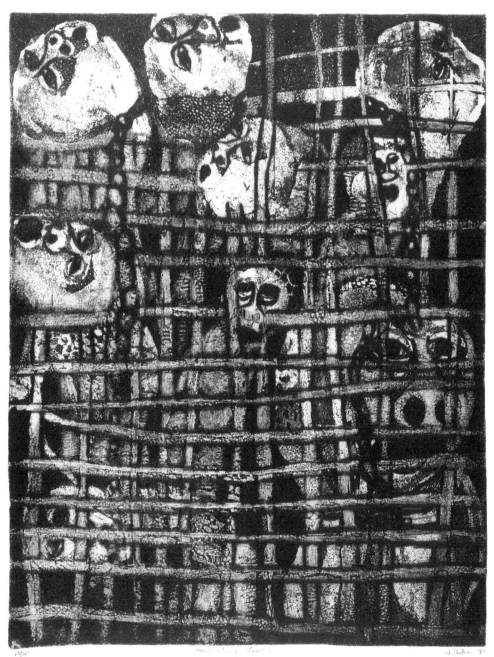

Vuminkosi Zulu, 'Awaiting trial', 1976, etching, 41.3 x 32 cm, Unisa Art Gallery.

Thami Mnyele, 'Meditation', 1976, 63 x 44 cm. (Courtesy of Nomathamsanqa Mnyele-Kaunda; photograph by Melita Moloney)

Thami and his daughter Nomathamsanqa (Thami) in Tembisa township at her
first birthday party, April 1978. (Courtesy of Naniwe Ramatsui)

which made them feel, Nape says, very 'motivated'. They cautiously scrambled the letters of the ANC,
though, pronouncing it publicly as 'Ankh' or 'CNA', the acronym for the country's largest stationery store.
This extreme care turned out to be fully merited the following year. Nape was arrested and sent to
Modderbee Prison (Criminal Section) for three weeks because he owned a poetry book with the ANC
colours – black, green, gold – on the cover. While Thami was constitutionally averse to confrontation, the
inescapable nature of South African politics was apparent all around him.

At work a new, popular project preoccupied Thami. In March *The World* began putting out an educational supplement every Sunday, produced by Sached and called 'People's College'. Thami helped lay
out and illustrate articles designed to educate readers in basic matters of modern life. Since accessibility
was the key, there wasn't much scope for creative flair. In an effort to compensate for abysmal township
education the supplement presented school subjects like South African history, geography, and English.
More innovative were articles of practical concern like 'breast and bottle feeding', how to write a business
letter, cross a busy street, buy a second-hand car, get papers to work in town.

The effect was that the contents of Sached workbooks could now be purchased by anyone with a few
cents to spare, though 'People's College' granted no degrees. The paper's stated aim was 'to provide a

foundation on which people can build an understanding of the world around them'. Sometimes the left-wing retelling of South Africa's past annoyed donors. Dave Adler had to fend off an angry phone call from a manager at Anglo American after Luli Callinicos's 'Social history of South Africa, from farms to factories' appeared. The mine executive may have found her ungrateful for dwelling on 'the struggle for survival of those whose hands made the wealth …'[32]

Among the less incendiary articles were ones on artists. Thami was featured on the cover of the seventh issue. Under the headline 'He's an artist of Africa', he laid out four core, cautiously stated beliefs: society was perhaps partly to blame for the dissolute behaviour of artists; they could ignore neither apartheid nor the painting of flowers; township art was limited and limiting; African art could be social commentary or it could be religious. The article closes with the line 'His first exhibition will be in the townships'.[33] Instead, his work appeared three months later in an indoor shopping mall in white Pretoria.

The contradiction between Thami's stated desire to exhibit first in the townships and his actual show in a suburban shopping mall can be explained by two events. First, he had become a father again. In April Naniwe had borne their daughter. They gave her the feminine version of Thami's Xhosa name, Nomathamsanqa. (A family photograph around her first birthday shows him holding her tenderly, meanwhile wincing as she tries to whack his eye with a spoon.) He had

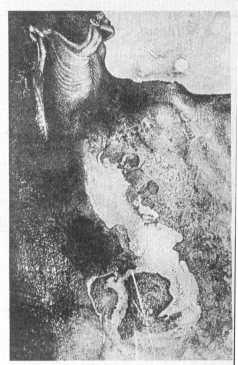

HE'S AN ARTIST OF AFRICA

● "There is a sad myth that to be accepted as a good artist one must be a socialite, a hard drinker, a militant, and indulge in affairs. Perhaps the society is to blame for part of this."

These are tough words; surprisingly so, seeing as they come from Thamsanqa Mnyele (above) the small soft-spoken artist who was born in Alexandra.

We asked Thami what artists should be doing. "I do not say that artists should paint flowers or paint apartheid, but I think that they cannot ignore either," he said.

Thami developed his talents through the encouragement of good friends. "In several respects these friends are still contribut-

ing to my development," he said. "Together we discuss our problems and discoveries in art, whether it is poetry, music, painting or sculpture.

Is there anything like township art? "I don't know about that," said Thami. "If it exists, it's a limited, limiting kind of art."

'There is, however, African art — art from the African point of view. This art can be a social commentary. It can also be religious drawn from the African experience."

Thami plans to hold an exhibition of his work. He may do this on his own, or together with friends. His first exhibition will be in the townships.

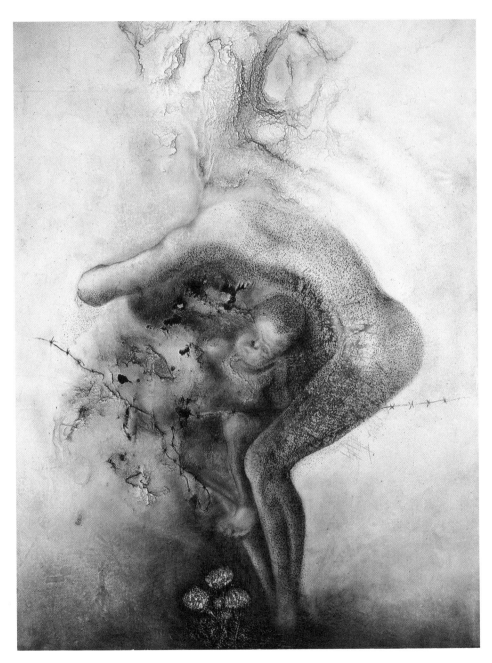

Thami Mnyele, untitled, 1977, 120 x 90 cm (picture), Chabani Manganyi and Peggy Sekele-Manganyi Collection. (Photograph by Wayne Oosthuizen)

new responsibilities, ones he was determined to fulfil more faithfully than those he had left behind with the mother of his first child in Makapanstad.

Second, Thami was already deep into planning an exhibition that, in the words of 'People's College', would take 'Soweto by storm'. The exhibition was called *A New Day*, after a poem by Don Mattera. Its genesis lay in a disappointment: Fikile complained to Piero that his exhibit had been cancelled by the Goodman Gallery a few months after the Soweto uprising, so, along with Themba Miya, they decided to found the Soweto Arts Association (Soarta) as a way of avoiding the white gallery world.

Piero and another architect did the rounds of Johannesburg corporations and banks, saying: 'You are the modern equivalent of a pope or a lord in terms of artistic patronage. You've exploited the workers. Now it's time to give something back.' The donations, especially from Anglo American's Zach de Beer, whom Piero found 'a beautiful soul', allowed them to take what they hoped would be the first step toward a Soweto public art gallery. They booked the Dube YWCA and showed the work of three artists: Ben Arnold's sculptures, and Fikile's and Thami's drawings.[34]

Because it was the first show of its kind in the township and came towards the end of a difficult year, the public responded rapturously. Thami estimated that a thousand people crammed into the hall on opening night, 15 September 1977, with more waiting outside. Dube tycoons wanted to buy the work, but the three young artists refused to sell, thinking it should go into the future Soweto museum. 'These products had to be exhibited where people are,' Thami said, rather than in white galleries. His lifelong hope was to safeguard South Africa's black art as a resource for the people.[36] The show moved on to Regina Mundi church, a centre for activist meetings in Soweto.

Soarta was explicitly hostile to the gallery world, stating that one of its aims was to 'protect black artists from exploitation by profit-making art merchants'. Thami agreed, accusing art dealers of becoming 'an extended arm of the cruel government' because they promoted apolitical art. He thought the galleries served, not the black community, but white interior decorators and that they encouraged standardised art. And yet, as Neil Dundas of the Goodman Gallery has argued, galleries were allowed an expressive latitude in the 1970s that was not possible in museums or in publishing. The security police tended to ignore galleries and, when they did ban or confiscate art, they actually stimulated broader interest in it than ever before. The members of Soarta, nevertheless, suffered from a pervasive sense of being cheated.[36]

Fikile called his ten large-scale drawings 'Dance of a second creation'. The charcoal and graphite works show a new man being born. He is growing out of escarpments, arid plains, and clouds. A human foetus

Architect Piero Cuzzolin and one of Fikile's drawings, *New Day* exhibit, Soweto, September 1977. (Courtesy of Ben Arnold)

Fikile Magadlela and one of his drawings exhibited at the *New Day* exhibit, Soweto, September 1977. (Courtesy of Ben Arnold)

emerges from the white of a broken egg. A planet breaks open to drop liquid and unfurl cloth. Inspired partly by Dali, Fikile's world is mystical and improbable. The figures are not situated in history but in some ideal, extraterrestrial vision of Africa. A pyramid represents the continent, and the figures sport Afro hairstyles and wear flowing robes as well as expressions of surpassing calm and dignity. Despising pictures of Africans wearing 'torn trousers', Fikile chose to draw 'beautiful, handsome' black men and 'heavenly' black women.[37] He executed them in precise detail, but their provenance seems to lie more in dreams than in nature or time as we know it.

The ideals of Black Consciousness censored what its adherents felt they should depict. Murder, rape, or shopping were unfit subjects for their art. The figures who populated their surreal landscapes tended to be idealised. Mothers were perfect. Birth was loaded with the meaning of a free South Africa. Unlike European surrealism, their art bears no trace of Freud's influence: the drawings are almost prudish in their asexuality. Thami and Fikile both chose to express their manhood artistically in ways that could hardly be called erotic.

Ben Arnold exhibited 14 sculptures, some named after a strong emotion – 'Grief,' 'Depressed', 'Supplication' – but generally their mood was composed, as in the solid 'Family' (see p. 91). His work conveyed the same elegance he displayed in his own bearing and clothes, his embroidered skullcaps and vests bearing African abstract designs. Arnold was trying to cut away the rawness of experience and aimed to communicate its essence. Having just returned from FESTAC, the festival of black diasporic arts and culture held in Nigeria, he carved two heads that resemble the iconic Africanness of the Benin bronzes.

Thami was thrilled that his ten drawings 'clicked' with the community. In appreciating the series based on Wally's *No Baby Must Weep*, Sowetans cut into his loneliness, enlivening him with the same sense of communion he had felt when performing in Mihloti as Malcolm X. In the exhibition brochure he stressed the religious rather than the political impulses behind his work. He mentioned his early musical ambitions and Wally's inspiration, but his first and last statements addressed the spirit: 'the spiritual aspect of life is ultimately more enduring than the physical and the mental', he began, concluding that his goal was 'to preach the human religion, to tear down walls and fences, and thus make a contribution towards reconciling and uniting the universal family'.[38]

The emotional opening of *A New Day* was given macabre energy by a terrible event that had occurred three days earlier. Craig Williamson, an overweight, shaggy-haired security agent posing as a left-wing student, had bought Steve Biko a ticket to Botswana, where he was to meet ANC president Oliver Tambo.[39] En route to Cape Town, where he wanted to consult the noted intellectual and activist Neville Alexander about his plans to meet Tambo, Biko was picked up by the police. His interrogators beat him senseless and then transported him, dying, 1 400 km to Pretoria in the back of a police Land Rover. He died on the floor of an empty cell in Pretoria Central Prison. The news of his death rocked Thami's new-found domestic and professional stability.

On 25 September Thami travelled with a few friends to the small Eastern Cape town of King William's Town for the funeral. They all dressed in black. Nape thought Thami was lucky to get through the police blockades, as he knew some fellows had been stopped en route and threatened. *The World* reported that the authorities attacked travellers at the Dube YWCA and tried to interfere with their travel. Still, 20 000 people managed to attend the funeral. Biko's words kept coming back to Thami: 'If there's a disease in a village that a doctor has to treat and the source of the disease is a river, then the real source of the

Thami Mnyele, 'Things fall apart', 1977, Botswana National Museum and Art Gallery. (Photograph by Mark Henningsen)

disease is the political system. That's why I decided to go into politics.'[40] Like many of his most deeply felt experiences, this death elicited few words from Thami. Nor did it have any discernible impact on his art, as it did on that of his fellow artists Ezrom Legae and Dikobe Martins, both of whom memorialised Biko. Nevertheless, he absorbed the blow, and it changed his life in hidden ways.

After the *New Day* exhibition an intense young artist named Mpe Figlan sought Thami out. Mpe admired his art and his way of projecting the 'unique air of an artist' with his polished boots, corduroy trousers, and nice shirts. Thami took pleasure in this admiration and in passing along what he had learned. When they met, he was drawing his second interpretation of 'Things fall apart'. A woman is poised above a cracking, arid landscape, and she has just let a pot slip from her grasp. She watches as it plummets, her face composed in mute but unmistakable dread as the disaster approaches. Watching the patience with which Thami worked, Mpe was struck by his absorption in technique, to the extent that he didn't talk about the meaning of the drawing at all. He explained his decision to depict the moment before the crash by posing a question, 'If you walk in the street with your girlfriend and she is stabbed by a thug, how would you express your strong feeling in art? Would you show the hand raised or the woman lying on the ground?' He decided to heighten the drama and render it more subtle by leading the viewer to imagine the consequences.[41]

Thami took care to teach his technique to the younger man. Mpe watched him as he drew with soft (6B, 7B) pencils, constantly sharpening them with a razor blade. He mixed paint thinner, water and charcoal ash, and then spread or threw the emulsified solution on to paper fixed to a tilted board with masking tape. On top of the designs that emerged from the solution he developed his own patterns, often building them in tiny dots. He also used conté crayon in black and various shades of brown: brick, earth, rust, burnt sienna. 'Draw everything as you see it,' he advised Mpe. 'Put leaves of grass in a glass and draw them.' He posted near his drawing board a magazine photograph showing one person in various moods, urging Mpe to experiment by sketching a similar range of emotions.

Thami particularly emphasised the importance of knowing the structure of the body, advising Mpe to feel his arm as he drew. He said he admired Michelangelo for going to the mortuary to study anatomy, and he called attention to the fall of drapery in Michelangelo's sculptures. Mpe remembers Thami studying X-rays and books on anatomy. Sometimes he rubbed the paper so hard he broke through, and he liked the effect. At this point in his life Thami worked with both deliberation and abandon. He was willing to follow the lead of his tools and the random patterns made by processes he had initiated.[42]

Through reading the letters of Van Gogh, Thami discovered a soul mate in the Old World. He talked about him passionately with Naniwe and young, aspiring artists like Jaki Seroke, a Tembisa poet, and Dikobe Martins. Dave Adler also noticed that he 'was sensual about' Van Gogh's art. He remembers Thami appreciating that the Dutchman 'spends the time' to make a picture with the right texture.[43]

Despite the century and the continent separating them, the circumstances of the two young artists – the Dutchman and the African – bore some similarities. They had both witnessed the brawling side of urban life at close quarters. In their late twenties they felt estranged from established religion, finding the Bible oppressive when read for simple rules of morality and immorality. Their spirituality was, nevertheless, lively. Van Gogh wrote that a man who seriously loves Rembrandt will surely believe there is a god; Thami was prone to weep at church services. They were continually short of money, though Van Gogh received remittances from his devoted brother, an art dealer, while Thami increasingly scorned art galleries and had no family member to help him. They both suffered from periods of 'melancholy'.

Thami drew solace from Van Gogh's words that the first period of a painter's life was necessarily dominated 'by a feeling of not being able to master the work ... by a great ambition to make progress, by a lack of self-confidence'. They found music a consolation; Van Gogh wrote to his brother, 'in a picture I want to say something as comforting as music is comforting'. Having felt frustrated in formal art institutions, they studied anatomy on their own. Both frankly wondered how long they would live. Thami had alluded to his sense that time was brief when he titled his 'remember me / I am going / time calls me' drawing in 1974. (Mpe thought he lived as though he knew he was going to die.) Van Gogh, at the age of 30, felt that he might not have more than five or ten years in which to 'finish a certain body of work'.[44]

Thami understood Van Gogh's ambitions. He nodded in stunned agreement when reading that Van Gogh believed the word 'artist' meant 'I am seeking, I am striving, I am in it with all my heart'. The word 'heart' was crucial to Thami's artistic vocabulary. He recognised that Van Gogh was, like him, trying to make feelings visible. How long would Thami be able to hold on to Van Gogh's corollary: that art meant seeking without absolutely finding? He was captivated by Van Gogh's use of 'stream' as a metaphor for what he was trying to achieve. 'I have a sure *faith* in art, a sure confidence that it is a powerful stream, which bears a man to harbour ...' When he arrived in that harbour he would have gained a sense of reality more true than literal truth. Both men felt intimate sympathy and respect for what life had written on people's faces, for what bodies expressed about work.[45]

Leabharlanna Fhine Gall

Thami drew Mpe's attention to how miners' hands had been enlarged and distorted by their hard labour underground. He was fascinated by the large, rough hands of 'The Potato Eaters', peasants who expressed their connection to one another with gestures rather than words. They had dug the potatoes with the gnarled hands that were now passing the food. Van Gogh was then eager, in an unusually didactic way, to show that the meal had been 'honestly earned'. He didn't want people to admire the painting without knowing that he meant to show respect for people not yet caught up in urban, bourgeois life.[46]

Thami was surprised that Van Gogh had worried at the age of 30 that he had made no progress with colour. In nearly every letter the man's passion for it spilled out. Thami, who had still not studied colour, must have envied the Dutchman's ability to act on his belief that 'if someone does not learn to have a feeling for [tone and colour], how far from real life he stands'.[47] In fact, he could only have imagined the vividness of Van Gogh's paintings. The sole original available for him to see locally was a charcoal sketch, 'Orphan man with top hat', owned by the Johannesburg Art Gallery. Van Gogh had sketched the old war veteran in 1882 when he was living in The Hague, where most people regarded the 'Orphan man' as an eccentric. The painter wanted his work to show that in the heart of that disagreeable 'nobody' – himself, and possibly the veteran – there were deep and tender feelings. But his motive was not fundamentally vain or personal. 'The feeling for the things themselves, for reality' was to him far more important than the feeling for pictures. This trait is what critic John Berger has called Van Gogh's ideological nakedness: he did not refer 'to salvation by way of an ideal which the things embody …' Instead his drawings derived from his 'capacity to love, suddenly and at any moment, what he saw in front of him'. For Van Gogh, art *was* life's essence. At this point in his life Thami shared that expressive goal. Reading Van Gogh's letters he determined to work, as the Dutchman said, persistently, continuously, 'in spite of everything' to achieve it.[48]

The *New Day* exhibition had come at a 'crucial' time. It was the 'most interesting' and 'most important' exhibition in his life to date.[49] Because it coincided with Biko's death, it forced him to face the question: was he involved in the struggle and life around him, or was he merely producing pictures? Recent events suggested that, if he continued his present life, the correct answer would surely be the latter. While his own circumstances were stable, the world around him was emphatically not. On 17 October 1977, a month after the 'New Day' exhibition, minister of justice Jimmy Kruger, the man who had announced that Biko's death 'left [him] cold', banned *The World* and the *Weekend World* without giving any coherent reason.[50] A few months later Dave Adler himself would be banned.

Work at Sached had, in any case, grown stale for Thami. He felt that his 'pretty little illustrations' mainly benefited 'a small number of sophisticated [Sached] students' who hoped to win an overseas scholarship. He recognised 'with a creeping feeling of wasting away' that he had grown bitter. 'I had the financial source of income, so what! What had this to do with being a committed artist?'[51] Just before Biko's death, two of Thami's friends had left the country. He may have known that one of them – Zinjiwa Winston Nkondo – was already an ANC member. Nkondo, a poet and former copywriter at a leading advertising agency, had been director of the Black People's Convention in Johannesburg, but had spent most of 1976 in prison. (Dikobe says he seemed to be arrested every other day.) Upon his release, while working for Sached, he had become increasingly allied with the ANC. He fled the country for Swaziland the month before Biko was arrested for the last time. In December 1977 yet another Saso member, Ngoako Ramatlhodi, who also came from Tembisa and had been inspired by Thami, crossed into Botswana and underwent an intensive ANC course in underground work and propaganda. The ANC was proving to be good at recruiting BC people within Thami's immediate world. Many felt that mobilising against a common enemy was more important than maintaining loyalty to a particular grouping.

Meanwhile, Soarta stopped functioning, some said because of financial mismanagement. There was no longer any Mihloti or MDALI to replace it, as most of their members had left. Piero even lost his large Troye Street apartment because, he said, the landlord objected to his 'coloured' visitors using the elevator. In truth, these lovers of loud music, often drunk, cannot have endeared him to his neighbours. Piero moved to two studios in a Bree Street building that was already looking rundown.

Thami began to feel trapped in his marriage. He expressed his ambivalence in a drawing called 'Families' that he gave to a young Sached colleague, Chris van Wyk, one weekend when he invited Chris to Tembisa. (Delighted to serve as host, he bought a small bottle of brandy for Chris and insisted he sleep in the marriage bed vacated temporarily by him and Naniwe.) There are three families in the drawing: a nest of birds in the upper right, a cluster of ants on the lower left, while the paper is dominated by a grim man standing beside a nursing woman. While apparently celebrating domestic life, he was also deriding it as something thoughtless and obligatory, devoid of emotional content.

Naniwe did not share his artistic sensibility and believed in soldiering on through hardship, rather than surrendering to strong feelings. He stunned her by saying that divorce made sense when people no longer liked each other. She wondered if they were growing apart because they spent too little time alone. People who are not free, she thought, are lonely, so they gather compulsively to draw strength from each other. Naniwe would try to figure Thami out by reading the Van Gogh letters he spoke about with such passion.[52]

At a train station he met Rhona, the shy, 20-year-old sister of Alex Segale, a highly politicised Tembisa friend he had met the previous year. Like Thami, she had been born in Alex and her mother, like Mamanyena, worked as a domestic servant. Her family, though, was intact. Her father walked to his job each day in a Kew steel factory until the family was moved to Tembisa in 1971. Thami began courting her with chocolates. Twice he took this tall, slim girl with the radiant smile to visit an old man who was dear to him in Makapanstad. He was ashamed of his adultery and kept the fact secret even from his friend Alex. Rhona fell in love with Thami, becoming yet another woman who, as Wally would later write, 'ran to him their hands flying in the air'.[53]

Thami secretly began to plan his escape from a life that fell far short of allowing him to become 'an articulate artist'. Wally was now nearby, having left New York and arrived in Gaborone against the advice of Steve Biko, who was 'not very confident' about the move. The poet once again seemed to offer a solution to Thami's feeling of aimlessness.[54] Publicly, Wally was working to revive the spirit of Mihloti in the form of the Pelindaba Cultural Unit, but privately he was developing other plans.

After entering the country in the northern town of Francistown with a half-empty suitcase, indicating how little of his prior life he wanted to preserve, Wally met armed guerrillas from the war in Zimbabwe whose sense of purpose he admired. This contrasted with his feelings about the African intellectuals and professionals he met once he moved to Gaborone at the end of 1977. He despised their snobbery, their obliviousness, and their habit of 'drinking his and her money to death'. Wally, previously a 'reckless' drinker, stopped drinking.

He was also meeting South African exiles, who were drawing him into the ANC. Cassius Make, from MK military headquarters, gave him a book on Che Guevara and a volume of Vietnamese poetry. These conversations and insights led Wally to think that Black Consciousness, because it excluded allies simply on the basis of their skin colour, had become too negative. He was imbibing a more class-oriented analysis, one he had resisted in the 1960s when he encountered it through his friend Joyce Sikakane, and now believed that a people's history and culture depended on 'their material life'. In 1978 he wrote the auto-biographical essay the ANC required of its new recruits and joined the movement.[55]

Thami visited Wally in Gaborone early in 1978. Listening to the complaints of the young artist who longed to return to the articulate and communal days of the early 1970s, Wally responded with the most

Thami Mnyele, untitled, 1978, Andrew Orkin Collection.

reasonable advice he could offer. He told him to go home and advised him not to try to leave South Africa until he was leaving for the right reasons. Thami's current logic seemed negative; he seemed to be in flight. He should move to Botswana only from a position of strength, when his reasons were positive. Upon his return to Johannesburg Thami remarked with awe to Mpe, 'Those guys outside are working, while we inside [South Africa] are not doing any work.'[56]

At that point ANC leaders were contending with rival movements. The PAC still behaved like a competitor, setting up military training camps in places like Libya and cultivating its own allies. The Cold War was setting the stage with new, more threatening rivals. In part because the ANC was fighting with Russian arms in Angola alongside Cuban allies, Pretoria and its Western allies were trying to foster anti-ANC forces. The Zulu movement, Inkatha, was one of them. Inkatha's sworn fidelity to foreign investment won American support, making it a particularly dangerous rival. Some people believed that the BCM in exile had won support from elements in the United States who were anxious to shore up non-communist factions. To wage a war for South African hearts and minds against these competitors, the ANC had to convince people at home of its continued pre-eminence. Its cadres in Botswana were part of this effort.

The ANC was evaluating its strategic choices. When Tambo visited Botswana's president Seretse Khama, a few months after Thami's visit to Wally, the two men spent an entire day discussing how to activate the struggle. Should the ANC focus on mass political mobilisation or the armed struggle? Tambo received the same reply from Khama as he had had during his recent trip to Vietnam. Key figures within the ANC and among its Soviet contacts – Joe Gqabi and Vladimir Shubin, respectively – believed that the ANC should devote more energy to political mobilisation within South Africa and pay 'secondary' attention to the armed struggle.[57] Too many impatient young cadres expected, against all reason, that they would ride into Johannesburg atop Russian tanks.[58] Tambo lamented that the ANC had failed to make the Soweto uprising the 'spark', to use Lenin's word, that would lead to revolution.[59] Wedded to the idea of rural warfare, the movement hadn't been prepared for township revolt. Three years later it was still not sufficiently organised to carry out military operations to avenge the hanging of MK cadre Solomon Mahlangu. The ANC managed only to distribute leaflets, leading one activist to complain, 'It is not enough to call people to join MK when it is doing nothing that warrants joining it.'[60]

In 1979 the ANC's 'new thinking' about how to achieve 'a socialist order' elevated 'political mobilization and organization' to the 'main task'. This message was publicised within the movement by the 'Green Book', a report on strategy drawn up by a small, high-level committee after their fact-finding visit to Vietnam in late 1978. The following three years would be dedicated to political mobilisation as preparation for an all-out people's war in 1982. In the meantime, cadres in Botswana, as in the other frontline states, would be charged with giving 'day-to-day attention to the internal situation' so that political and military activities could be coordinated effectively. They would facilitate 'armed propaganda' within South Africa in order to 'support and stimulate political activity and organization rather than to hit at the enemy'. Joe Slovo defined 'armed propaganda' as 'military activities … which inspired and gave people new courage inside, and hope'.[61] A Special Operations unit under Slovo's leadership was formed to select symbolic targets, such as an army base, and mount spectacular armed attacks on them.

These attacks would answer 'the enemy's counter-insurgency tactics' by imbuing 'especially the working and student youth, with a deep pride in and respect for the fighting traditions of our people'. The expression 'fighting traditions' sounded inspiring, but a considerable number of the movement's strikes within South

Africa since the late 1960s had simply involved exploding leaflet bombs in railway and bus stations. Few MK cadres had engaged in actual combat. The ANC leadership had to inspire a population faced daily with news photographs of the new prime minister, P W Botha, inspecting state-of-the-art weaponry. It needed to assert a glorious military heritage in order to prevent a relapse into the pre-1976 'demoralisation'.

Botswana depended too much on South Africa to resist demands that it curb ANC activities. Three months after Tambo's visit, Botswana police raided the homes of four activists and imprisoned them for possessing war materiel. Even though the ANC had recently created a department of intelligence and security to try to weed out informers, the information leading to that raid had probably come from within the movement itself. There was no shortage of agents eager to collect monthly salaries ranging from R300 to R1 000 by telling everything they knew to the security police. Botswana received refugees, but it was no refuge.

Thami nevertheless began to plan an orderly, though clandestine, exit. First, he resigned from Sached, a decision that caused him great sorrow. He had grown so attached to people there that he 'fought back tears' the afternoon he said goodbye. To support his wife and child in the interim he went to work for Crownwoods Cash and Carry, where his job was to draw advertising banners, some featuring pictures of money flowing. The pay was good. The task depressed his spirits so deeply that he nearly stopped making his own art and slept for long hours.

He drew two pictures in 1978 as he was sliding into depression. One was for Andy Orkin, his former Sached officemate, whose daughter had just been born in Canada. In a rocky landscape under a pulsating sky a man sits on the ground. His small figure is overwhelmed by the solidity of the rocks and the enormity of the space above. He leans against a peculiar tree, its bare uppermost branches extending into the sky like roots. The only leafy branch is growing down toward the soil. The world seems to have been turned upside down, and the man may be dreaming.

Thami drew one other picture for a friend at that uncertain time. Chris van Wyk was publishing his first book of poetry and asked Thami to design the cover. Because Thami, always a painstaking worker, was slow to produce it, Chris considered transferring the task to someone else. Thami was adamant. He eventually drew a rock face situated between a calm body of water and a sky in tumult. Celestial energy radiates outward in concentric circles while two mysterious forces collide in the sky and drip boulders onto the landscape. Something is happening, but it is not clear what it is. Perhaps the drawing lacks definition because it expresses a moment of stalemate. Thami drew the pale, unaccented scene without offering the viewer any sense of resolution or direction.

In private Thami deliberated over the drawings he wanted to keep near him in exile. Which ones expressed best what he had to say? Half-a-dozen pictures eventually made their way into the neatly wrapped roll that he kept to one side: 'Brotherhood on Ninth Avenue' and 'The best of our kind' from 1974; two illustrations for *No Baby Must Weep*, from 1975; and 'Things fall apart' and the woman giving birth, from 1977. He left behind 'Meditation', his drawing of a man ruminating in 1976, the year when things in his wider world had started to fall apart.

NOTES

1   David Adler, interview (22 Jan 2000).
2   Peder Gowenius, quoted in P Hobbs and E Rankin, *Rorke's Drift: Empowering Prints* (Cape Town: Double Storey, 2003), 197.
3   'Staffrider profile of Fikile', *Staffrider* (June 1980), 24–5.
4   David Koloane, interview (July 2001).
5   Dikobe Ben Martins, interview (31 Dec 2005).
6   Pat Williams, 'Last paintings by Bill Ainslie, 1934–1989' (Wolfson College, Oxford, 1990), 3; Bill Ainslie, interview (14 July 1989).
7   Ainslie, quoted by Williams, 'Last paintings', 7, 10.
8   'Graduation speech by O R [sic] Tiro at the University of the North, Turfloop, April, 29, 1972', in Karis and Gerhart, *From Protest*, 497–9.
9   'Bomb-case man tells of flight to Botswana', *Rand Daily Mail* (12 July 1974), Karis-Gerhart Collection, reel 4.
10 Bill Ainslie, interview (14 July 1989).
11 Wally Serote, *No Baby Must Weep* (Johannesburg: Ad Donker, 1975), 55, 50, 30.
12 Nel Erasmus, 1968, quoted by Joyce Oyzinski, in 'Peanuts for the gallery', *Snarl*, 1, 2 (November 1974), 10–11. This European bias also excluded most white South African artists until the 1950s. Anton van Wouw, a sculptor, was the first South African artist whose work was bought by the JAG.
13 Ibid, 4.
14 Mnyele, 'Observations', 3; David Koloane, interview (July 2001).
15 Montshiwa Moroke, interview (13 July 2001); Mnyele, 'Observations', 2–3.
16 Mnyele, 'Observations', 5; Molefe Pheto, *And Night Fell: Memoirs of a Political Prisoner in South Africa* (London: Allison and Bushby, 1983), 54–5.
17 Pheto, *And Night Fell*, 121. Hamilton had actually written a letter revealing that he found Molefe untrustworthy, so the idea that the two men were comrades seems to have been baseless, 195.
18 Joyce Ozynski, 'Black art and black lives', *Sunday Express* (16 Oct 1977).
19 Naniwe Ramatsui, interview (8 Jan 2003).
20 Brigitte Mabandla was to become Minister of Justice and Constitutional Development in 2004.
21 Biko, *Black Consciousness*, 22.
22 Interviews: Luli Callinicos (20 Dec 2003); Carohn Cornell (17 Jan 2000); e-mail from Janet Ewing Callinicos (14 Jan 2004).
23 David Adler, interview (4 July 2001); Vesta Smith, interview by Karis-Gerhart, Political Documents I, Folder 35, and interview by Julie Frederickse (July 1985), SAHA, Cullen Library, Wits.
24 Piero Cuzzolin, interview (Johannesburg, 13 July 2001); Ben Arnold, interview (Johannesburg, 7 July 2001).
25 Naniwe Ramatsui, interview (8 Jan 2003).
26 Biko, *Black Consciousness*, 21.
27 Ibid, 32, 145, 57, 176.
28 Luli Callinicos, *Oliver Tambo: Beyond the Engeli Mountains* (Cape Town: David Philip, 2004), 384.
29 Lindi Mnyele Binca, interview (5 Jan 2005).
30 Shubin, ANC, 176, 174, 183, 172.
31 Nape Motana, interview (7 Jan 2005).
32 *Weekend World Educational Supplement*, 'People's College' (6 March – 23 Oct 1977); David Adler, interview (4 July 2001).

33 'He's an artist of Africa', *Weekend World*, 'People's College', 7 (17 April 1977).

34 Cuzzolin, interview (13 July 2001).

35 Mnyele, 'A new day', *Staffrider*, 3, 3 (Sept/Oct 1980), 42.

36 'SOARTA will bring art to the people', *Weekend World*, 'People's College', 31 (16 October 1977), 1; Mnyele, 'Observations', 6; Neil Dundas, interview (14 July 2001).

37 'Staffrider profile: Fikile', 24–5.

38 Soarta, *A New Day* exhibition brochure (15 Sept 1977), Ben Arnold personal archive.

39 ANC statement to the TRC (Aug 1996), 53 n75, quoted by Luli Callinicos, *Oliver Tambo*, 650 n75; Karis and Gerhart, *From Protest*, 313.

40 Pauline Malebo Thamane, interview (4 Jan 2005); Mpe Figlan, interview (11 July 2001).

41 Figlan, interviews (2001, 2004).

42 Ibid.

43 David Adler, interview (25 May 1989).

44 Mark Roskill (ed.), *The Letters of Vincent van Gogh* (New York: Athenaeum, 1985), 182, 286, 201

45 Ibid, 188, 141.

46 Van Gogh, quoted in Cynthia Saltzman, *Portrait of Dr. Gachet: The Story of a Van Gogh Masterpiece. Money, Politics, Collectors, Greed, and Loss* (New York: Penguin, 1998), 9–10.

47 Ibid, 200, 132.

48 Ibid, 156; John Berger, *The Shape of a Pocket* (New York: Vintage, 2003), 88.

49 Mnyele, 'A new day', 42.

50 Harvey Tyson, *Editors under Fire* (New York: Random House, 1993).

51 Mnyele, 'Observations', 5–6.

52 Naniwe Ramatsui, interview (8 Jan 2003).

53 Wally Serote, *Freedom Lament and Song* (Cape Town: David Philip, 1997), 10.

54 Serote, autobiographical essay.

55 Serote, *Hyenas*, 12.

56 Figlan, interview (11 July 2001).

57 Report of the Politico-Military Strategy Commission (the 'Green Book') to the ANC National Executive Committee (August 1979), Part 2, Annexure B, section 11, in Karis and Gerhart, *From Protest*, 731.

58 Lynda von den Steinen, 'Soldiers in the struggle: Aspects of the experiences of Umkhonto we Sizwe's rank and file soldiers. The Soweto generation and after' (MA dissertation, University of Cape Town, 1999), 217.

59 Callinicos, *Oliver Tambo*, 382–3.

60 Unidentified activist quoted by Shubin, *ANC*, 204.

61 'Green Book', 720–34; Callinicos, *Oliver Tambo*, 523.

Chapter 5

Roots

The border between Botswana and South Africa looks from the air like a long surgical incision in the brown plains of the bushveld. Two dirt roads run along a fence, allowing military vehicles to patrol, protected on each side by a line of electrified wire. In the 1980s brilliant lights flooded the official crossing points at night. If any purposeful sounds came from the bush, German shepherd dogs rushed and snarled. The areas around the border gates were so tightly monitored that Thami's friend Alex Segale called them 'savage'.[1] Elsewhere it was easier to cross undetected.

Thami crossed the border at Tlokweng Gate on 10 August 1979, in the conventional manner, without menace or alarms. He filled in an entry form, presented his travel document, and was waved ahead past the raised barrier. His suitcase contained the signature wardrobe he'd carefully selected for his old Johannesburg life: crisp white T-shirts and chinos, a couple of designer shirts, corduroy jeans, a lumber jacket, and boots for the surprisingly cold winter nights. As he left the car that had driven him to his chosen place of exile, he carefully lifted out the roll of his half-dozen best pictures, neatly wrapped in brown paper. They meant more to him than any other possession, even if, for the time being, he wasn't quite clear how he could use them in his new home.

In some ways he knew what to expect in Gaborone. The couple of dozen shops in the city's two shopping malls carried the same merchandise he was used to buying across the border. In fact, many local businesses – Guys & Girls and Standard Bank, for example – were branches of ones at home. The acacia-studded plains and dry air reminded him of his time at school in Makapanstad. Since those years had taught him to speak rural Setswana without an accent, his speech didn't advertise his difference, though his graceful and urbane manner often did.

He was amused by local humour, smiling at laconic Tswana stories about things going awry, like the unravelling of a recently purchased shirt. He smiled, too, at what he called the Tswana tendency to make incongruous or dishonest remarks with a perfectly straight face. He was even more amused by styles of courtship. Young men from home would woo local girls with lines like 'my black tulip', dumbfounding and antagonising Tswana men whose approach was less poetic. He knew that Wally, already resettled in Gaborone, would help him to adjust socially and logistically.

In other ways he was facing the unknown. The reassuring familiarity of land and language compensated somewhat for the extraordinary mystery that lay before him. How would he support himself? He had lunged toward Botswana partly as a way of escaping personal turmoil, but he had no clear idea how he could resolve his problems. He had emerged from the depression of the previous year when he could scarcely draw anything. He had 'run away' from his unhappy marriage, an act he was not proud of, one which surely shook his confidence in himself as an ethical man. What he was running towards wasn't yet clear.

Thami Mnyele, 'Consequences', 1980, 76 x 113 cm with blood stains, Botswana National Museum and Art Gallery. (Photograph by Mark Henningsen)

Thami's mood may be gauged in his portrait of his new friend, Tim Williams, drawn soon after he arrived. Tim had grown up in Soweto and hadn't met Thami prior to landing up in Gaborone. The two men shared quiet and introspective natures and quickly found they could spend hours silently in each other's company, Thami drawing and Tim reading. Thami worked on the likeness of his temperamental soulmate so hard that Wally and Tim joked he would break through the paper, but he said he wouldn't stop fussing over Tim's arm until there was life in it. The drawing, called 'Consequences', shows Tim leaning over a barbed wire fence, gazing into space and apparently into himself, his arm slack. To the right Thami printed in his careful, slanting script three lines from a poem, 'Death alone', written by Pablo Neruda when he was precisely Thami's age, 31: 'like a wreck we die to the very core, as if drowning at the heart or collapsing inwards from skin to soul'.[2]

Within a few weeks of Thami's arrival in Gaborone his father, now a minister of the AME Church in the township of Vosloorus, moved house within greater Johannesburg. His new home was a brand-new, ranch-style residence, far more spacious and gracious than its neighbours or than any house he had ever lived in.

Thami wrote an anguished letter to the new address. His trademark slanting script is free of error; he worked hard to produce a precise final draft. He pleads for peace in the family. He expresses such keen remorse at having abandoned his wife and child that he suggests a reconciliation is forthcoming, 'as soon as possible please'. He calls his difficulties with Naniwe 'minor' and says she and their daughter will join him in Botswana 'as soon as they've made up their minds'. He seems to be begging his father's forgiveness for having betrayed his own paternal responsibilities. He is longing to enter the shelter of his father's embrace. 'It will make me happy', he wrote, 'if you understand that I still love you and respect you as a father and my parent, despite the fact that we seldom [sat] and felt each other.' He hopes his father will allow his younger brothers and sisters to visit him in Botswana and even come himself.[3] He never suggests that he will return to South Africa.

Thami's friends initially arranged for him to stay in Broadhurst, a one-time farm being developed as a suburb. Two- and three-bedroom homes sat there on small plots of land, occasionally decorated with a lawn and garden. A tiny outbuilding, called the 'quarters', or a servant's bedroom-plus-toilet, was typically located at the back of each house. Thami stayed in several of those quarters while gaining his bearings. He was no doubt struck by the similarity of this tract housing to the homes of his mother's employers. One significant difference lay in their occupants. Batswana businessmen and bureaucrats tended to rent them while working in the capital. On weekends and holidays they often decamped for their true homes and cattleposts in the countryside, giving the town an even more provisional air than its raw newness and lack of landscaping already conveyed. Mixed among these newly urban Batswana were foreign aid workers. They were fulfilling contracts meant to develop the country's economy so that Botswana could gain greater independence from South Africa. Like the young refugees of 1976, the foreigners tended to be both idealistic and hostile to the regime next door.

Gaborone was so new that it seemed to have dropped directly on to the bushveld from the drawing boards of British town planners. It bore few signs of having been shaped by its residents. It had no apparent history. A government enclave and two malls – one for grocery stores and boutiques, and one unpaved and unplanned 'African mall' for cheaper shopping – made up the town centre. Fresh from rural areas, secretaries, 'dressed for success' in cocktail dresses, teetered across the malls on high heels. There were no traffic lights. Sometimes you could hear a cow bell rattle in the heart of the city. The dry land of Botswana could seem as vast and flat as the ocean on a calm day, its steep hills rising up like islands. The refugees were used to a wetter, more billowing landscape, and to women who dressed smartly.

Under the city's blandly unpromising surface, though, people were constantly moving about in search of community, and finding it. Expatriates, discovering no restaurant scene, met to swim, drink, and play tennis at the Gaborone Club. Refugees mainly gathered at each other's homes, while those with cash could meet for drinks in the city's two main hotels, the President and the Holiday Inn. Outside these formal settings lay the same kind of tightly packed and unmapped squatter communities they knew so well from South Africa. These shantytowns had unaccountably encouraging names like Naledi ('star'). The least privileged refugees, those without skills or connections, could find themselves exiled yet again to Dukwe, a camp in the north-east set up by the Botswana government in 1978 to hold young men fleeing the war in Rhodesia.[4]

After a few months in Broadhurst limbo, Thami found more permanent lodging across Mobutu Drive from the university. The new arts community in Gaborone – made up of South African exiles and sympathetic foreigners – functioned as his conduit for information. In his case it worked in this way: Albio Gonzalez, a dynamic Spanish-speaking expatriate, who had arrived in Gaborone two years earlier as part of the Swedish aid mission (Sida), met writer Mandla Langa, who in turn introduced Wally Serote, who eventually asked him to put up his friend Thami. Albio, born in Cuba to Catalan parents, had trained as an architect and city planner, eventually setting up home in Sweden, and SIDA had sent him to work at the Department of Town and Regional Planning. His pretty young wife, Teresa Devant, had trained as an actress at a progressive theatre school in Barcelona and in Sweden.

The couple invited Thami to stay in the garage to the right of their house at 2935 Pudulogo Crescent. Thami thereby acquired not only a place to sleep and set up his drawing board, plus access to their kitchen, but over the next five years, throughout his early thirties, he gained beloved friends. In part because all three devoted their considerable energies to creative expression, they struck what Thami would call a deep rapport. They would work side by side within a cryptically named organisation dedicated to the arts, and it became the public centrepiece of their lives.

Thami arrived in Gaborone seven months after a small group of South Africans had founded Medu Art Ensemble. (Outsiders would puzzle over the word 'medu', thinking it was an acronym, though it is actually the Pedi word for 'roots'.) He was already familiar with its ethos. Medu was built on efforts to foster black South African creativity and political consciousness dating back to the founding of Mihloti in 1971, and it even included some of the same members.

The Soweto uprising had provided the catalyst for this latest ensemble effort, and the University of Botswana supplied the initial venue and founding personnel. When the student revolt began on 16 June 1976, South African lecturers – Bob Leshoai and Mbulelo Mzamane of the English department, and the Rev. Gabriel Setiloane of Theology – organised poetry and dramatic readings and song-and-dance performances where students and their Batswana friends could express outrage at what was happening back home. These efforts attracted exiled artists who lacked formal ties to the university, like trombone player Jonas Gwangwa, artists Phillip Segola and Lefifi Tladi, and, eventually, Wally Serote. In various configurations they founded a succession of proto-Medus, called Dashiki, Pelindaba Cultural Effort, and Tuka Cultural Unit.[5] Why did Medu survive, unlike these similar efforts which had been rising and subsiding for nearly three years? Perhaps the force of Wally Serote's personality and his vision set Medu apart. Many remarked on his genuine humility, his ability to listen intently and respectfully to the concerns of ordinary people. These traits existed in close harmony with his egalitarian political vision. However, as Lefifi Tladi tells the story, Wally deliberately set out to abolish both Pelindaba and Dashiki in order to create Medu. Thami took a more diplomatic view, saying that Medu resulted from a merger of the two groups.

Exiles readily fell into mutual recrimination. In 1979, for example, Lefifi, who was involved in Tuka, had organised an art exhibition that caused controversy by including only artists from Pretoria. There was no ideological tension between the Johannesburg and Pretoria artists. They were simply intensely competitive for recognition and prone to feeling excluded. Even though the art travelled to Sweden, the show may have destroyed Tuka by creating enmity.[6]

These squabbles were symptomatic of quarrels that went on regularly among the highly insecure exiles, black and white. They may have talked romantically of solidarity but they lived in what sometimes seemed to be a nest of vipers. They were rarely certain whom to trust.

Nor did the Botswana government make them feel welcome. It avoided encouraging the exiles in any way that would invite South African interference. Although President Seretse Khama had allowed the ANC to set up an office in Botswana in the early 1970s, his government opposed the movement of arms into or out of the country. When in 1978 University of Botswana students threw stones at policemen to protest against the detention of a man charged with the death of two suspicious white South Africans, it deported the two South African lecturers – Leshoai and Setiloane – accused of having stirred the students up.[7] In the late 1970s as many as 30 000 people fleeing regional turmoil had joined Botswana's one-million population. They poured in from South Africa and Rhodesia. During the Soweto uprising, up to 50 refugees a day had crossed the border and the South African government subsequently accused Botswana of harbouring ANC terror squads.[8] After the Zimbabwean peace accord was signed in December 1979, only the South Africans were left.

Refugees knew they had to report to a police station and request asylum. The police would ask if they wanted to be put in touch with the ANC or the PAC. Some young newcomers were so unaware of events just prior to their birth that they needed first to be instructed in the difference between the two organisations. Thami's new friend, Tim Williams, had initially chosen the PAC as the most likely embodiment of Black Consciousness values but, disillusioned by training at a PAC camp in Libya, had switched his allegiance to the ANC. To evaluate their skills as well as their sincerity, the ANC representative would ask potential cadres, especially those with no known history, to write autobiographies and also to decide if they wanted to join MK or be sent abroad to study. Those choosing MK tended to be flown to Lusaka and sometimes Tanzania to get in shape for the real MK training camps in Angola. People would hint at their ANC membership by calling each other 'comrade'.

While in Botswana the refugees lived on small subsistence grants from the United Nations High Commission on Refugees. About half of them, more than 200, lived in Dukwe, but that site struck fear into the hearts of most refugees. To them it meant being marginalised. The few youth who actually enjoyed camping in the bush and raising chickens embarrassed the more urban refugees, who feared being seen as, and maybe even becoming, country bumpkins if they were forced to live in the bush because of the lack of a job. When Thami arrived in Botswana, he needed to find a legitimate role in Gaborone quickly in order to avoid that fate or, far worse, detention by the Botswana police and deportation back to South Africa. An artistic, not a political, organisation would provide the necessary cover. The South Africans rarely succeeded in hiding their urban origins in Gaborone. Some might don blue coveralls in an attempt to appear to be simple workers, but the speed of their step and their electric alertness gave the game away. They looked as if they were on a mission. One never knew, though, if they were working as agents of the security police or if they were the hunted.

Medu had to dance around the forces arrayed against it, avoiding any compromising revelations. Its most general statement of purpose had to be unimpeachable, and it was: Medu said it trained 'artists interested in … theatre, music, dance, photography, film, graphic arts, publications and research'. Its policy declaration went on to state that the group was 'committed to the belief that artists have a duty and a responsibility to assume a didactic role in developing and promoting cultural progress within their community and country, towards the ideal of a progressive, just and democratic cultural order'.[9] Thami subscribed ardently to these sentiments.

Medu was in the vanguard of the community art centre movement in Southern Africa. Radicals in the United States and Britain had begun the popular movement in the 1960s in reaction against the awesome power of government and big business. In the broadest possible terms they aimed to encourage ordinary people to reclaim their responsibilities and rights from experts. The heart and soul of the centres lay in cultivating collective action. People could see their own potential power when they made murals and community gardens. They gathered in groups to criticise each other's work in progress. Ideally this dialogue would make the arts more democratic. The first South African art centres initiated by community members – as opposed to those run by missionaries, like Rorke's Drift, or by local government, like Polly Street – were founded just a few years before Medu.[10] Being based outside South Africa gave Medu greater freedom to admit to working toward social change.

Medu's freedom was, none the less, limited. Public political affiliation was a fraught issue. At its founding it revealed, vaguely, only that it aligned itself with 'cultural bodies within liberation movements recognized by the OAU'.[11] It called itself, blandly, 'a cultural group of artists living in Botswana' and took care to appear welcoming to the citizens of its host country by belonging to the Botswana National Cultural Council. It had to do so despite Wally's initial impression that Gaborone's African intellectuals were sunk in their own pleasures 'oblivious to all that was happening around them'.[12] At first, Medu wanted to avoid driving away the more committed followers of Black Consciousness and asked no whites to join. (Late in 1979 Albio Gonzalez and Teresa Devant proudly became the first white members.) Medu's policy declared unambiguously, 'All our relations [are] to be on the basis of mutual and equal respect and recognition of our people's cultural identity, dignity and right to freedom, peace and progress.'

'Our people' meant black and, for some, only Bantu-speaking Africans. And yet the group was alluding to the non-racialism of the ANC when it swore 'to relate to all non-African bodies' committed to eradicate 'the cultural domination inherent in colonialism, imperialism and racism'.

In secret, as first Tim and then Wally had done before him, Thami joined the ANC soon after his arrival in Botswana. This act set him apart from some of the younger Soweto refugees who preferred non-alignment to affiliation with a movement they knew barely anything about. Because of his close relationship with Wally, he probably did not have to write an essay or supply references in order to be accepted.[13] Thami knew he was committing himself to support the armed struggle. The ANC had decreed 1979 the Year of the Spear, the first in a planned three-year advance to 'all-out people's war'. The rhetoric was grand. Fulfilling it posed extraordinary challenges. The movement was still debating whether to give priority to urban or rural theatres of battle. It hadn't ironed out the relationship between its political and military wings, so military strategies tended to dominate.

One reason for this military dominance is that exile made it hard for the ANC to connect with and organise domestic political structures. In 1979 exciting new community movements were afoot inside South Africa: workers at the Fattis & Monis factory were on strike, which led to a nationwide boycott of the company's pasta; there were consumer boycotts of red meat; a new unregistered union called the Port Elizabeth Black Civic Organisation (Pebco) organised a strike against the Ford Motor Company. Workplace grievances were inevitably bound up with political ones and unions became the means for expressing opposition. Pebco, for example, opposed the imminent independence of the nearby Ciskei homeland because it saw the homeland government as an enemy that would recruit cheap and compliant labourers to replace any who went on strike. So Pebco members raised their clenched fists and sang union songs to taunt the homeland police. Even though they knew the police might shoot at them, they refused orders to disperse. When Ford did dismiss them, the newly emboldened Pebco members demanded that they be reinstated.

In Botswana ANC members charged with gathering intelligence would try to establish contact with such activists, interview them to get an accurate picture of their political and strategic leanings, and then transmit the information to Lusaka. Pete Richer was one ANC intelligence agent. After fleeing the threat of detention when a student at Rhodes University in 1976 and training in East Germany in 1979, he kept a low profile in Gaborone while gathering and passing on information from home. He worked under the cover of reporting for Solidarity News Service, whose simple office was located in one of Gaborone's poorer neighbourhoods. In this way the ANC was trying to garner energies it was legally prohibited from organising.

Attempting to insert itself into the newly militant spirit at home, the ANC adopted new tactical principles the month Thami arrived in Botswana. The movement advocated the boycott of all South African elections and aimed to develop the insurrectionary potential of the townships. These two resolutions suggested that Thami's revolutionary role would be, at least, to send to the townships propaganda that could detonate a popular revolt: he would propagate 'the main campaign slogans and issues around which the people can be mobilised to organise and act'.[14] He would inspire the majority to have faith in their own powers, and in the liberation movement. But all these activities had to be hidden.

Was Medu simply a front for the ANC? Wally, Tim, and Mandla Langa had founded it after consulting with Raymond Mokoena and Henry Makgothi, two ANC representatives sent down from Lusaka, who helped them think through how to fit a cultural organisation into the political and armed struggles.[15] But Tim is adamant that the art ensemble did not use art as a cover for political and military activities. Medu was a serious artistic organisation, he says, not a convenient ruse. He and Thami and Wally effectively constituted an ANC unit within Medu, but when they put on a play they were not parroting a party line. Uriel Abrahamse, who left law school at the University of Cape Town in 1982 to develop links between the ANC in Botswana and progressive organisations at home, notes that the ANC sent no directives from Lusaka to the artists in Gaborone. The only people the movement ever sent to Medu were poet Willie and singer Baleka Kgositsile, who also arrived in 1982. Further, because Medu had a high profile, the movement could not use it as a conduit for clandestine funds. Rather, the ANC helped Medu raise money for art outreach by supporting its applications to Scandinavian and Canadian aid agencies.[16] In any case, Uriel says, the art ensemble and the exiled movement influenced each other. Vectors of inspiration flew both ways, not simply from Lusaka.

The barriers to creating a collective that actually lived up to its name looked insurmountable. Medu had little money beyond occasional grants from the aid agencies of Norway, Sweden, and Canada.[17] It lost its workplace. Its members sometimes lacked discipline. In 1979, for example, when the group managed to buy a white minibus, pleasure-seeking members drove it to 'unholy places at ungodly hours', at one point crashing the vehicle.[18] These same members could be lax about showing up at scheduled meetings or keeping an up-to-date file of newspaper clippings about South Africa. Sometimes people disappeared with money entrusted to them for furthering Medu's aims.

The youth who had fled South Africa after 1976 were wrestling with a daunting range of dilemmas: they were afraid of being sent to Dukwe, where they would be vulnerable to both boredom and attack; their education had been spotty to poor; many had imbibed from the BCM an anti-white racism that made working with Medu's expatriate members seem counter-revolutionary. Some accused the group's non-racial orientation of being 'too ANC'. On top of everything, South Africans weren't always welcomed

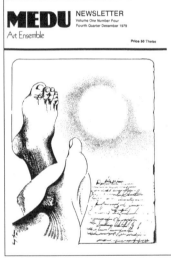

by Batswana. Tswana men, in particular, resented competing with refugees for the attentions of Tswana girls. It didn't help when some cocky young refugees said publicly that they didn't need to compete with local men: the girls were theirs. Thami laughed with delight when he learned that Wally had rebuked some Tswana men in the most withering terms after they made the mistake of instructing him to keep away from their women.

Thami alluded to the generic insecurity when he drew the cover for Medu's September 1979 newsletter. His design depicts a man looking up from a mysterious console toward a moon which has dripped three dark drops, like the motif he had used on Chris van Wyk's book of poetry. No sign of exaltation or hope lights up the man's face or the design itself. On the following issue, his cover (a drawing of an exile's crossed feet) is only slightly more optimistic. To the right, beneath a sun-like floating orb, he scribbled a partially legible text entitled 'Notes for home', with only the words 'Something like this' standing out clearly.

Yet Medu had already achieved a good deal. By the time Thami arrived, it had set up its basic structures. A publications and research unit aimed to publish the newsletter four to six times a year, while overseeing graphic design, photography and film projects. The theatre unit staged two plays in 1979 alone, and took responsibility for dance and music projects. Having grown up in the repressive atmosphere of Franco's Spain, Teresa believed theatre should lead people to 'question why things are like this'. She was not afraid to stage Wally's *Take a Look at the Child* and Kush Mudau's *Marumo*, which celebrated the British defeat by the Zulu in 1879, in a 'didactic' way so as to 'change society'.[19] Inevitably, some of the plans foundered on lack of funds and expertise. The film unit produced one script, *The Flower of the Earth*, though it was never filmed, while music and dance events took place mainly when artists visited from South Africa. Despite its insecure circumstances, Medu palpably thrilled its members, making them feel they were in the vanguard of achieving something big and new.

Thami interviewing Petra Röhr-Rouendaal after her successful wire-car exhibition, Phuthadikobo Museum, Mochudi, Botswana, in the early 1980s. (Courtesy of Petra Röhr-Rouendaal)

This esprit de corps was never more evident than when making posters. The printers first met in June 1979, prior to Thami's arrival, when Petra Röhr-Rouendaal, a German graphic artist, spent one Sunday afternoon instructing them in silkscreen technique. A graduate of a Hamburg art school, Petra commanded more technical skills than most Medu members. Throughout her working life she would demonstrate her commitment to popular education by sharing those skills with disadvantaged people like children in squatter settlements. Without formal political affiliations she was free to make political points in surprising and often humorous ways. She liked playing graphically with ambiguous identity: she drew a woman's face so that it dissolves into a Tswana landscape, and she designed a tableau entitled 'South Africans', in which the white and black figures interlock like pieces of a puzzle. Her creative flair made political points with greater subtlety than the Medu poster unit required.

When the small, ardent group of silkscreeners had absorbed the basics, they set about developing a truly collective ethos. Wally usually decided the issue of each poster and newsletter cover. Then one member would venture an idea for expressing that concept, and the others would critique it. What kind of image was appropriate to mark 16 June? Was a photomontage too cluttered? Should you allow a photograph to control your artistic decisions? How big should a fist be? Were fists, after all, a cliché? Had someone inadvertently drawn the open-palmed sign of PAC membership? Was it too provocative to depict a gun or to disrespect the Voortrekker Monument, that radio-shaped icon of Afrikaner nationalism, by

Petra Röhr-Rouendaal, 'South Africans', n.d. (Courtesy of Petra Röhr-Rouendaal)

drawing an ANC flag smashed into its top? Wally thought it was.[20] In the first two years many of the posters were designed by Albio (Thami was too preoccupied with preparing for his one-man show to venture his own designs).

After an image had been modified, up to 200 copies would be printed over the course of four or five hours. They were folded twice over to become the same size as a newsletter page and sent across the border. Swedish diplomats and other friendly individuals brought some early issues across the border clandestinely, while later issues managed to travel by mail. Progressive organisations in South Africa like the Federation of South African Women and the Five Freedoms Forum took out subscriptions after Uriel assumed responsibility for distribution in 1982. All told, at least 14 posters travelled inside the newsletters. (The newsletters distributed in Botswana never carried posters as they would have exposed Medu as a political organisation.) While former Medu members can still name the primary author of each poster, the production process was truly collective. Wally was proud of that. Thami likened their work to musicians playing off one another's ideas.

Thami and his comrades argued that black South Africans needed strong, even heroic, images in order to imagine another possible reality. Many of their intended audience were illiterate. What better way than graphic art to inspire hope? Thami's young friend and fellow artist, Dikobe Martins, remembers people in South Africa photocopying the posters and carefully sharing them as 'treasured objects' that needed to be kept 'safe'. A particularly popular poster, he says, bore the profile of 23-year-old MK cadre and martyr, Solomon Mahlangu, grasping an AK-47.[21] South African censors sensed their power as well and banned most of the newsletters carrying the posters. At the time the South African police were pursuing visual symbols of African nationalism so zealously that they confiscated even coffee mugs and bedspreads bearing the green, gold, and black colours of the ANC. They probably would have been incensed, just as Wally imagined, by a poster showing the Voortrekker Monument cracking under the impact of an ANC flag.

Medu was growing to express its affiliation to the ANC ever more boldly. By early 1980 the BC members had flushed themselves out. Wally

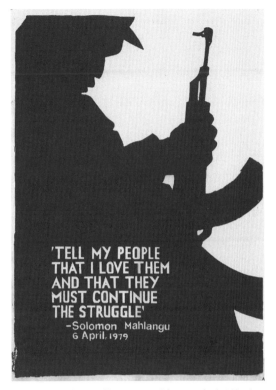

Judy Seidman, Solomon Mahlangu poster, n.d. (Courtesy of Judy Seidman)

referred to their departure from the ensemble when he wrote that some members had disagreed with the principle that Medu 'as a Cultural group must be open to everyone', and that it was regrettable that they had to be 'shaken off along the path and lost'.[22] References to Mandela slipped onto some posters. In 1980 Albio executed Tim Williams's idea of scrawling on top of a photograph of Robben Island the graffiti-like words 'Free Mandela! Free our leaders!' In 1981 Judy Seidman, a new, politically committed American member, drew '… and the people vote for Nelson Mandela' on a red and black poster of valiant workers. (Judy went on to design many of Medu's posters, including the one of Solomon Mahlangu.) Only in July 1981 did Medu record in its minutes an unambiguous statement of affiliation to the ANC: 'It must be the duty of MEDU as a body to identify the organisation that is leading the people. Through mass media in South Africa, apparently the ANC has come to the fore as the right organization.'[23]

Everyone knew it was risky to claim fervent allegiance to the ANC, hence the hedging word 'apparently'. Even Swedish diplomats, whose country had been giving humanitarian aid to the ANC's Botswana office

Thami speaking in the library of the Swedish embassy, Gaborone, on 9 August 1981, Women's Day (commemoration of the 1956 South African women's anti-pass campaign). (Photograph by Albio Gonzalez)

since 1975, didn't want to be seen supporting an overtly ANC project. Thami worried that South Africans would be roughed up and interrogated as if they were comrades when they returned home after visiting Medu members.[24]

The censors were not the only nemesis of Medu's poster-makers. They saw commercial advertising as an even more insidious rival for popular attention. Pictures of Africans modelling evening dress around bottles of Richelieu brandy were the stuff of a different kind of dream from the one they had for South Africa's future. Wally scorned advertisements 'tell[ing] us that the height of female existence is to spend three hours at the hairdresser, a month's salary on a dress, and then drape oneself over a very expensive stereo set'.[25] He might have been referring to a recent ad for a Supersonic console, headed 'That's class, man', though Wally was developing a somewhat different perspective on the word 'class'. The ardour of both Wally's and Thami's attacks on consumerism has the ring of repentance for the period they had each worked for the J Walter Thompson advertising agency.

The newsletter educated readers about radical ideas on race and African liberation by citing Paolo Freire, Samora Machel, Frantz Fanon, James Baldwin, Fidel Castro, and Julius Nyerere. Its articles attacked the capitalist values of the West. The fear of being seduced by Western riches led writers to adopt a puritanical language directed even at frothy commodities like the film *Saturday Night Fever*. They voiced 'disgust' when black John Travolta contests were held in South Africa.[26] Jonas Gwangwa, who had lived in the United States for fifteen years, warned readers against thinking they would gain something from living there; Africans in America risked becoming African-Americans and losing their cultural roots.

These unapologetically didactic articles aimed to marshal support for a cultural boycott of apartheid South Africa. They sharply attacked African-American singers like Millie Jackson, whose visits gave a patina of normality to that warped society. They rebuked South African groups like Juluka, which hoped to gain international exposure by accompanying American performers like Brook Benton. Medu extended the boycott to Botswana, campaigning against the visit to Gaborone of the non-political

That's class, man.

The Supersonic Chesterfield is a record player, a radio and cassette deck in one big, beautiful set.

When the day is done and the night begins, that's when a man needs a Chesterfield. A Supersonic Chesterfield. You can play it hot, play it cool, play it your own way. Because the Chesterfield combines a record player, an FM, MW and SW radio and push-button cassette deck all in one handsome wood console.

And, man, what a sound the Chesterfield makes. The Supersonic sound - crisp, clear and beautiful. But that's not all. In the middle of the Chesterfield there's a deep cabinet where you can store your records, tapes even your drinks! It's the classiest looking, best sounding music set around.

More music for your money. SUPERSONIC

South African musical *Ipi Tombi*, effectively banishing it, and winning the right to stage Mudau's *Marumo* instead.[27] (The high-stepping dance routines and boisterous township jazz of *Ipi Tombi* would surely have given Gaborone audiences more fun.) People jokingly called the newsletter '*Staffrider* in exile', after the glossy South African quarterly that, since 1978, had been printing the poetry, photographs, drawings, and short stories of the angry young generation.[28] While the production values of the unsubsidised, roneoed Medu newsletters were necessarily weaker than those of *Staffrider*, both had a tendency to shout.

After Medu started to produce posters and newsletters on a regular basis, Wally flew to Lusaka to meet ANC president Oliver Tambo, a meeting arranged by Cassius Make, a senior commander in MK and deputy secretary of the ANC's Revolutionary Council. Make had travelled to Vietnam with Tambo and Joe Slovo the previous year to study guerrilla war, and had drawn Wally into MK itself. For the time being, Wally thought Tambo should learn first hand about Medu's cultural initiatives. The poet and the president met in the Revolutionary Council offices for an hour and a half. Wally walked into the office awestruck that he was finally meeting, seated at a file-laden table, the 'large' man who carried the 'dignity of

Africa'. Pulling himself together, he explained Medu's philosophy and activities, while Tambo listened intently, raising many questions and occasionally laughing. When Wally had finished, Tambo told him that 'the important thing to remember was that culture had the strength to unite South Africans'.[29] Wally cherished these words, repeating them over and over to himself and his comrades in Botswana.

On Radio Freedom eight months after Medu was founded and the month after Thami arrived in Botswana, Tambo elaborated on this idea, urging artists to uplift the masses by 'depict[ing] our world of optimism and hope'. By stressing positive values, he believed, art could draw people together. (Tambo felt this power whenever he conducted choral groups; he could famously lose himself for hours in this beloved pastime.) Art could help create a new nation that would, of course, honour African traditions; but Tambo was so open to European influence that the only authority he quoted in his broadcast was the 19th-century British designer and socialist, William Morris. South African artists, he believed, were already contributing to 'the emergence of a world culture and art'. Despite having been 'long denied an outlet for true cultural expression by the racist system our people, our youth, our intelligentsia, our artists have succeeded in piercing the dam wall … [They] are articulating the feelings, hopes and dreams of the impoverished millions of our land.' Their art, he stressed in his clipped, reedy voice, 'can serve as a power-ful weapon in the struggle for national liberation' by merging the people into a united whole.[30] While taking care to urge artists not to hide the 'inhuman conditions' inside South Africa, he saw their primary task as rallying people by celebrating the positive.

Tambo's words gave Thami and all the Medu poster-makers guidelines they respected. They rarely depicted poverty. Thami did so only twice. He drew the back of a malnourished baby under the heading '… scourge of the "bantustans"… kwashiorkor'. He also used captions in 'Fragments: a brief comment on black lives in South Africa' to draw attention to miserable conditions. On a foldout sheet, a man stretches forth his arm to indicate to his female companion and to the reader that schools are 'extremely poor' (children are seated on the floor) and South Africa is 'ruled by force' (a body lies at the feet of policemen). In the middle of this didactic illustration a hand holds aloft a book in front of an AK-47.[31] Even in this rare foray into depictions of poverty Thami inserted symbols pointing the way out. Both the book and the gun seem necessary, though the context suggests that the gun was to be used mainly for self-defence – to prevent more bodies lying at the feet of more policemen. He drew his images from news photos, but he had not abandoned his devotion to his former exploratory style and dreamy subject matter. For the time being, he was managing to combine the two.

Medu members were realising that it was 'vital [for Medu] to be committed more to the local scene'.[32]

fragments: a brief comment on black lives in South Africa

Thami Mnyele, 'Fragments: a brief comment on black lives in South Africa', 1981. (Courtesy of SAHA)

They had to reassure the Batswana that they respected them and that the organisation posed no threat to their country. In peripheral villages Wally performed in dramas about health as part of the mobile museum's lecture series and Thami drew the illustrations. Wally held creative writing classes for high school students and published some of the better stories in the newsletter. He put his Columbia education to work by starting to shoot a film in the village of Kanye, intending to develop a script based on the Kanye audience's reaction to the initial footage.

Petra volunteered to teach poor schoolchildren how to draw at the Trade Fair grounds under the auspices of the Botswana National Museum and, when she moved to Mochudi in 1980 to work at a new museum, Thami replaced her. The Gaborone museum eventually provided a classroom and material but paid neither teacher. In some ways Thami didn't mind. He needed the respectability of being associated with the museum so he could avoid being regarded as a candidate for Dukwe. From August 1980 Thami and another South African exile, Gordon Metz, took over the programme founded by Petra and taught art to poor children from Bontleng and the Old Naledi shantytown. Their classes proved so popular that they had to split them in half so each child could get the requisite attention every two weeks. They invited schoolteachers from Gaborone to attend so they, too, could begin to instruct the deprived children in the use of pencils, coloured pens, powder paints, and making collages. When Medu's undisciplined members crashed the minibus, the classes ground to a halt until it was repaired.[33]

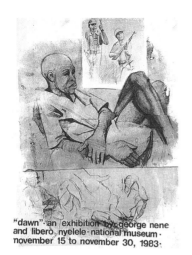

"dawn": an exhibition by george nene
and libero nyelele · national museum ·
november 15 to november 30, 1983·

Medu Art Ensemble, poster for exhibition of
George Nene's art, 1983. (Courtesy of SAHA)

Thami also taught art for a year and a half to inmates of Gaborone prison. One of his students, a Zimbabwean African People's Union (Zapu) guerrilla named George Nene, adopted elements of Thami's sketching style. He soon went on to exhibit in a two-man show at the National Museum, even while serving an eight-year sentence for armed robbery.

Botswana had only three local artists at the time: Victor Moremi, from the royal family of Ngamiland; Jack Mazebedi; and Phillip Segola, a South African by birth. The younger generation of artists needed an inspirational figure and they found one in Thami.[34]

While these educational efforts were part of Medu's attempt to appear helpful to their host country, they also reflect genuine engagement with Tswana institutions like the museum and issues like literacy. Thami approached these tasks with his customary gentleness and sincerity. He enjoyed the children. He murmured encouragement to a slender, long-limbed girl intent on painting a mural of a playground. One small boy amused him by showing up religiously for class but never, though coaxed, daring to draw. Thami travelled to Mochudi to view Petra's exhibition of her students' wire cars, like those he himself had made as a small boy. He shared Petra's big-hearted spirit and appreciated her skill and engagement. Petra, in turn, recognised Thami's own 'greatness and generosity'. He treated her as an equal, instead of making her feel bad about being white. He had the heart of a giraffe, she thought, though he lived in a landscape of jackals.

These personal connections and his generosity with his time may have helped assuage his guilt at having abandoned his two-year-old daughter. She visited Gaborone in her mother's arms in December 1979, but Thami's new life was so full of broadly defined social duties that he could not return to his particular responsibilities as a father. (He did send his daughter one drawing, which, Naniwe reports, his mother tore up for unknown reasons.) He waved goodbye to his wife and child at the Tlokweng gate, turned, and walked back to the new life he was embracing so ardently. And yet he worried that he had wounded his daughter.

Thami lived alone in a one-car garage, though his new love Rhona, having sought him out and found him soon after his arrival, often visited from Johannesburg. She became pregnant at about the time of Naniwe's visit but had to keep up a peripatetic life, shuttling between Tembisa and Gaborone as Thami's life offered her no prospect of settling down.

Thami takes a class of his students to a show of George Nene's watercolours at the Swedish embassy, June 1981. (Photograph by Albio Gonzalez)

The garage accommodated a single bed near the roll-up door, which was never raised, plus a drawing board, bookshelf, and desk. Upon arriving in Gaborone he had borrowed household items from Naniwe's aunt, returning them abruptly when he no longer needed them, as if he wanted to cut all ties with his past married life. Entering the room from the Gonzalez's backyard he first encountered his desk on the right, above which he posted memorabilia. He tacked up a short poem by Dennis Brutus describing the apparent flight of the strelitzia flower, as if it really were its common name, the bird-of-paradise. Nearby he posted a list of Spanish words Albio and Teresa were teaching him. Odd clippings from South African newspapers found their way there, too, drawn from the piles of discarded papers on the floor. He cut out and posted one news photograph of a couple of African actors portraying drunks gesticulating on a staged stoep; it amused him to find this illustration of a friend's remark that drunks tend to move exaggeratedly, as if they were actors on a stage. The bookshelf held a series of books by Lenin, as well as writings about Africa by Aimé Césaire and Ngugi wa Thiong'o. Above the tilted drawing board he strung up a beetle and a mobile of leaves he had collected in the garden in order to draw them. He turned on his tape recorder every single morning to greet the day with the music of Abdullah Ibrahim.

Thami's curiosity about the visual arts and literature was global in its reach. Long intrigued by Salvador Dali's mixture of fantastic images, he had asked Albio to buy a book about Dali's art when he went on holiday to Barcelona and became absorbed in the coffee-table book Albio brought back. He could borrow anything from Albio's personal library, like the big book on the Afro-Chinese Cuban artist, Wilfredo Lam, that Albio had bought for a good discounted price at Exclusive Books in Hillbrow, then Johannesburg's slightly Bohemian quarter.[35] While he chose most frequently to read black writers, he balanced his political commitment with curiosity and respect for the life of the mind without reference to race. He openly envied an internationally eclectic pile of novels on a friend's table.

While some hardline BC ideologues might deride appreciation of Western art, Thami was alive to music without reference to borders. He was actively searching for a modern African aesthetic at the same time as he enjoyed listening, with Albio, to the SABC's classical lunchtime concerts. He loved *Carmen*. He had, of course, listened to Dvořák and Vivaldi at Sached, so the sounds weren't completely new to him. His young comrade Mike Hamlyn, a clarinet player who had evaded the draft by leaving his studies at the University of Natal and crossing the border to study science at the University of Botswana, would often play Prokofiev.

Meanwhile, Thami determined to find a renowned Tswana traditional musician named Ratsie Setlhako, and directed a companion to drive through the bush west of Gaborone one day on a fruitless search for the old man. He greatly admired the jazz of Keith Jarrett and was shocked, even disdainful, when an American friend one day revealed ignorance of her compatriot. How can you be a good American, his raised eyebrows seemed to say, if you don't know your great musicians? He adored Nina Simone. He took double bass lessons in Gaborone.

Above all, he loved music from home. A friend travelling to Johannesburg was instructed to buy him a copy of Abdullah Ibrahim's new record *African Marketplace* at his old Diagonal Street haunt, Kohinoor Records. When the shop's owner, Rashid Valli, learned the record was destined for one of his most devoted former customers, he sent back, as a gift, a long-playing record of South African music he had recently produced. Music was not only the sound of freedom. It could erase Thami's sense that he had left home at all.

His efforts reflected more than attempts to assuage the exile's restless longing, expressed by poet Arthur Nortje in the words, 'who[ever] escapes / a lover's quarrel will never rest his roots'.[36] Like Molefe Pheto before he went into exile in London, Thami was setting out to find old and neglected African musi-

Albio González (far left) films Basil Jones introducing Thami (far right) at the opening of Thami's one-man show in the Botswana National Museum and Art Gallery, September 1980. (Photograph by Teresa Devant)

cians. He listened to music tapes in Gaborone for the purpose of rescuing traditional African sounds from oblivion. They might prove useful in forging a culture for the new South Africa. He committed himself to finding an alternative vision to the dominant white one, and to the re-creation of old African culture, which had been destroyed by colonialism. He both admired and defended African arts, as may be seen in his description of a dance he saw in rural Zimbabwe: 'I was alone in harsh circumstances in Zimbabwe. There was a dance near [the] Mozambique [border]. The women danced in one line and the men faced them beating blocks of wood together fast – they were like an orchestra – and then one man and one woman would meet in the centre and dance gracefully.'

The body of work Thami was putting out in Botswana wasn't very large, although Wally kept urging him to produce. Wally even tried to provoke him by complaining that he could listen to jazz all day long and not bother about anything else. Thami was distracted not only by the shifting events around him but also by his own health. Perhaps to compensate for mysterious bouts of immobility, his work habits were extreme. When he was working flat out in 24- or 48-hour bursts of energy, he wouldn't sleep. (He taped the same beloved songs over and over so he wouldn't have to interrupt his drawing to start them again.) At other times he might sleep for long stretches, particularly when migraine headaches obliged him to spend three or four days continuously in a darkened room. Judy Seidman remembers a doctor telling him he needed a heart valve replacement but, fearing the operation would oblige him to live near a medical centre, he decided to endure the sporadic headaches and chest pain. Sometimes he attributed the headaches to tension and arranged to run to the Gaborone dam with fellow painter and Medu member Gordon Metz in order to relax.

His headaches and anxiety worsened in the months leading up to the first week in September 1980.

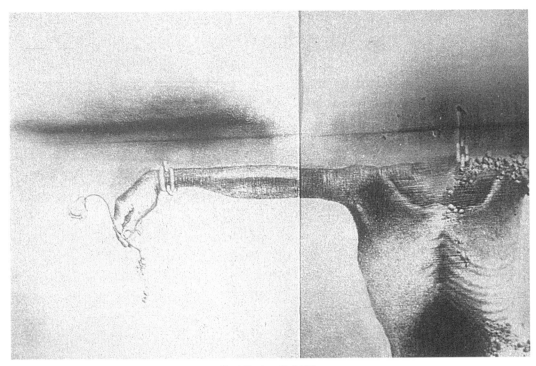

Thami Mnyele, untitled, 1980.

He felt, in Wally's words, 'prematurely pushed' to mount his first one-man show at the National Museum and Art Gallery.[37] While honing his skills, he would have preferred to participate in group exhibitions for quite a while longer. Instead, he rushed to fill the wall space by putting up sketches alongside finished works, plus the six he had brought over the previous year. His days were bursting with new demands and new life. Rhona gave birth to their son, Sindelo, the same week as his show opened.

He called the show *Statements in Spring*. The statements were a mixed lot. He drew a few peaceful images, such as a couple of workers talking. He assembled a more abstract design called 'Hard times – some seasons' by soaking cartridge paper in a turpentine bath containing carborundum powder and then imprinting leaves and thorns (he gave this piece to Petra). He took Teresa's photograph of dancers and drew the man and woman without heads, their linked arms so taut they seemed in combat.

Many of his images commented explicitly on violence: a headless torso holds a drooping flower in its outstretched arm; a trio of heads scream; a body lies on the ground while a helicopter hovers in the distance. The diptych 'Zimbabwe' could be a revolutionary sequel to 'Consequences', his 1979 portrait of

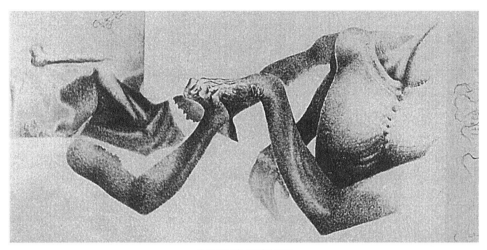

Thami Mnyele, untitled, 1980.

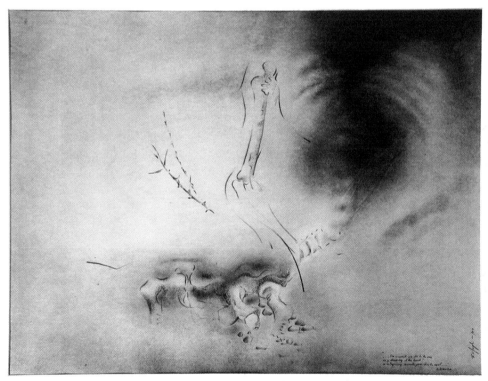

Thami Mnyele, untitled, 1980. (Courtesy of Nicolaas G. Maritz)

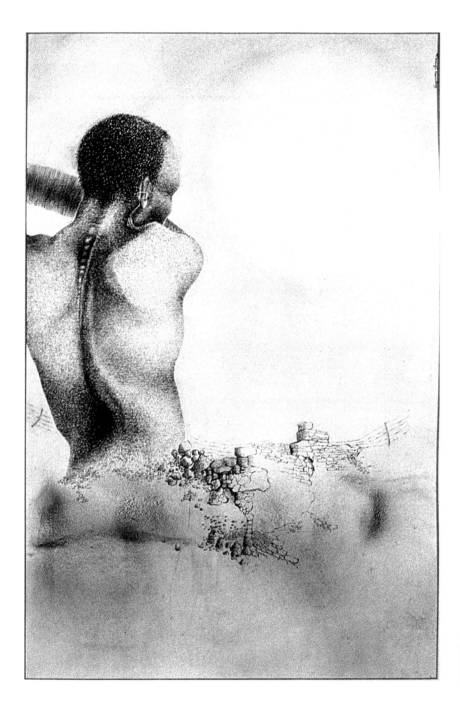

Thami Mnyele, 'Zimbabwe',
1980, 86.4 x 62.2 cm,
Author's Collection.
(Photograph by
Michael Hamilton)

141

Thami Mnyele, untitled, 1980, 62 x 58 cm, Chabani Manganyi and Peggy Sekele-Manganyi Collection. (Photograph by Wayne Oosthuizen)

Tim Williams: a naked man's back has risen from a crumbling stone wall; he has laid his right palm on top of his left fist, as if to say 'amen, the violence is over'.

His fellow South African graphic artist, later a co-founder of The Handspring Puppet Company, Basil Jones, wrote an essay for the show's brochure calling attention to the layers of Thami's symbolism. Some symbols, Jones wrote, were conventional, like the chains holding up the arm of the headless torso. More personal ones, like stony ground, alluded to hardship, while the body parts suggested alienation, and the chasms represented 'an impending threat of disaster'. Jones found the spaces and skies far more complex and significant: they were 'the transcending index of an infinity of suffering and insecurity … sublime nausea … neglect and absence … the feeling of soiled second-handedness … the terrifying medium in which all suffering and loss is steeped'. Thami redeemed this negativity by his 'manifest love of human forms' that he guided with 'care and reverence' into the picture space. Jones had correctly perceived that Thami's sworn affection for 'the people' was based on deep feeling.[38] Alec Campbell, founder and director

Thami Mnyele, 'Somewhere in our hearts', 1980, 73 x 51 cm, Botswana National Museum and Art Gallery. (Photograph by Mark Henningsen)

of the Botswana National Museum and Art Gallery, bought four of Thami's works for the museum.

Through the first half of the following year Thami still entertained the idea of developing his talents by studying art at, for example, the Pratt Institute in New York City. He had taken life-drawing classes at the museum along with Petra, Albio, Adrian Kohler, a couple of Americans, and a few Batswana, all of them working on Medu-made easels. (Each of them posed as models for life drawing, though only Adrian, soon to co-found with Basil The Handspring Puppet Company, and the American man agreed to pose naked.) He openly longed to be a great artist, not just a good one. 'I don't believe art should be separate from feeling,' he told a friend in 1981. When the same friend showed him Michelangelo's self-portrait as a bag of flesh in 'The Last Judgment', he responded solemnly, 'I want to be that good.' The sheer simplicity of his yearning to be excellent stripped his statement of any possible grandiosity. He knew he would have to study to gain technique that he hadn't yet acquired through his own spotty education. He was also resisting members of the movement who tried to dictate the company he could keep in his private life.

The times, on the other hand, were calling for total dedication to the goal, as Radio Freedom put it, of seizing power from the oppressor. Wally, for example, counselled Judy Seidman to omit all elements of 'defeat or non-resolution' from her posters. He cared enough about this point to write her a letter, even though they lived in the same town and saw each other all the time. Artists, he wrote, should avoid showing misery, fear, and sorrow, and instead concentrate on depicting 'a determination to fight on' so that others would follow.[39] Tim Williams remembers Thami making the same point in an oblique way. He would seem to be joking when he derided bad art as 'caricature', but he was deadly serious: 'Those people [in the painting],' he would say, 'why do you portray them without dignity, as if they were defeated? There's no life in those people.'[40] The Medu poster-makers celebrated resistance, as did most politically conscious writers of the time. Nadine Gordimer, for example, saw resistance even in a maid's shocking red nail polish.

As Mac Maharaj, a key ANC strategist, explained it, ' I saw, to be quite frank, propaganda as a detonator … I saw propaganda distribution as enabling [us] to go into the community and probe and listen [to] who was impressed by it and how they were reacting to it – to guide [us] to who we could consider for cultivating, to recruit.'[41] Seen in this strategic light, Thami's turn away from the style and content of his early art becomes easier to understand. If he depicted the emotional consequences of being dominated, he was doing nothing to end the demoralisation. If he illustrated the reasons for the armed struggle, as he did in 'Fragments', he might win a cadre.

Thami knew that total commitment was a life or death matter. On 16 June, upon hearing a young Medu member use violent language at an event commemorating the Soweto uprising, he shook his head. 'That fellow can't call the South African government "fascist" like that. Those people are serious.' He meant that the enemy was too formidable to taunt with loose language. The youth was deluding himself if he thought his bravado would not excite a vicious response. Still, in 1981, Thami had the temperament of an artist more than of a cadre. He was prone to dreaming, and he was inattentive to practical details like where exactly he had left his address book. In October, disturbed about the arrest of two comrades, he observed, without identifying his act of negligence, 'If we lose people and gain little or nothing, that's bad, but if we are carried forward, even though we lose people, that's all right. I was very upset when I felt personally responsible for two guys being picked up – they're on Robben Island now – until I realised that the fault is in the whole situation, outside my control. They've sent out messages saying they're all right.'

What role did Botswana play in the recruitment to and deployment of cadres in the ANC? Initially, it was a place where refugees and visiting South Africans could learn about the movement. The generation of 1976

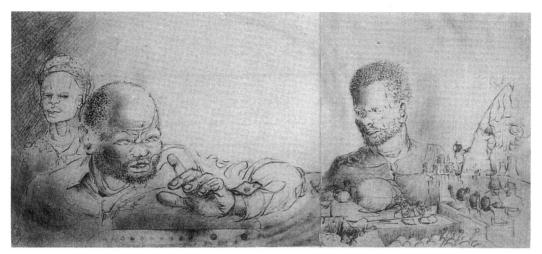

Thami Mnyele, illustration for an article in *Staffrider* (1981). (Original in Alex Segale Collection)

knew little of the culture of protest that came before it. In 1979, for example, Wally had to explain to Dikobe Martins why the ANC had resorted to revolutionary violence. Martins, like many young recruits, had known only vaguely about the ANC and the PAC in the 1970s; political reading groups focused then on Black Consciousness readings, but found Marxist literature 'too advanced'. Martins went back to South Africa and disseminated what he had learned among his friends.[42] Uriel Abrahamse remembers introducing visiting MK figures to local exiles and then walking away so he couldn't overhear their conversation.

Botswana was also the place where some people learned their first lessons in how to conduct a 'people's war'. In 1981 Martins, with two other men, received, in Botswana, a 'short [circa one month] crash course in the use of firearms and explosives'. Then he returned to Pietermaritzburg, where he knew only about three or four ANC members.

Choosing to work as director of the youth department in a lay ecumenical centre, Martins recruited about 20 young men whom he had identified as mature and skilled at organisation and communication. He asked them if they would find military training palatable and, when six answered yes, he transferred them to outside 'structures', usually in Lesotho, for short bursts of military training lasting only a weekend or a week. Similarly, Alex Segale remembers walking around Tembisa at night, putting revolutionary documents – about the Freedom Charter and the ANC leadership – in letterboxes. When people responded positively to them, he would gather them into units of three to spirit out of South Africa. They would drive to the border, perhaps watch schoolboys play a football game in a nearby field. Then they would slowly filter through the fence into Botswana. They would ask to be taken to meet Alex's friend Thami, who would pass them on to their instructors.[43]

Botswana increasingly became a conduit for arms. They arrived in the country hidden in false compartments built into long-distance trucks, large and small, and had to be secretly stored before being transported into South Africa. Thami never said anything about armaments to Albio, though he sometimes asked Teresa and other white friends to carry mysterious items across the border to Johannesburg. They took care never to ask questions, so they would have nothing to reveal if stopped. Upon the advice of a Swedish diplomat, Teresa once carried material hidden in a sanitary napkin. Another friend carried papers wrapped up as a wedding present; on arriving in Johannesburg she slid them under a bench in a restaurant where she had arranged to meet Thami's friend James Molaya, a graphic artist employed in the advertising world and a natty dresser with a taste for fancy cars. On one occasion the Botswana police were sent to dig up Albio and Teresa's yard, but found nothing. Thami asked Albio to obtain for him the most accurate maps of the long Botswana border and, when he obliged, succinctly murmured, 'The movement is grateful.'[44] (Thami used the maps to do 'border reconnaissance' with Tim.) The maps, like 'safe houses', would enable MK cadres returning from military training in Angola to find safe routes home via Zambia and Botswana.

The country was also a site for diplomacy, a meeting place for people inside the ANC to learn what was going on in South Africa. Cars bearing telltale TJ (Johannesburg) licence plates drew up outside Thami's garage and out spilled old friends, as well as activists like union representatives, eager to discuss strategy. The exiles put people up in safe houses, sometimes the homes of Scandinavians gone home on holiday. They publicised ANC values, traditions, and history. As Wally, who had become a member of the ANC's 'Botswana Senior Organ' or joint political-military committee, later observed with pride, 'We penetrated the rural areas and townships, white suburbs, Indian and coloured areas from an underground position. There was not a single day when we were not in touch with people from South Africa for debriefing and briefing.'[45] Since they all used *noms de guerre* – Riaz Saloojee was known, incongruously, as 'Calvin Khan' or 'Cal' and Thami may have been called 'Sipho' – no one was ever precisely sure whom they were meeting. Among them, inevitably, were spies.

Race, of course, provided no guide to who was trustworthy and who was not. Some white South Africans joined the ANC in Gaborone and supported a wide range of activities whose function they didn't always know. Mike and Carol Kahn secretly joined the ANC the year after they arrived in Gaborone so Mike could teach science at the university; Wally had chatted with them until he determined they were worthy of trust. They housed draft resisters and, on one occasion, two top ANC officials, Mac Maharaj and Reg September. Carol, a specialist in early childhood education, used books to make coded messages, whose meaning she never knew. On their trips home she and Mike would scout for dead-letter boxes, like toilets in suburban Cape Town railway stations typically ignored by the police. They organised picnics in villages like nearby Mochudi, where people with something private to impart could wander into the bushes to talk. Exiles used their telephone, even though they assumed it was tapped. Whenever they crossed the border carrying presents, border guards would rip them open, looking for, but never finding, messages like the ones they hid in the Cape Town toilets. Carol, whose code name was 'Farida', drew this attention partly because her cousin was Cape *Argus* newspaper sub-editor David Rabkin, then serving a prison term for preparing and distributing ANC pamphlets.[46]

Midway through 1981 Thami unambiguously threw in his lot with the movement. He sacrificed private longing and artistic ambition for the movement's definition of the greater good and how it was to be achieved. He never complained again that he ought to be able to trust his instincts when choosing his friends. Nor did he express bitterness, even to Wally, his confidant and one-time muse. Developing his own commitments and faith, he openly disparaged his father's tendency to quote the Bible. When young comrades like Dikobe visited from South Africa, they earnestly discussed 'the totality of the struggle and the need to give all your skills to advancing it'. They stressed the imperative of putting the collective above the needs of the self.[47] Thami was learning to become a comrade.

NOTES

1   Alex Segale, interview (25 Sept 2004).
2   Pablo Neruda, 'Death alone', *Selected Poems* (Boston: Houghton Mifflin, 1990), 89.
3   Mnyele to father, letter (n.d.), property of Lindi Mnyele Binca.
4   Jenny Zetterqvist, *Refugees in Botswana in the Light of International Law*, Research report no. 87 (Uppsala: Scandinavian Institute of African Studies, 1990), 22. Dukwe was designed by a newly arrived British town planner, Tony Gregory, who was then put in charge of the decentralised Department of Town and Regional Planning office at Francistown. Albio Gonzalez, pers. comm. (16 Dec 2005).
5   Lefifi Tladi, interview (21 July 2001); Boitumelo Makunga, 'Introducing Medu', *Medu Newsletter*, 1, 1 (March 1979), 5-7; Pheto, 'Mihloti black theatre', 41–6.
6   Notes of a meeting regarding the Swedish Project held at A Gonzalez's home on 11 June 1980; T Mnyele, Secretary for Medu Work Committee, to Sir/Madam (17 August 1980), Gonzalez Collection.
7   'Students are released', *Botswana Daily News* (18 Sept 1978).
8   Roger Southall, 'Botswana as a host country for refugees', *Journal of Commonwealth and Comparative Politics*, 22, 2 (July 1984), 156, 162.
9   Medu Policy Declaration (n.d.), Seidman Papers.
10 Lize van Robbroeck, 'The ideology and practice of community arts in South Africa, with particular reference to Katlehong and Alexandra Arts Centres' (MA, University of the Witwatersrand, 1991).
11 Medu Policy Declaration.
12 Ibid; Serote, *Hyenas*, 12–13.
13 Dikobe Ben Martins, interview (31 Dec 2005).

14 'Green Book', 730.

15 Serote, autobiographical essay. Serote notes that Medu also absorbed elements from the PAC, BCM, and Unity movements, even though he and his fellow two founders had by then severed their connections with the BCM and with Pan-Africanist thinking.

16 Tim Williams, interview (7 Jan 2006); Uriel Abrahamse, interview (23 Dec 2005).

17 The Medu project proposal (1979) noted that it initially received some financial support from the International University Exchange Fund. Elizabeth Gron ('South African cultural exiles in Botswana' (MA dissertation, University of Botswana, 1997), chapter 1) writes that Medu received ANC funds, as well as money from the donor agencies Cida, Sida, and Norad. Tor Sellstrom (*Sweden and National Liberation in Southern Africa* (Uppsala: Nordiska Afrikainstitutet, 1999), vol. 2, 675–9) writes that from the late 1970s the Swedish government received the ANC's requests for politically motivated 'home-front' assistance in a positive spirit, and the Botswana government never requested that Sweden suspend its non-military support for the ANC inside Botswana; by 1985 Sweden and Norway were the only countries channelling official support to the ANC in Botswana, including by helping to support 100 ANC members, half of whom were refugees in transit. Sellstrom believes Medu and the Botswana National Museum organised the 1982 Culture and Resistance conference 'on the ANC's initiative'.

18 'Report on transport', Medu Art Ensemble Annual Seminar (1981), 2, Gonzalez Collection.

19 'Interview: Bachana wa Mokoena interviews Teresa Devant de Gonzalez', *Medu Newsletter*, 1, 2 (1979), 39–40.

20 Interviews: Judy Seidman (2003, 2004) and Albio Gonzalez (2000).

21 Dikobe Ben Martins, interview (31 Dec 2005).

22 Wally Serote, 'Editorial', *Medu Newsletter*, 1, 4 (Dec 1979), 1.

23 'Community development, policy/approach', Medu Art Ensemble Annual Seminar (1981), Gonzalez Collection.

24 According to Tor Sellstrom (*Sweden and National Liberation*, 611–15), Sweden was responding to an ANC request for help in 'expanding our network of organizers, who need transport, safe houses, visible means of subsistence', that is, money for dependants, bulletins, legal aid, printing, publicity, transport. Sellstrom notes that because Sweden did not monitor the aid, some of it must have gone to MK. Medu members' fears of harassment at the border are apparent in the June 1980 Medu minutes regarding early stages of planning the Culture and Resistance conference, Gonzalez Collection.

25 Wally Serote, 'Politics of culture', *Sechaba* (March 1984), 28.

26 Interview with Jonas Gwangwa, *Medu Newletter*, 1, 4 (Dec 1979), 29–38; Bachana wa Mokwena, Editorial, *Medu Newletter*, 1, 3 (Sept 1979), 2.

27 'Press release on Ipi Tombi', *Medu Newletter*, 1, 2 (June 1979), 28.

28 *Staffrider*, published by Ravan Press, was established in response to what it called the recent surge of creativity; it initially had no editor or editorial board, and the state banned three issues in the first two volumes because they depicted the police in an 'offensive' way, 'calculated to evoke [sic] hatred and contempt of them'. During his lifetime, Thami's drawings appeared in issues 3, 3 (1980) and 4, 3 (1981). The first two issues (1978) contained poems inspired by or dedicated to him, written, respectively, by his friends Nape Motana ('Village from the portion of my mind') and Chris van Wyk ('We can't meet here, brother').

29 Serote, *Hyenas*, 8.

30 'Comrade O.R. Tambo on people's art from a Radio Freedom broadcast, September 1979', Karis-Gerhart Political Documents 3, Folder 32, Cullen Library, Wits.

31 *Medu Art Ensemble* [Newsletter] Special Edition, 1981, between pp. 4 and 5.

32 Notes on meeting, 11–13 July 1981, Gonzalez Collection.

33 Interviews: Petra Röhr-Rouendaal (June 2003), Gordon Metz (30 July 2001).

34 The following were members of this younger generation of Botswana artists: Steve Mogotsi, Keitse Bogatsu, Moitshepi Madibela, Neo Matome, Mokwaledi Gonthwanetse, Velias Ndaba.

35 Albio Gonzalez, interview (2000).

36 Arthur Nortje, 'Cosmos in London' in Barry Feinberg (ed.), *Poets to the People* (London: Heinemann, 1980), 149.

37 Wally Serote, 'Introduction', *Statements in Spring* catalogue, 3.

38 Basil Jones, 'Meaning in Mnyele's skies', *Statements in Spring* catalogue, 4–5; Basil Jones, interview (8 Jan 2002).

39 Wally Serote to Judy Seidman (4 or 5 Nov 1981), Seidman Collection.

40 Tim Williams, interview (7 Jan 2006).

41 Mac Maharaj, interview by Howard Barrell, quoted in Barrell, 'Conscripts to their age: African national Congress operational strategy, 1976–86' (DPhil thesis, University of Oxford, 1993), 171.

42 Dikobe Martins, interview by Howard Barrell (20 Nov 1990), Karis-Gerhart Collection, reel 2.

43 Ibid; Alex Segale, interview (25 Sept 2004).

44 Interviews: Albio Gonzalez and Teresa Devant (2000).

45 Serote, *Hyenas*, 8.

46 Carol Kahn, interview (30 Dec 2005).

47 Dikobe Ben Martins, interview (31 Dec 2005).

Chapter 6

Making the Sun Rise

Thami was finally ready to produce his first poster and he worked very hard on it, according to Albio. He copied from a postcard the image of two South West Africa People's Organisation (Swapo) guerrillas, outlining them in red. Above their faces he drew guns. Wally scoffed at his slogan 'SWAPO will make the sun rise …', saying the words reminded him of an advertisement for detergent. Given Thami's sensitivity to criticism, he cannot have been pleased. Albio understood that people like the Swapo guerrillas needed to be idealised for propaganda purposes. His training as a draughtsman, as well as his familiarity with the history of Soviet, Chinese, and Cuban posters, undoubtedly helped him to formulate strong designs. Thami's education had failed to give him this historical perspective, and there were no Soviet posters available to study in Botswana.[1] In any case, he had long approached paper with the intention of sketching a finely detailed image in pencil. His first poster looked tentative.

Thami's political commitment was deepened by what happened to Joe Gqabi. He had crossed paths with Gqabi in Gaborone, and what he learned of the life story of this man, portly and deliberate in manner, struck him with awe. A long-time communist, Gqabi trained as a guerrilla for 18 months in Nanking, China,

Thami Mnyele, Medu poster, 1981. (Courtesy of SAHA)

149

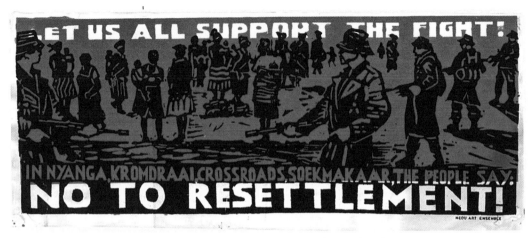

Thami Mnyele, Medu poster, 1982, 73.7 x 29.2 cm. (Courtesy of SAHA)

in the early 1960s. The Rhodesian police arrested him in 1963 for channelling exiles into MK and he spent the next 12 years as a political prisoner on Robben Island. Upon his release, reporter Nat Serache interviewed him for the *Rand Daily Mail* and received his 'first political education'. While Serache remained publicly identified with the BCM, he immediately joined the underground because he was so moved by Gqabi's 'honesty' and 'humility', as well as by his revolutionary logic. (In 1976, for example, Gqabi urged Soweto students not to attack shebeens because they would thereby drive their owners into the protective arms of the police.)[2] Going into exile in 1977, Gqabi served on the ANC's Revolutionary Council, becoming the chief ANC representative and MK commander in Botswana until South Africa pressured Botswana to expel him in 1980. In 1981 he became deputy director and head of intelligence within the ANC's Department of Intelligence and Security.

On 31 July 1981 Gqabi was shot dead in Harare through the back window of his car. Thami was stunned. He stood in the middle of his room and stared into space. What made this event most pressing was that Gqabi was a senior leader of MK, whose death deprived the movement of real talent and knowledge, as well as personal integrity. ('You [must] never lie to your organisation,' Serache remembers him saying.) Along with Mac Maharaj, Gqabi was working on building a Political Reconstruction Committee whose goal was to recruit new ANC members rapidly inside South Africa. Because Gaborone was near the big cities of the Rand, it was an important staging area for that effort.

Gqabi's murder was not the first of its kind in 1981. South African forces had attacked three ANC houses in a Mozambican suburb called Matola, outside the capital, on 31 January, killing 13 people. Even Botswana suffered losses at the hands of the security police. Exiles were sometimes kidnapped or handed over to the South African Police (SAP). Peter Lengene, for example, was abducted in February 1982 and subjected to a 'recruitment process' during which he was transported to Rustenburg where he was held in a private garage, fed alcohol, assaulted, and, after a week of this treatment, had 'turned,' that is, agreed to work for the Soweto security police.[3] Other victims proved neither so lucky nor so malleable. One angry young man who had visited Thami at Albio's house in April was picked up at the border upon returning to South Africa. The police interrogated him so roughly that he died. 'A lot of people are going to his funeral,' Thami said gravely, though he himself did not dare. The deaths of comrades like Gqabi and the angry young man made him sombre enough to say, 'I can't be happy at the moment because I might easily be hanging a still life in a sinking ship.'

MK's stated goal since 1977 had been to enhance the popular appeal of the ANC with dramatic attacks that brought the movement to national and international attention. The name for this strategy was 'armed propaganda'.[4] Given the improbability of MK overwhelming the mighty South African army, the goal was to mobilise popular resistance in the workplace and communities by demonstrating that apartheid society was nevertheless vulnerable. Slowly but steadily the campaign grew. The first major salvo was fired on 1 June 1980, when the ANC made a new foray into warfare by exploding a mine at the strategically important Sasol plant where coal was converted into petroleum. The brazenness of the attack was unprecedented. Pete Richer would learn years later how deeply this blast shook the confidence of the apartheid regime: National Intelligence Service analysts would tell him they were meeting on an island in the Vaal Dam when they heard the news, and from that moment they began wondering what time might be ripe for negotiations to begin.[5]

The second salvo came in 1981 when MK hit the Voortrekkerhoogte military base, home of the Special Forces high command just outside Pretoria, with a 122 mm rocket launcher. This was a spectacular example of 'armed propaganda' and the attack came ironically close to enacting the provocative poster Wally had vetoed, the one depicting the cracking of the iconic monument of Afrikaner nationalism high on a hill above Pretoria.

MK's successes emboldened the USSR to increase its military assistance. It packed container ships with timber, concrete, clothing, as well as arms, and dispatched them to Luanda, Angola, and to Dar es Salaam, Tanzania. From these ports the material travelled by road to states bordering South Africa. Within Botswana

THE PRESIDENT'S COUNCIL and

His Master's Voice

Albio Gonzalez, Medu poster, 1980.
(Courtesy of SAHA)

itself, though, the Russians had no contact with ANC members apart from the ordinary social occasions that every embassy hosted. Ronnie Kasrils, head of MK's military intelligence, described Vladimir Shubin, a member of the Soviet Communist Party's Central Committee, as 'our best Soviet friend … a bear-sized man, with a booming voice and bone-crushing embrace … like an uncle to us all'. Shubin writes that his government avoided ANC contacts in Gaborone partly because the city was simply too close to South Africa. Pete Richer, then a member of the SACP, agrees, imagining that the Russians didn't want to jeopardise their diplomatic mission by engaging with the ANC so close to the border.[6] Even if this diplomatic stance meant Thami had no ties to the Soviet Union, he felt some gratitude and chided an American friend who was amused by the sight of stocky and overdressed Russians, wearing fedoras and overcoats in hot Gaborone, snapping, 'At least they're doing something.'

The ANC named 1981 the Year of Youth, projecting it as the final year before all-out people's war. The changing names of its internal organs signalled its increasingly militaristic stance: from 1976 to 1980 its local units were called Internal Reconstruction and Development committees, charged with re-establishing the political underground and organising propaganda inside South Africa; from 1981 the units were called Senior Organs and consisted of military and political personnel in the 'forward areas'. And yet, while MK had made 1981 its best year since 1963, 21 of its combatants were killed or arrested in the 55 attacks it had launched. The losses were due, in large part, to the web of spies within the ANC, many uncovered in March. Since the movement was 'madly' recruiting new members, as Pete Richer remembers, it had accepted into its midst many paid agents of Pretoria.

Thami was worried that P W Botha's strategy for winning support by giving benefits to the black middle class might work. Would Africans fail to support the ANC because they lived in upgraded urban neighbourhoods? Would they be mollified by their ability to vote in their own local government elections? Would coloured and Asian voters embrace the nominated President's Council, set up in 1980, and the two new houses of Parliament it would open specially for them in 1984? Would neighbouring countries withdraw from the sympathetic nine-nation Southern African Development Coordination Conference (SADCC) and belong instead to Botha's Constellation of States because it promised foreign aid and freedom from South African attack?[7] In 1981 the Medu posters addressed each of Botha's proposed reforms with the intention of mobilising domestic opposition.

Thami's 1982 poster 'No to resettlement' (see p. 150) strikes a less exhortative tone than many Medu posters. It makes a statement of fact, one that is unusually ambivalent about the prospect of success. More than a dozen women and children stand in the background, stalwart in their opposition. Their figures are upright. The five soldiers are armed, so the situation looks, for the time being, like a stand-off.

For the most part, though, Thami was leaving behind the searching and sometimes surreal style that marked his one-man show. He grew suspicious of what he called distortion, abstraction, and mysticism, all of them signs of 'our alienation'. The impact of his decisions is made clear by a comparison of the images in his one-man show with those he drew shortly afterwards.

In 1982, for example, he illustrated Medu's only published book, Wally's long poem entitled *The Night Keeps Winking*, drawing the cover and the illustrations that separate each of the three portentously titled sub-sections: 'Time has run out', 'The sun was falling', 'Listen, the baby cries and cries and cries'. Thami had wanted Wally to choose him as illustrator because, he said, it was time for him to reflect the struggle as it really was. His drawings recycled his own familiar imagery – barbed wire, thorns, barely legible words – but he assembled them to reveal a narrative of sorts. The barbed wire runs in front of a protesting, uni-formed schoolgirl. He portrays a man on either side of two jail scenes: on the left he is simply reflecting; on the right, having contemplated the prisoner's or his own suffering, he is wearing a bandolier of bullets and gazing at a map on which a power station appears to be marked. Miners and hard-working women complete the picture of a people who are stolid and ready[8] (see p. 154).

The drawings mirror Wally's text, which takes the reader from Steve Biko's murder back through the Soweto riots to 'exploitation', and asks, 'Who are we when babies die, bright boys get killed, fear blooms to hate[?]' The answer is: people who have learned 'how to hold a gun and a grenade'.[9] Wally has inserted the names of Mandela and Tambo in the poem, but Thami has not explicitly referred to the ANC. Nor has he depicted a hoped-for future. In 1982 the future still seemed so opaque that neither poet nor artist ventured any imagery suggesting what lay ahead, apart from the negation of what was. The South African government banned the book in 1983.

Probably because he was widely liked and trusted, Thami rose in the middle of July from being the head of the Medu graphic unit to chairman of the entire organisation and held that position until

Thami Mnyele, illustrations for Wally Serote's poem *The Night Keeps Winking*, published by Medu, 1982. (Courtesy of Wally Serote)

November 1982, when his friend Tim Williams took over. He thereby held a high-profile position during the Culture and Resistance festival, Medu's most celebrated achievement. The initial core organisers – Albio, Thami, and Wally – had originally called the festival 'the Swedish project' after its origins in an exhibit of South African art intended to travel to Sweden in October 1981. However, the idea grew more ambitious, eventually embracing poetry, drama, and music, as well as the visual arts. And it would be held in Southern Africa, not in Scandinavia.

First, links had to be forged with artists who weren't in exile. Albio took advantage of his Swedish passport and travelled to Johannesburg to meet with Thami's former comrades, exciting his envy and longing. (Thami was still so attached to the city that he asked a friend to take his boots for repair to a Johannesburg cobbler.) Albio met fellow architect Piero Cuzzolin, artists Ben Arnold and Ezrom Legae, and a young man whose immaturity caused problems. (He squandered the R200 Medu gave him to help organise the conference.)

Medu recruited help from foreign donors like Norad, Sida, and IVS, and Thami told the local representative of the Norwegian government that he was simply an artist and had no political agenda; Norad gave Medu a new car and money for its cultural activities.[10] Thami and Wally wrote to South African groups they thought might be interested – the names constitute a roster of the socially conscious arts organisations of the time: Ravan Press and the *Staffrider* staff, the Federated Union of Black Artists (Fuba), Mpumalanga Arts, the Open School, and MDALI. Colin Smuts, of Johannesburg's Open School, became Transvaal, and then national, organiser largely because he was asked to do so by other South Africans who couldn't.[11] The net effect of this chain of communication was that rural artists were largely left out.

The first event in the Culture and Resistance programme was the opening of the visual art and photography exhibit on 10 June. That evening an audience, split evenly between Africans and European and American expatriates, wrapped up against the cold of a winter night, gathered in Gaborone's museum, one of the exhibition venues. (The work spilled over from the National Museum on to the inner walls of the Anglican cathedral.) Thami's fellow compatriot Doreen Nteta was the new director of the museum, even though she was on record as thinking there wasn't 'much in Botswana in the way of art'. She introduced him and looked on admiringly as he spoke from a typed text on which he had penned a few amendments. He added, for example, the words 'imperialist institutions' when he referred to galleries in world capitals, the very cities where he often spoke of wanting to study.[12]

Thami, expressing Medu's creed, made the point that 'art and cultural workers cannot be divorced from this process' of struggling for liberation, as if he were saying to the ANC leaders, who had not established

Thami with Doreen Nteta (right), opening the Culture and Resistance art exhibition at the Botswana National Museum and Art Gallery, Gaborone, 10 June 1982. (Photograph by Michael Kahn)

a cultural wing, that Medu belonged in the heart of the struggle, that its members were ready for the party to guide them. He asserted that art was 'the work of many hands' rather than of individuals, warning that galleries in London, Paris, and New York were manned by 'extremely dangerous people' because they exploited South African artists and alienated them from their community. He went on to allude to core ANC principles, like the need to include 'all South African races' among 'cultural workers'. He added the mantra of the times: artists had to avoid expressing 'a dangerous sense of fear and despair'.[13]

He contributed five drawings to the exhibition, calling them 'Statement, workers, and country' (see p. 158). They were not for sale. He drew tools like wire-cutters, chisels, mallets, and even a book with the title 'Socialist Ideology on Culture' on its spine. He also drew dignified workers communing with one another. They looked like illustrations for a Medu newsletter or a book like *The Night Keeps Winking*. What do these drawings express, apart from a statement that workers triumph? Years later South African artist Paul Stopforth found them subtle, rather than didactic, and full of 'silences'; that is, they possess a sense of mystery allowing the viewer to move into them and not be forced into an agenda. Others were not as impressed. Critic Ricky Burnett remembers Thami's art as 'polemical cartoons – not particularly striking'. Thami was proud mainly of the egalitarian way the exhibit was mounted. 'The work wasn't put up on [the basis of] a professionalism,' he said. 'If you look around you'll find work done by very known artists and next to their work you'll find students. The basic principle here was to create a basis for discussion; a basis for dialogue.'[14]

Thami in the Department of Town and Regional Planning, Gaborone, framing pictures for the Art Toward Social Development (ATSD) show in June 1982, helped by Miles Pelo (left) and 'If' (right). (Photograph by Albio Gonzalez)

The second event was the opening on 2 July of a five-day symposium and festival of plays, music, and panel discussions. The 800 people in attendance generated an ecstatic air, as if they were declaring Gaborone a liberated zone. People broke all sorts of rules. They drank a lot, they didn't sleep, they had interracial sex, which was illegal in South Africa. They were aware of spies watching them. They knew some of the participants were armed. Some worried aloud that the event would be bombed.

Emotions ran high as old friends from home and abroad reunited. Wilson 'King Force' Silgee, veteran of 1930s jazz bands, played his saxophone with the vigour of a man far younger than his 70 years. Thami drew Silgee thrusting his right arm triumphantly in the air at the end of a number. When Abdullah Ibrahim arrived at Gaborone airport, Thami strode with a measured gait towards his musical hero, his shoulders thrown back. Greeting the world-famous pianist on behalf of Medu was probably one of the

Thami Mnyele, 'Statement, workers, and country', 1982. (Courtesy of Janet Pillai)

grandest moments of his life. He looked on, star struck, as the younger jazz legend was introduced to Silgee, the older one.

He enjoyed an even higher profile during the closing event when, as chairman of Medu, he introduced Ibrahim on stage in front of Ketumile (Quett) Masire, the president of Botswana. At the microphone, he said, 'The fundamental objective of this event has been to bring all cultural workers of my country together to explore the ways and means of achieving social justice, peace and harmony. These are the self-same objectives that your excellency is striving for as a member of the frontline states and SADCC … At tonight's performance we have cultural workers whose music has always inspired my people despite social injustice and deliberate destruction of our culture.'[15] For Thami the symposium, exhibit, and festival surpassed their path-breaking predecessor, the *New Day* exhibit in 1977. It gave new life to phrases like 'the breezing dawn of a new day', which he had previously heard only as words of hope in a poem.

The symposium papers frequently alluded to the standard white opinion that black people had no culture. That month's exhibits in South African art galleries prove the authors had not misjudged South African cultural attitudes. In Cape Town the four galleries displaying African art described it, with one exception (the linocuts of Azaria Mbatha), as tribal. During the Gaborone symposium the older speakers and those who had lived overseas tended to react the least stridently against what they considered European artistic values. Gavin Jantjes, based in Germany, said he didn't fully agree there should be no art for art's sake. 'But,' he went on, 'I cannot begin to argue the art for art's sake argument in a situation where children are being shot and killed for protesting at injustice.'[16]

Wally's friend Nadine Gordimer spoke with empathy of the profound alienation – 'divided from others and distanced from himself' – of the South African black writer. She was, in a sense, explaining the continuing need for black consciousness. '[The black writer] has now turned his alienation in the face of those who rejected him, and made his false consciousness the inevitable point of departure towards his true selfhood, to be found or rediscovered by no eyes but his own.' She affirmed that the 'relevance' of one's work to one's own people was the only way to break alienation. 'He cannot choose the terms of his relevance or his commitment because in no other community but … one which blacks have set up inside themselves are his values the norm.' In a society ordered and dominated by whites, a black person does not possess 'self-hood'.[17]

In noting the capacity of agitprop to ignore the artist's inner world, Gordimer was issuing subtle warnings relevant to Thami. She stated that black art had 'not really visualized itself beyond protest'. (She was sensitive to her audience's antipathy to lecturing, so she walked delicately around the point, saying, 'the

Nadine Gordimer delivering her conference paper in front of a wall of Thami's posters at the Culture and Resistance symposium, Gaborone, July 1982. (Photograph from Mayibuye Archives, UWC)

black writer *has* to assert the right to reject agitprop', rather than state outright that agitprop should be rejected.) After the 'heat of the present' had passed, artists would synthesise African traditions with 'the aspirations of people who still want TV and jeans'. She was effectively counselling those Medu members who scorned the advertisements and articles in slick magazines like *Drum* and *Pace* to accept that people would want to engage with the modern consumer world. She was raising a provocative question: what would revolutionary intellectuals do when the 'community', on whose behalf they claimed to speak, actually chose values they rejected?[18]

The poet Keorapetse Kgositsile proved to be the star speaker – it was his ideas that everyone quoted. He began his address by referring to the ANC and MK, then asked rhetorically what they had to do with art, and answered 'Everything'. He rejected artists who said they could not be involved in social issues, calling them 'charlatans, pimps and prostitutes'. There was 'no such creature as a revolutionary soloist' in a struggle for national liberation, he asserted.[19]

Thami introduces the keynote speaker, poet Keorapetse Kgositsile, at the Culture and Resistance symposium, July 1982. (Photo by Michael Kahn)

Abdullah Ibrahim took up this nationalist cry. When interviewed, the brilliant jazz pianist tried, archly, to erase his glamour by calling himself a 'piano player', a 'messenger boy', and, in the phrase of the moment, a 'cultural worker'. The symposium, he said, had to take place because Western 'cultural imperialism' had brainwashed artists and musicians, making them dream of using art to win money and fame for themselves as individuals. Trumpeter Hugh Masekela failed to echo this cry. Instead he urged musicians to develop a good business sense so they wouldn't be exploited by record companies.[20] Thami affectionately called Masekela a 'scatterbrain' because he was a man governed by his appetites, while Thami, a man becoming a soldier, was trying not to be. Perhaps the fame, as well as the exile, of the two musicians had led them to understand the goals of the conference in slightly different terms from those of its organisers. Wally had stressed that the event's target groups were South Africans involved in community projects at home.[21]

Thami's own conference paper was an autobiographical manifesto. He devoted the first two-thirds to the candid and sometimes wry story of his youth. Immediately after confessing that he left the Sached staff in tears of loss, he shifted his tone, recounting the story of his Medu years in the stern and principled voice of a member of 'the liberation movement'. He advocated a new educational system that bridged 'the gap between intellectual and practical labour'. He rejected critics who, by dismissing political art as clichés, deliberately ignored 'the actual meaning and intention of the work'. These critics failed to see that the artist's role was 'to heed the people's word'. Taking a leaf from Ernst Fischer's *The Necessity of Art*, a book he was discussing in Medu, he repeated the word 'need' so his listeners could sense the urgency: 'We need to clearly popularise and give dignity to the just thoughts and deeds of the people.' The impractical and the mystical were, at best, frivolous, because they did not 'inspire change'.[22]

The neatness of Thami's model shows how well he had imbibed the movement's lessons and how agreeable he found them. Nevertheless, there are moments in the essay when glimmers of his own dilemma and unresolved contradictions shine through. He derided artists who wanted to go overseas, though he still yearned to do so. He praised the recent acts of community resistance – 'workers' strikes, student revolts, peasant revolts, rent strikes, commemoration services' – yet, in the same breath, lamented 'a growing lack of the spirit of the community'. Further, he seemed conflicted about the precise role of the cultural worker: on the one hand, heeding the people and, on the other, inspiring them. He offered no guidelines on how to balance the two.

His stand on 'fine art' was also ambiguous. He still seemed to regard it with longing. The previous year he had urged South African artists, 'Let's combine the warmth of fine arts with the popular immediacy of the graphics'. To the festival audience he said, 'I am not of the opinion that artworks must be sacrificed for political posters but in the same breath would demand to know the reason for the undesirability of political propaganda.' Looking back at his decision to leave Sached, he hoped the skills he had learned there would allow him to make posters, banners, illustrations 'whenever my community demands it', and, 'of course, I would still create my fine art for posterity'.[23] These tensions suggest he was still reluctant to surrender his artistic vision entirely to the revolution.

Thami had drawn the festival logo: two interlocked hands with flames rising from the fingertips. He based his idea on a photograph Teresa had taken of his own hand paired with that of a visiting Swedish girl. The origin of the poster, then, lay in a vision of interracial solidarity. Aspects of the conference belied this hope. Some Black Consciousness participants, like Durban playwright Benjie Francis, played the race card, attacking the presence of whites and, through them, the ANC.

Even Thami was moved to join the racial attack, accusing Bill Ainslie of having treated Dumile disrespectfully in the late 1960s by lodging him in his servants' quarters. Artist Anne Sassoon Pogrund went up to Thami after his public outburst and tried to set the record straight. She found him 'gentle, responsive … very smart; it was a friendly encounter'. Ainslie remembered Thami later making a major effort to apologise but, as it was not a fresh and open apology, he seemed to be doing so under duress. David Koloane understood Thami's outburst as typical of young people's resentment of white privilege. Thami, he said, was expressing pent-up anger at what he had left behind in South Africa.[24]

Racial tensions permeated even Medu. Photographer Mike Kahn remembers two discussions soon after the festival ended in which blacks attacked whites for playing an overweening role in organising it. Thami joined in during the second discussion. There are several possible reasons for his unusually racial outbursts. The high visibility of whites in an African

Thami Mnyele, logo for Culture and Resistance festival, July 1982. (Courtesy of SAHA)

cultural organisation may have irritated him; he may have found some of the whites intrusive and overbearing; he may have been voicing his own version of the resentment he had heard Steve Biko explain six years earlier: 'You may be as intelligent but not as articulate [as a white]. You are forced into a subservient role of having to say yes to what they are saying, talking about what you have experienced, which they have not experienced, because you cannot express it so well.'[25] Perhaps he regarded artists like Bill Ainslie as linked to the formal demands of the New York art world and therefore hostile to the dreamscapes drawn by artists like Dali, Wopko Jensma, Ezrom Legae, and, formerly, himself.

One hint that Thami had not repudiated an artistic perspective informed by Black Consciousness may be found in the way he disposed of three of his best drawings. During the festival he gave them to former associates. Jaki Seroke, a young Tembisa man leaning toward the PAC, bought one drawing when Thami asked him to take his work back home. Dr Joel Matsipa, a comrade from Mihloti days and former medical school classmate of Steve Biko, drove back from the festival with the 'woman giving birth' and the 'screaming heads' in his car. Thami told Matsipa not to sell them as he wanted the drawings preserved inside South Africa, an indication perhaps that he foresaw danger in Gaborone. The gift was certainly a sign that he still valued that phase of his art. One comrade suggests that Thami never gave up Black Consciousness 'as an intrinsic part of [his] revolutionary stance'.[26]

Some felt that the brave talk and good feeling fell short of the symposium's promise. Did they succeed in defining the next step? Albio regretted that no book or resolutions resulted, as planned. He was stung by those who failed to recognise the initiating role played by the Swedes and the hard work he and Teresa had put in. Wally found the film of the event superficial in overstressing whites' relief that blacks were talking to them. The art travelling north for exhibit in other Southern African venues was mysteriously lost. Energies dissipated without much visible issue.

What did the symposium actually achieve? It led to great South African musicians playing frequently around Gaborone, at Julia Helfer's Woodpecker restaurant on the Notwane River and at the Blue Note Club in the nearby village of Mogoditshane. There people could 'jol' the night away as if they were at home; they could also grow careless about whom they consorted with and what they revealed. The symposium did prove to be a recruiting ground for the ANC. Tim Williams notes with pride that cross-border contacts proliferated after July, not only boosting ANC recruitment but also providing South Africans with new ideas for propagating activist ideals on T-shirts and posters. In January the annual message from the ANC's National Executive Council was inserted in the *Medu Newsletter*.

While the tone of militancy overwhelmed and alienated some conference participants, other cultural workers grew more politically active. They were determined to disseminate a set of values different from those of apartheid. They resolved to stage a sequel in Amsterdam. Because South African community projects tended to operate at cross-purposes, Wally said, the symposium had been designed to help them work toward a common goal. In this sense, the festival contributed energy toward the creation of the United Democratic Front the following year. Among the exiles in Gaborone it gave rise to the exultant, even giddy notion 'we're going home'.

Culture and Resistance produced one tangible fruit. By early 1983 the ANC had inaugurated, in Lusaka, its Department of Arts and Culture DAC, headed by Barbara Masekela, Hugh's sister. By using cultural organs like a singing group (Amandla Cultural Ensemble) and a magazine (*Rixaka*), the movement hoped not only to raise its profile internationally and publicise the cultural boycott, but also to disseminate its own values. As the 1982 festival made clear, those values were radically egalitarian. Social distinctions were levelled so that everyone, including artists, was called a worker.

Artists would ideally work alongside unions and civic associations within communities, articulating their grievances and hopes, free from the pollution of Western pop culture. Self-expression was 'naïve' and 'foolish'.[27] Paul Stopforth would reflect later on the unworldly purity of the times: people were saying that fame and money were unclean; they were claiming that simple, unadorned greatness never required spin or publicity to be recognised.

Culture and Resistance immediately spawned a sequel: a similar arts festival in Holland organised by the Dutch Anti-Apartheid Movement. This event – the Cultural Voice of Resistance festival – ran from 13 to 18 December 1982 and bore the joyful sub-title 'The doors of culture shall be opened'. Certainly it opened the doors of Europe to Thami for the first time. In December 1982 he travelled to Amsterdam as a Medu delegate. Bundled up in wool and corduroy against the damp chill of a northern winter, he presented a backdrop he had designed and painted for the stage where the Amandla Cultural Ensemble would perform 'revolutionary' songs and dances.[28] In frank reference to MK he fashioned an arm holding aloft a spear. The squiggly outline of the arm and fist gave the image a remarkably stylish air.

Thami Mnyele, backdrop, 1982.

The words spoken on stage at the conference were more bellicose than Thami's design. Poet Cosmo Pieterse, for example, spoke with relish of the ANC using guns, and told the Dutch to boycott the country 'under Nazi apartheid culture'. The Dutch minister of culture, who had just urged dialogue with the South African government, looked abashed. The 50 Dutch and South African artists rejected his argument and voted for a cultural boycott of the country and a cultural agreement with the ANC instead. One woman asked the minister if he would have recommended dialogue with Hitler. It was a heady experience, even in the safety of Amsterdam, to speak about propagating new values in the interests of humanity, as poet Willie Kgositsile urged. The audience applauded angry black speakers when they derided a white South African for speaking lovingly of his white and black 'mothers'. A Dutch choir director proudly wore a T-shirt bearing the image of Thami's MK fist.[29]

The Amsterdam festival gave the ANC a far higher profile than had been possible at the Gaborone conference. Barbara Masekela, as representative of the brand-new ANC Department of Arts and Culture, even mentioned 'ANC and Medu delegates' in the same breath. A group from Somafco, the ANC school in Tanzania, performed *Dear Sir*, based on a letter written by Nelson Mandela, while Medu staged a two-man play, *Shades of Change*, by a Medu member, Bachana Mokoena, based on a poem by Wally about the anguish of two captured freedom fighters. 'Remember, these are extremely abnormal conditions,' the actors said, '[but] they can't stop the people's will.' Four thousand people attended the opening night, when 'future cultural exchange with the ANC was visualised'. Actor John Matshikiza met Thami there and found him a new breed of exile: focused, disciplined, and confident that he would be going home.[30]

Patrick Fitzgerald, who directed *Shades of Change* in Amsterdam as well as in Rotterdam and London, remembers Thami's seriousness during this trip. He was six years older than Patrick and far less wild. He did not drink and dance all night, as Patrick did. He seemed depressed.[31] He was distressed by the 12 December raid by the SADF on Maseru, the capital of Lesotho. Forty-two unarmed people died in their homes during that raid, 30 of them ANC members. The Lesotho army did not intervene. He cannot have avoided wondering if this attack foretold Medu's fate … and his own.

Thami also struck his Amsterdam hostess, Moira Whyte, as depressed and unhappy. He confessed he had been disturbed by an unfriendly encounter at the home of a South African exile during a side-trip to London the previous week, but didn't want to talk about it. (In addition, he had gone to Brixton to visit Molefe Pheto, still loyal to Black Consciousness; when they talked about the arts, they grew confused about who belonged to which group, leading Thami to ask sorrowfully, 'Why aren't we all in one political organisation?') Though he did speak of wanting to study art in Amsterdam one day, he worked so hard on the backdrop that he saw little of the city, and he seemed, in any case, focused on home. He spent one whole day listening to Moira's tapes of African music.[32]

Moira's husband took him to the Rijksmuseum where he wanted to see only one painting – Gerard Dou's 17th-century portrait of Rembrandt's mother. He stood in front of the old lady's image for about 20 minutes, drinking in the fur-swaddled figure staring devoutly at an illustration of the gospel. Then he bought several postcards of the painting and sent one to his own mother. On the back he wrote, 'Dear Mum, when I went to Rijksmuseum in this city of Amsterdam I was deeply moved by this painting you now see on the postcard … I was moved very very deeply, and felt very humbled to a point of near tears. And I thought, and I thought of you, Love, Mnyele.'[33]

Thami's confidence had been growing in Botswana as he succeeded at each new challenge. The young man who had dropped out of school with chronic 'feelings of failure' was now presenting conference papers. The Mihloti member who walked away unnoticed from conversations now talked easily with people from around the world. He had followed his first tentative poster with increasingly bold designs. At great cost to Wally's nerves, he had been taught to drive. He had learned to swim. He was trying to become less sensitive to criticism. This newly confident 34-year-old man was now walking up the grand central staircase in Amsterdam's palace of Dutch culture, past the 17th-century oil paintings of venerable burghers who had made fortunes shipping goods to South Africa and the East Indies, irrevocably changing the lives of Thami's ancestors. He genuinely wanted to be a great artist, not only for himself, but also for 'our people', giving them greatness to be proud of. Faced with dazzling oils painted by artists who had not been distracted by his sort of social commitment, he felt humbled.

Thami also felt depressed because Cassius Make and Joe Modise had been arrested earlier that year. The two MK leaders had been carrying plans for the year's attacks, so a hiatus in armed activity ensued. This lull interrupted the ANC's recent string of armed successes, after years of searching for an effective military strategy. In 1983 the ANC began extending its principle of using violence to embolden the people and advertise its own pre-eminence: it set up 'suicide' squads who would carry small arms or grenades into the country and, ideally, choose targets in consultation with the 'community'.[34]

Thami embodied two major paradoxes: he was a gentle man endorsing war and he championed the community despite experiencing the abundant violence within it. How did he reconcile these contradictions? He accepted an ideology – first from Black Consciousness, then from the ANC – that explained the broader context and origins of the disorder and poverty within black communities. Black people, as he told the Gaborone conference, had suffered 'the deliberate destruction of our culture', but now they were on the brink of a new culture based on new ways of living and working together. With an adequate material base the community would, like 'a stream', feed a cultural flowering that was truly liberated. He had relinquished the belief he had shared with Van Gogh in the 1970s that art itself was the stream that bears a man to harbour. Thami readily idealised the collective because he found the socialist interpretation new and exciting, because he possessed a deep humanism, and because there was no plausible alternative, especially once he had gone into exile.

Reading a Marxist cultural history, *The Necessity of Art*, helped Thami articulate his project. Much of the text, written by Ernst Fischer, an Austrian intellectual, recounted European cultural history in greater detail than Thami found relevant. When he skipped around, he stumbled upon insights that clarified the big picture. He earnestly discussed this utopian vision with Medu comrades like Judy Seidman and visitors from Johannesburg like Jaki Seroke. They were all living in 'the late bourgeois world' where artists dehumanised men either by distorting them or making them disappear from their work altogether; man had become nothing, and success was all. Capitalism had destroyed all fundamental human relationships and turned art into a commodity, so the close bond between artist and consumer had been lost and the artist was now isolated. Socialist art, on the other hand, anticipated the emerging socialist world. Like 'the sorcerer in primitive tribal society', the committed artist would 'guide individual life back into collective life, the personal into the universal'. It would 'restore the lost unity of man'. Even music would express entirely new and unforeseeable ideas: 'the collective of the working class'. Thami was interested to learn that Fischer approved of Van Gogh because he depicted the 'bowed backs, bent heads, humiliation and degradation of workers and peasants'. Thami, of course, had moved on to championing the upright posture of defiance.[35]

Although he had left Van Gogh's letters behind in Tembisa and had not sought out his art in Amsterdam, he may have remembered the Dutchman's yearning for a new 'consoling' religion, such as Christianity used to be, one that ought to be born privately and secretly in the hearts of men, 'whatever happens in the way of violent revolution'. Van Gogh found that religion in nature. For the time being, Thami could not afford to be, like Van Gogh, indifferent to 'whatever happens in the way of violent revolution'. As an exiled member of an illegal organisation, attacking and under attack, his attention was turning toward violence as a means of ending the 'late bourgeois world'. Its death, he thought, was the necessary prelude to bringing about a new human-centred, because collective, society.

Between 1981 and 1983 Thami drew five designs with guns in them. He made the poster of Namibian soldiers in 1981 and also sketched a man with a machine gun to the extreme right of a newsletter pull-out. In 1982 he drew a gun behind a book in 'Fragments', plus an armed woman carrying a child as the letterhead for the ANC Women's League's 'Voice of Women'. He drew in 1983 an awestruck child greeting an armed cadre, and also a gun emerging from the roots of Medu as the logo for a T-shirt, though this was considered too provocative to distribute at the time. The graphic unit produced about five other armed posters from 1979 to 1983, three of them commemorating martyrs. These guns expressed the emotional needs of the young refugees and their visceral sense of the task at hand.

Front commanders and commissars held a conference in Luanda, Angola, in April 1983 to discuss the

"let us arm ourselves with the fearlessness of Shaka; the vision and endurance of Moshoe-shoe; the dedication and farsightedness of Sol Plaatjie; the military initiative and guerilla tactics of Maqoma..."

DECEMBER 16
HEROES-DAY

Thami Mnyele, Medu poster, 1983.
(Courtesy of SAHA)

Thami Mnyele, letterhead for ANC Women's League, n.d.
(Courtesy of SAHA)

Thami Mnyele, Medu T-shirt logo, n.d.
(Courtesy of SAHA)

still ineffective coordination of the political and military wings of the struggle. They decided the ANC had to build military structures inside South Africa so that it could sustain military operations, 'rather than carrying out a string of one-off "pot-boiling" actions'. In addition, the Senior Organs were yet again redefined, because of what the ANC called the 'number of cross-border attacks and severe infiltration by the enemy'. They were now organised into Regional Politico-Military Councils. Wally served as a head of the Botswana 'political machinery',[36] becoming a 'commander' in MK, a responsibility that made him feel isolated and sometimes very lonely. Thami's muse had become his commanding officer.

Grenade squads began training in Botswana in 1983 because the 'all-out people's war' projected in 1982 had not broken out. 'Throw a grenade, not a stone – freedom or death,' the new saying went. Small cells were being trained in Botswana to filter across the border and, in turn, teach community activists how to throw grenades at perceived collaborators and their offices and homes. The government seemed to be seducing people to accept the status quo by offering them jobs as urban councillors. Perhaps if people inside South Africa had weapons to attack those new offices and the people who held them, the revolution would finally begin.

ANC leaders were wary: they didn't want the squads to identify themselves as ANC until they could assess how South Africans reacted to them. By targeting civilians who worked in black local government, the squads were breaking away from the definition of legitimate targets – those inside enemy structures, like the police – laid down in 1976. The leaders in Lusaka were also not happy with, but accepted, the term 'suicide squads', which some cadres liked precisely because it signalled their extreme determination.[37]

Two 'solutions' to the crisis – one armed with grenades, the other with organised demonstrators – were growing at the same time. In August 1983, 10 000 people protesting against the political 'reforms' of the National Party – especially the tricameral Parliament – launched the United Democratic Front (UDF). Like the ANC, the UDF openly accepted white members and rejected any collaboration with the apartheid regime. At first, the UDF did not dare to align itself publicly with the ANC. It chose yellow, red, and black as its colours, instead of green, black, and gold. It did not call for the adoption of the ANC's Freedom Charter or voice anti-capitalist sentiments.[38] No one had a clear sense of whether the diverse student, civic, and even sports organisations making up the UDF had the potential to confront the state.

The spies who infiltrated the MK network inhibited the work of the grenade squads. Too many of the operatives were either captured by the police before they could do any damage or were injured when the grenades exploded. Some people thought the grenades were booby-trapped. Others, like Mike Kahn, who made detonators, thought people might have carelessly communicated instructions on how to use them.[39] In any case, operatives based in Swaziland and Mozambique had a history of launching more successful military actions than those in Botswana, but this pre-eminence was coming to an end, and not just because of spies. In February 1982 Swaziland had secretly signed an anti-ANC pact with South Africa. General

Thami Mnyele, 'Angola', 1982, 85 x 39 cm, Theo Derkx Collection. (Photograph by Melita Moloney)

Magnus Malan, South Africa's defence minister, was aiming to use military intervention to destabilise the frontline states so that by 1987, he hoped, the ANC would have no home in them. Botswana was looking more and more lonely and vulnerable.

MK training camps had existed in Angola since 1976, the year after the Popular Movement for the Liberation of Angola (MPLA) took power from the Portuguese. In the late 1970s graduates of those camps carried out attacks on township police stations and rail lines. Graduates of MK camps also fought, aided by Cubans, alongside the MPLA army against the rebel movement, Unita, supported by South Africa. MK lessons in field artillery proved useful there, as they had not in South Africa.

Thami drew Angolan scenes in 1982 based on word-of-mouth testimony about these bloody encounters and on his own empathetic imagination. (Wally and his wife, Phethu, had gone to Angola to train after the Culture and Resistance conference, though Wally later confessed that he was 'very sad indeed' to discover that he wasn't essentially a military man.)[40] In what may have been the last trace of his grief-stricken style, Thami drew a man covering his face with his hands. The words he has written near the figures are strangely vague: 'episodes' are depicted for purposes of 'guidance', and the phrase 'bits of mortal …' trails off. Soon he would move closer to the action.

In mid-1983 Thami left for Angola, followed soon by Rhona, who was so preoccupied that she locked Albio and Teresa's cat in the garage and kept the key. (Forced to go to a locksmith, Albio was worried, because he suspected they kept guns and bombs in the garage.) They left their son, Sindi, with Rhona's parents in Tembisa and travelled on UN passports to Harare and then Lusaka, where they kept out of sight in safe houses, before flying to Luanda. From there they went by road to a camp for workers in the underground. At nearby Caxito camp, where they were housed in different barracks, they would learn the skills necessary to complement their roles in Botswana.

Thami Mnyele, 'Angola', 1982, 84 x 26 cm, Theo Derkx Collection. (Photograph by Melita Moloney)

Caxito, founded in 1979, seldom had more than 100 cadres training for deployment on the home front. Their time there was short, in contrast to the 18-month periods that many other recruits spent training in Angola, as well as in the USSR and East Germany. Thami would later tell Judy Seidman that he had worked with two South African printers in Luanda, learning how to set up a press so he could later do so in Lusaka.[41]

MK trainees received both military and political instruction. They learned how to use explosives, firearms, and artillery. They were taught how to orient themselves in a landscape 'in the middle of nowhere'. And they learned how to fight 'as a barefoot soldier, moving next to a tank and so on, being in a trench or manning a post as a guard'. Rhona initially found the food 'difficult', but a new commander improved it by bartering for local produce and getting tinned food from the USSR and Tanzania.[42] Thami observed that mosquitoes provided the music in the camps.

Some instructors at the Angolan camps passed on an evolutionary Marxist view of the stages of human history that they had learned in the Soviet Union. More specifically, they studied the history of the Bolsheviks and the Soviet Communist Party. The teachers, all South Africans, generally did not criticise the USSR.[43] The cadres studied the Russian, Vietnamese, and Cuban revolutions, as well as the long history of South African 'wars of resistance since 1652'. At Novo Catengue camp trainees had watched Soviet films for entertainment in the evening. The black and white footage of the Soviet army repulsing Nazi invaders in 1943 must have struck many of the young cadres as antique. Political instructor Jack Simons, a SACP member and, formerly, a distinguished University of Cape Town academic, doubted that the Soviet experience gave much insight into the South African struggle. The Bolsheviks, he wrote, had developed 'a small but tight, influential party organization, skilled in agitation & propaganda inside and capable of giving leadership'. The ANC had so far been unable to do so.[44]

These lessons addressed students whose level of education ranged from none to tertiary level. One stated goal was to erase the authoritarian heritage of Bantu Education, based on learning by rote. Another purpose was to ensure that the guerrilla force being shaped in the Angolan bush actually followed the political line laid down by the alliance of the ANC with the SACP. Commissars were appointed not only to foster morale but also to ensure that this ideology was transmitted. 'That's class, man' was henceforth to have a new meaning.

The ANC's ideals – 'the immediate content, strategies, and tactics of the South African revolution', in the words of Joe Slovo – did not differ significantly from those of the SACP. Both the movement and the party supported the creation of a workers' democracy in South Africa. Thami did have Lenin's work on his bookshelf at home, but his partisanship derived more from his hopes for the future than from any text. He frequently described his dreams as 'socialist', but his attitude to the Soviet Union was similar to that of most other young cadres: 'If they support us, they are the best people in the world.' And yet, cultural differences between the two societies could be frustrating; some cadres lamented that the Russians had got 'stuck' on classical music.[45]

The USSR gave arms to the ANC, according to Soviet contact Vladimir Shubin, in order to make the ANC dominant in case anything happened to divide the black population; Shubin particularly feared that an economic upsurge would win black acquiescence to the status quo. The armed struggle was also necessary, Shubin thought, because there was no legal way within South Africa to end apartheid. The ANC gratefully received arms: Shubin calculated that between 1963 and 1990 the USSR sent, in total, 'several thousand AK-47s of various modifications, over three thousand SKS carbines, over six thousand pistols, 275 grenade-launchers, 90 Grad-P missile launchers, over 40 Strela 2M anti-aircraft missile launchers, 20 Malyutkas, over 60 mortars, etc.'[46]

The Soviet Union did not post a single person to Gaborone specifically as an ANC liaison. The Russians knew Gaborone was a highly dangerous place, permeated by informers. (The wife of SACP member Dan Tloome told Shubin that a shop clerk from Gaborone shocked her by appearing suddenly, without explanation, at her interrogation by the South African police.) High-profile Soviet aid would have endangered everyone. Therefore, the Russians met with the ANC leadership in Lusaka instead, and Thami may have encountered them there.[47] Thami's contact with the Soviet Union thus amounted to a few encounters and books, gratitude for arms, and the odd lesson at Caxito camp. The first two words of his remark, 'At least [the Russians] are doing something [for us]', hardly suggest enthusiastic affiliation. There is no doubt, though, that he was deeply drawn to the ideals of community solidarity and the high courage of simple people. Nat Serache, who did join the SACP, says Thami behaved and lived like a communist – he was honest, humble and didn't tolerate indiscipline – even if he was not a card-carrying member.

After the South African Air Force destroyed Novo Catengue camp in 1979, the conditions in all the camps deteriorated. Projectors and radios were no longer available and the political instructors lost touch with events at home, and so political consciousness declined. The young, mainly urban recruits were so eager to fight that they disliked any hint that negotiations could lead to a political settlement. Occasionally they heard stories about developments at home like murders of ANC activists by Inkatha, and concluded that 'the masses are ready for the armed struggle and [we] question why MIC [military intelligence] is not intensifying the armed struggle and not there to protect the masses'.[48]

While they were proud of the military action that had taken place, they grew impatient with the pace of the struggle. Some frustrated cadres had lived in the camps for years. Even though Tambo had asked to hear their opinions in 1982, they found that the national commissar, Andrew Masondo, reprimanded them for expressing their views.

Thami and Rhona were in Angola for too short a time to have deep and disquieting experience of the problems brewing there. Other cadres reported tense relations with the Cubans who lived and ate apart from them, seeming to enjoy superior conditions. Commanders, commissars, and higher-ranking officials appeared exempt from the monotony of the camps, eating more palatable food than powdered eggs and yellow mealie meal. Unlike the ordinary cadres, they might even visit Luanda for entertainment. Rank and file members resented harsh punishments – solitary confinement, flogging, being tied or partially buried or starved – for infractions like smoking dagga, drinking liquor or simply bartering for fresh food from neighbouring villagers. The security department was tough and unpopular. It punished them for expressing any sort of criticism, such as having had to study ANC history for years without seeing any action. Cadres sometimes died as a result of their punishment, a few by committing suicide.[49]

Months after Thami and Rhona left Angola, morale in the camps reached its lowest point. Too many cadres were dying assisting the Angolan government's army in battles against Unita, far from home and with no apparent prospect of getting back there. At the end of 1983 most of the cadres in the camps began to mutiny, demanding that Tambo, Slovo, and Chris Hani address their grievances. An internal commission of inquiry affirmed the grievances of the protesters. The commissioners found that the 'total isolation' of the camps from the outside world coupled with 'the desperation and frustration of not being deployed' had made it 'practically impossible for cadres to survive (politically, morally and psychologically) in the camps for several years'.[50]

The news from Angola troubled Thami, but his commitment did not waver. He would explain that the fault lay not simply among the perpetrators of abuses but more generally in 'the situation': the ANC's security department had committed abuses because the South African government was trying to under-mine the liberation movements by invading southern Angola.

Nevertheless, violence and anger visibly upset Thami, wherever he witnessed it. When a married couple quarrelled publicly, he shrank away. He rarely displayed anger himself, not even to Naniwe during their worst days together. Once, though, when he visited an art supply shop during a trip to Harare, his resentment at years of indignities burst out in an uncharacteristic explosion. The old white proprietress urged him to stop looking and buy. When he asked her for a detailed receipt, she replied that the till receipt was good enough for him. He crumbled the receipt in his hand, threw it at her, and stormed out of the shop.[51]

Fatalism pervaded the times, as if Guevara-like martyrdom were likely. The government paid so many informers that basic human trust was eroded. When Thami's half-brother, Desmond, urged him to come home, he believed the security police had instructed him to do so, just as they had been pressuring Naniwe and manhandling his mother. The sense of being hunted hardened the cadres, making them close ranks protectively and reveal as little as possible, even to each other. When Thami returned to Gaborone he lied that he had been in France. Because Rhona had contracted malaria in Caxito, like so many of the trainees in that notoriously infected camp, and spent some time in a hospital, she returned looking emaciated. Albio and Teresa asked what had happened and where she had been. She hadn't prepared a story and grew flustered. The South African Police (SAP) probably knew where they had gone in any case. General Herman Stadler, in charge of the SAP for seven years, bragged that he had a photo album containing portraits of 6 000 people, 4 000 of whom were known to have undergone military training.[52] Thami's and Rhona's pictures were undoubtedly among them.

They returned to a world in Gaborone where, as Jonas Gwangwa remarked, they talked 'the struggle' all the time. (Thami gave Gwangwa a dense, apolitical drawing which merged a woman's face with a landscape; the red colour came from his own blood.) They gathered with other exiles in the President Hotel, the Holiday Inn, the new music clubs, aware they were being watched across the room by the enemy who would hunt them at night. There was bravado and romance in the drama. Thami enjoyed laughing with cautious Baleka Kgositsile as he taught her to drive, saying, 'Sissy, drive as if the boers are after you.' Carol Kahn remembers that the mood of the time was characterised by a peculiar mix of tension and partying. A drunk could reel through a party blurting secrets. It therefore made sense to organise into small cells so that the damage from indiscretions could be contained. In Botswana the cells were 'loose' as members moved in and out, depending on the task at hand, and they tended to be small, limited to three or four people. But, of course, safety could never be ensured. Dikobe Martins had been careful to communicate only 'need-to-know' information, yet he was picked up by the Pietermaritzburg police in November 1983 and spent the next seven months in solitary confinement, before he was berated by a judge for betraying the trust of his employers by recruiting youth into the ANC. Then he went to prison where he would remain for the following eight years.

Thami was skilled at recruitment. He could draw on a wide range of people inside South Africa who respected him. By telephoning, sending messages, and inviting visitors across the border, he stayed in touch with the Johannesburg art world and township friends, trying to draw in people he esteemed who, in turn, trusted his humility and sincerity. Sometimes he would send a friend to South Africa bearing the simple message, 'Tell him I still care about the same things I used to believe in.'

Pete Richer thinks MK's military, political, and intelligence networks all flourished in Botswana because Thami was 'an important recruiter'.[53] Chris van Wyk, then editor of *Staffrider*, remembers him apparently taking pleasure in the drama of ANC membership and the act of recruitment. Thami invited Chris to visit him in late 1984 and asked him to become a member, saying the movement was a 'good' one that took care of people, sending them abroad to study. He made this revelation solemnly inside a car near the Oasis Hotel in Tlokweng, a village rapidly becoming a suburb of Gaborone, to which he had recently moved. Thami and Wally then took Chris to a *braai* (barbeque) at an African bar and, sitting under a tree, Thami took notes while Wally pressed home the advantages of membership.[54]

Thami had begun secretly teaching visitors from South Africa how to use grenades and limpet mines. They returned home and taught others how to remove the pin and how to take security precautions. In this way revolutionary skills were meant to ripple out from the thin chain of exiles and allow people inside the country to act without becoming exiles themselves. Thami not only taught fighting skills; he also inspired people. The story of Shimane, a slightly built, aspiring poet and dramatist from the northern Cape, throws light on Thami's new role.

Shimane was sent to visit Thami in Gaborone by one Bushi Maape, an energetic recruiter in Vryburg, a dusty and remote crossroads whose flat skyline is punctuated only by monumental maize silos. Bushi and his comrades were fiercely opposed to a trio of local councillors who seemed to be traitors, ready to do anything the government wanted: the three men showed anti-ANC videos; they were believed to travel overseas to Canada as government apologists; they recruited youth into a state-sponsored military organisation called The Eagle; and, most important, they were trying to convince the people of Vryburg's African township, Huhudi, to move 55 km away to land within the Bophuthatswana homeland.[55] They had to be stopped.

Shimane arrived in Gaborone with one other comrade, and they moved straight into a house in Tlokweng where Thami would visit for an hour or two at a time. For a fortnight the two visitors never opened the curtains or left the house. They would simply wait for Thami to arrive and teach about politics and weapons. Then he would leave to give similar lessons in other 'safe houses'. These sessions were called 'crash courses'. They included not only how to handle the weapons but also how to discover if you were being followed and how to determine who was trustworthy. Bend down to tie your shoelaces and look behind you, Thami would say; write a coded response if you find a letter suspicious.

Thami was 'poetic … a very powerful speaker', Shimane remembers, especially when he told 'how the boers exploited us and how oppression affects us, how brutal the government was', as when it shot schoolchildren in 1976. 'We must be brave enough to fight,' Thami would say. As he spoke, he became so overwrought that his voice broke and tears flowed down his cheeks. Moved beyond words, Shimane wept, too. He went away 'very angry and couldn't value the lives of the people [who killed our children]'. These lessons enabled Shimane to go back to Vryburg and receive four grenades and two limpet mines that someone else had transported across the border inside a car door. He hid them in the township and then moved them to the even more remote town of Taung until the moment was ripe to punish the councillors for their betrayal of their own people. 'The masses', says 'Tiger' Ramorwagadi, a comrade whom Shimane went on to train, had decided on the targets. Thami had simply given them the means to act.[56]

Was Thami ever directly responsible for anyone's death? I don't know that he was, though because he trained people to throw grenades, he may well have been indirectly responsible. Searching the records concerning ANC activity in Vryburg, the focus of Thami's MK work in 1985, I find no mention of a death that could possibly be attributed to him. Most of the action there was carried out by youth from Huhudi township, and it amounted to throwing stones and grenades at perceived collaborators. The first person to die there, according to Truth and Reconciliation Commission testimony, was an activist, set on fire by government-sponsored vigilantes when there was 'intense conflict in the Huhudi community' in late 1985. During this same period, a 15-year-old girl, Frida Mabalane, also died, apparently stabbed and then burnt to death after a gallon of paraffin or petroleum was poured over her and set alight. Her mother believed that Frida, a UDF member, died because two of her great-uncles were policemen.[57] At UDF meetings people told her that they thought she was a spy, and so a mob of youths killed her. Thami would have been deeply pained by this turning of revolutionary violence into homicide.

The struggle had become Thami's life. Bill Ainslie ruefully observed that it had become like his father's church, a matter of blind faith. Thami confirmed this impression by tending to break into tears both in church and when he heard MK troops marching.[58]

In March 1984, a vice closed tighter on Botswana. The governments of Mozambique and South Africa signed the Nkomati Accord, pledging not to help each other's enemies. Radio Freedom reported that the accord 'temporarily won our ally to [the South African] side'. Thami cryptically remarked on a postcard to Teresa, on leave in Spain, 'There's a new song called The Inkomati Accord'. He knew Botswana was now uniquely vulnerable. One week after the accord was signed, Botswana's foreign minister, Archie Mogwe,

SOUTH AFRICAN CONGRESS OF TRADE UNIONS· 1955-1985·
ORGANISE FOR ONE UNION, ONE FEDERATION IN ONE COUNTRY

Thami Mnyele, Medu poster, 1984/5. (Courtesy of SAHA)

went to Cape Town to discuss 'purely economic' topics with his South African counterpart, Pik Botha. Mogwe's entourage belied this stated focus; it included the minister responsible for security, the commissioner of police, the head of the security branch, and the attorney general.[59]

After Nkomati, MK was seriously inhibited. Botswana was now the only staging area for raids into South Africa that had not been compromised by attack or non-aggression treaties. The grenade squads were being infiltrated and their losses were high. The vanguard role in the struggle was increasingly played by grassroots organisations within the UDF, boycotting schools, refusing to pay taxes and rent, rejecting the new tricameral parliament. The ANC leadership was coming under pressure to talk to representatives of South African organisations like churches and businesses.

In retrospect, Shubin calls 1984 a very difficult and tragic year for the ANC, but also the time when a political solution first began to seem possible.[60] Cadres were receiving very confusing signals. While Shubin found the visit of an Afrikaner academic to Lusaka highly significant, Thami saw less promising signs. His suspicions of Afrikaner recalcitrance were confirmed when he read that a conservative Pretoria city councillor objected to the local art museum buying black art. His worst fear – that the enemy was depraved – was stoked by the death of Jeanette Curtis (known as Jenny) in June. Thami had known Jenny, a former trade union activist, when she lived in Gaborone with her husband, Marius Schoon. Because the couple worked clandestinely for the ANC, they became targets for the kind of action that had killed Thami's friend Tiro ten years earlier. Craig Williamson, a police spy, sent a parcel to the Schoons at their new home in Angola, and when Jenny opened it, the explosion killed her and her six-year-old daughter, Katryn. Because Thami had known both mother and child, he was devastated by their deaths.

In 1984 Thami saluted the South African Congress of Trade Unions (Sactu), the venerable third of the Congress alliance, in his first colour poster. He portrayed the silhouettes of workers, their strong arms

Thami Mnyele, Medu posters, 1984/5. (Courtesy of SAHA)

bared, their fists grasping tools and flowers. That year he drew four different posters depicting workers, all bearing the acronym Sactu, and he drew hands holding aloft tools as the design for a 1985 calendar. He did so, ironically, at the same time as both the SACP and the ANC were recognising that Sactu, based in Lusaka, could not coordinate the trade union movement inside the country.[61] Thami's posters seem like a wistful ANC gesture toward harvesting the energies of new domestic unions, making them affiliates of an exiled movement that the law prevented them from joining. Sactu wanted to show internal workers' organisations that they had an ANC-affiliated umbrella over them, albeit one based in Lusaka. The unstated message was that they didn't need to join a rival federation called the Federation of South African Trade Unions (Fosatu), which focused on workplace rather than community or political issues. The ANC and Thami's posters implied that Fosatu was a diversion from the task of seizing power.

The signature 'tune' on Radio Freedom remained an explosion of machine-gun fire overlaid by rifle shots. Strategists within the ANC were wedded to their longstanding hope that liberation could be won

DOROTHY NYEMBE
15 YEARS IMPRISONMENT
WELCOME HOME!

JAILED - 1969 • RELEASED - 1984
SYMBOL OF THE COURAGE AND
RESILIENCE OF OUR WOMEN

African National Congress

'85
for our
youth!

IN THE YEAR OF THE CADRE

UNITY IN ACTION

ANC
1912 ● 1982

by an MK army, despite abundant advice to the contrary that had been piling up over the years from the governments of Vietnam and Mozambique, Soviet diplomats, and even insiders like Jack Simons. Some said the Nkomati Accord enhanced a kamikaze spirit in the ANC, which was already characterised by machismo. Others argued that the on-going strategic shift from mass mobilisation to open insurrection was 'adventurist and premature'. It exposed 'carefully nurtured organizations to massive reprisals ... and [missed] opportunities for a more calibrated engagement with a divided white establishment'. Martin Legassick, a member of the Marxist Workers' Tendency of the ANC, saw landmines and explosions in milk bars as 'merely inflam[ing] and enlarg[ing] the white ultra-right'.[62] And yet, when a bomb went off in Johannesburg's Hyde Park shopping centre, for example, many black people greeted the explosion with joyful cries of 'Viva MK!', suggesting that armed propaganda could indeed function as a political 'detonator', reminding people of the ANC's work on their behalf.[63]

Is this strategic debate apparent in Thami's art? Thami continued to draw dignified men working and women caring for children, pictures that were not particularly revealing of strategy and debate. He paid special attention to their hands on tools. Their expressions are grave. He was depicting the conditions of people's lives: children drawing water from a well in a desiccated landscape, adults building a shanty, children suffering from malnutrition. The style and content of his posters, on the other hand, reflect the heightened militancy of the grassroots movements from September 1984, when the tricameral parliament first met.

Thami's faith in the community was mightily affirmed by the growth of the UDF. He wrote that the graphics produced by grassroots organisations – like Community Arts Project, Mpumalanga Arts

Thami Mnyele, untitled, 1985, Author's Collection.

Project, and the Johannesburg silkscreen workshop – amounted to 'the birth of a new culture'. T-shirts publicised confrontational images and slogans. Banners and posters gave colour to large rallies. Thami urged his fellow artists to use 'huge and complex graphic means to match the efforts of our people's resistance'.

UDF posters made bold use of primary colours – especially its signature red, black, and yellow – to announce meetings and actions: 'Make your mark against apartheid' shouts a man on a red poster urging people to gather a million signatures against whites-only elections. A crowd of working people advances smiling under yellow initials, framed above and below by the words 'UDF unites – Apartheid divides' and 'Forward to people's power'. These posters radiate the sense of urgency that Medu had been trying to inspire. There are fists galore. In what may have been an unintentional admission of the expressive limitations of struggle art, Thami observed, 'There can never be artistic freedom or freedom of expression from a people in captivity.'[63]

A popular uprising began in August 1984, when people took to the streets of the greater Johannesburg area townships to protest against rent and service charge increases. They were angry that they themselves were paying to upgrade the townships. In retaliation, troops killed 33 people in Sharpeville on 3 September. (Because South Africa was now a country on the boil, these deaths excited far less shock than the killings in the same township nearly a quarter-century earlier.) The soldiers evicted rent strikers and ended rubbish collection. Troops also entered Sebokeng township near Vereeniging.

Although initially reluctant to court confrontation for fear of repeating the failure of the narrow-based 1976 revolt, senior UDF leaders began to see there was indeed scope for revolutionary change. People were already burning tyres in the streets of some townships, as if the stench foretold their power to drive the military away. The revolt spread from these greater Johannesburg townships to other parts of the country, leading the government to arrest UDF leaders and charge them with treason.

Radio Freedom urged a more general uprising. Following its opening burst of machine-gun fire, an announcer spoke of the 'seizure of power from the oppressors', while singers intoned MK's hymn-like anthem. 'Our task', a commentator went on, 'is to make government "impossible" by attacking community councillors and other "puppet institutions".' By the beginning of 1985 Tambo had endorsed popular insurrection as part of a conscious ANC strategy to 'render South Africa ungovernable'. To this end, Thami worked to set up mass mobilisation units within what was then called the PWV (Pretoria-Witwatersrand-Vereeniging) area: he helped recruit cadres, gave them tasks after assessing their political maturity, and taught them why they had to be carried out.

MK divided up the South African map among its cells in the frontline states, although the PWV area was open to action by anybody. Cells based in Botswana planned actions in the areas they could most easily reach: the western and northern Cape, and the northern and western Transvaal. In September 1984, as part of the broad ANC strategy to disable the South African power grid, MK cadres from Botswana attached limpet mines to the Trident power station in Rustenburg. When they exploded, they destroyed three transformers and disrupted power to that West Rand town and a large part of the Bophuthatswana homeland. Attacks on policemen ensued: a hand grenade was thrown at a Constable Molete at Stilfontein on 28 September; a Major Laubscher from Counter-Intelligence and a Constable Clau from Makeking were killed on 3 January 1985; a border guard named David Motlala was murdered at Kopfontein on 3 February; and a Mrs Joubert and a Mr Soon, farmers at Swartruggens, were killed on 13 March.[64]

Thami was the operational commander of a command cell that included two other people. Probably in early 1985 he travelled without them to Vryburg. Shimane, his grenade student, thinks Thami crossed the border to give lessons in how to operate more advanced arms, like Makarov pistols. He may have been preparing the local comrades for a grenade attack on the house of Councillor Dikgole, chair of the Huhudi Community Council; the houses of a security policeman and Councillor Thiba were attacked at the same time. He walked across the border at Pitsane-Molopo, was collected, stayed in safe houses, but

Thami Mnyele and Rhona Segale at their wedding, 31 May 1985, in the Magistrate's Court, Gaborone Village, Botswana. Mrs. Tim (Stella) Williams, a witness, sits on the right. (Photograph by Tim Williams, courtesy of Sarah Mamanyena Mnyele)

was so tired on the return journey, when he was apparently driving, that he overturned his vehicle. The second trip he made in the company of Wally.

Comrades frequently crossed the border at night, disguising themselves in the ragged clothes of peasants. Either walking or riding suitably humble transport like a bicycle or a donkey, they approached a point where the surveillance was poor and, their nerves jangling, pressed on toward home. They might simply be meeting contacts. Sometimes they carried out operations on their four chief targets: power stations, policemen, soldiers, and councillors. Nat Serache stresses that they were very selective about whom they attacked, targeting figures known to terrorise people. Lusaka didn't send commands to eliminate anyone in particular. 'When we were trained we were taught to use our own discretion,' he says, though he notes that some comrades 'did go overboard'.[65] MK cadres, Wally affirms, 'chose the target'.[66]

Thami may have been in two minds when one of the first grenade squads from Botswana firebombed the Rev. Sam Buti's shop and parsonage in Alexandra, destroying the theological library he had been building up for 30 years. Molten glass hung like icicles from the window frames, the *Sunday Star* reported,

Rhona, Thami and their son Sindi in Gaborone. (Photograph by Albio Gonzalez)

and four days later the library was still smouldering.[67] Thami knew that Buti had joined other black NGK ministers in declaring there was no biblical justification for apartheid, and he had fought, aided by David Mnyele, against the removal of families from Alex. But Buti lost radical support when he agreed to serve as chairman of the Alexandra Town Council in 1983. The firebombing was punishment for this dangerous act of collaboration, one the ANC believed fell right into the National Party's plans to co-opt the black middle class. And yet, Buti was hardly a collaborator pure and simple. Under his chairmanship, for example, an art exhibit was hung in Alexandra's stadium to celebrate the township's 70th anniversary. This event not only honoured the arts in an unprecedented fashion, it also signalled that Alexandra was unlikely to be removed. Buti himself blamed the bombing on the government, explaining, 'When people do not take other people's lives seriously, you get frustration, a loss of reason, and a resorting to violence.'[68]

Some argue that the grenade squads were inadequately briefed on their political goals. Riaz Saloojee, an ANC member involved in training them, later complained, 'None of the top guys in the political leadership actually sat down with us to discuss what the problems were.' The targets were chosen in a 'really ad hoc' manner, he thought, and sometimes individuals used the squads to enhance their personal power.

Local 'structures' had power struggles within them, leading people to defend and accuse certain individuals. By the middle of 1985 they were heavily infiltrated, and the political 'structures' in the ANC – angry that the military wing was resisting their guidance – eventually wiped their hands of the squads. Saloojee thinks the military wing resisted political control because its members had a vested interest in the 'myth' that MK was a highly trained professional army capable of liberating South Africa.[69]

Tambo said in September 1984 that the ANC 'had got over the shock' of Nkomati, but there was still a long way to go.[70] One ANC goal was to ensure that the ANC was not outshone nationally or internationally by Inkatha, whose leader, Mangosuthu 'Gatsha' Buthelezi, had been received by both President Ronald Reagan and Prime Minister Margaret Thatcher. Radio Freedom broadcast one song with the lyrics 'Hey you, Gatsha, it's only a matter of time. We will meet with a bazooka.'[71]

On 31 May 1985 Thami and Rhona were married in the district commissioner's court in Gaborone's Village, witnessed by Albio, Teresa, Tim Williams and his wife Stella, who lent them her wedding ring. Paying inadvertent homage to his father's taste in clothes, Thami looked dignified in a white suit, purchased for him by Phillip Segola. Rhona's tall elegance was sheathed in a slim navy-blue suit. They broke the sobriety of the event by opening a bottle of champagne immediately afterwards on the porch of the court. Thami looked across the street and joked when he spotted a man in a parked car, who had been following him for weeks, 'Maybe he'll be in our wedding photos, too.' The Botswana government was warning many of their friends to leave the country for their own safety.

Their five-year-old son Sindelo had stayed with Rhona's parents in Tembisa, as Thami and Rhona were preparing to move. Within two weeks Rhona would travel to Zambia, so their first days as a married couple were brief. They hoped, during that short time, to re-experience some hint of the weeks in March the previous year when they had stayed in the Gonzalezes' house. Thami had written to Teresa, then visiting Spain, to communicate the happiness they had found in those 'normal' but rare domestic circumstances, 'Our beloved Sindelo is around us here and he's contesting the territory I mean the yard with Pepe [the dog] … My loving lady Rhona is at her best around, trying hard to make us the best meals (thanks to your pressure cooker!) Oh how we miss you – our moments are spent sometimes recalling the amusing things you have said and of course we laugh a lot!' He sent the note on the back of a Medu postcard bearing the message 'Organise, Unite for People's Power'.[72]

Thami and Rhona yearned for a 'normal' family life, one with both parents living at home with the children. They knew how rare such families were in the townships of South Africa and believed they were helping to bring about the conditions in which such intimacy could flourish. Thami had warned Rhona not to be shocked in Gaborone by the dissolute behaviour of even dedicated cadres. Some cadres behaved as if 'liberation' meant freedom from all concern with domestic affairs, or even from accountability for personal behaviour. After all, they formed relationships with many people whose real names they never knew. They were not certain they would live to see the new South Africa. They were young, and they were used to accepting that men lived as free of domesticity as if they were butterflies.

Thami's life was strung up with tensions. He managed to live with them because it was necessary. Though he taught Baleka Kgositsile to drive by warning her that the 'boers' were after her, he told Gordon Metz on 12 June that he wouldn't be marching in a parade on the day of liberation; he would be at the airport trying to convince Afrikaners not to leave the country because the 'boers' helped to make South Africa what it was; they belonged there.[73] He could also grow too morose to mention victory parades at all.

A few months earlier he had told artist Bongiwe Dhlomo, while saying goodbye in front of the Gaborone museum, that he would see her 'next time north, or dead'.[74] By specifying north instead of south, he revealed pessimism about the speed, and perhaps even the success, of the ANC advance homeward. Only the previous year he had talked with her about his dream of reopening their alma mater, Rorke's Drift, under the auspices of the ANC or Medu. Bongi thought his remarks in 1984 revealed his sense of his own mortality. Many others, like Mpe, had noticed this trait long before. It had been apparent in the 1974 drawing, 'Remember me / I am going / Time calls me'. In that drawing, though, he had used red boot polish. Now he was using his own blood.

NOTES

1 Albio Gonzalez, interview (2000). Thami made his first poster in June 1981.

2 Nat Serache, interview (Oct 2006).

3 Abduction of Moleke Peter Lengene, 6 Feb 1982, Case H, Amnesty signed by Judge R Pillay, 31 May 2001, AC/2001/228, TRC.

4 Cal Saloojee, interviewed by Howard Barrell (Harare, 5 Aug 1989), Karis-Gerhart Collection, reel 3.

5 Pete Richer, interview (4 Jan 2006). Richer heard this story in the late 1990s when he was working for the National Intelligence Agency.

6 Ronnie Kasrils, 'Armed and Dangerous': My Undercover Struggle against Apartheid (Oxford: Heinemann, 1993), 272; Richer, interview (4 Jan 2006).

7 Nine states in the region belonged to SADCC at the time.

8 Wally Serote, The Night Keeps Winking (Gaborone: Medu, 1982), 10, 13.

9 Ibid.

10 Ellen Tveter Deilkaas, e-mail to author (Dec 2005). The abbreviations stand for: Norwegian Agency for Development Cooperation, Swedish International Development Cooperation Agency, International Voluntary Service (a British organisation).

11 Planning documents in Gonzalez Collection; Colin Smuts, interview (July 2001).

12 Mike van Niekerk, 'Gaberone's festival of arts hopes to attract SA artists', Cape Times (Dec 1981).

13 Mnyele, 'Opening remarks 1982 South African art exhibition' (10 June 1982), Seidman Collection.

14 Paul Stopforth, pers. comm.; Ricky Burnett, e-mail (1 Sept 2001); Saying No, Novib film, 1982, Mayibuye Centre, UWC.

15 Mnyele, Notes for spoken introduction, Gonzalez Collection.

16 Gavin Jantjes, Paper on fine art, Culture and Resistance Conference Papers (Cape Town: Michaelis Library), 8.

17 Nadine Gordimer, 'Relevance and commitment: Apprentices of freedom', Culture and Resistance Conference Papers (Cape Town: Michaelis Library), 2, 6, 9.

18 Ibid, 10.

19 Keorapetse Kgositsile, 'Culture and resistance in South Africa', 3, 8, 9, SAHA AL 2596, Cullen Library, Wits.

20 Transcripts of taped interviews with Abdullah Ibrahim and Hugh Masekela, Julie Frederickse Collection, AL 2460, File M1, Cullen Library, Wits.

21 'Botswana arts festival planned', Grassroots (Feb 1982).

22 Mnyele, 'Observations'.

23 Mnyele, 'Art can never be neutral' (23 Sept 1981), 3, Seidman Collection; 'Observations', 5, 7.

24 Anne Pogrund, e-mail (3 Dec 1999); Bill Ainslie, interview (14 July 1989); David Koloane, interview (July 2001).

25 Biko, Black Consciousness, 27–8.

26 Muff Andersson, interview (27 Dec 2001).

27 'Art and conflict in South Africa', reprinted from Social Review, for Culture and Resistance symposium, 2–3.

28 Willem Campschreur and Joost Divendal (eds.), Culture in Another South Africa (London: Zed, 1989), 158.

29 'The doors of culture shall be opened' (13–18 Dec 1982), The Dutch Anti-Apartheid Movement Video Archive, SAA. The catalogue incorrectly identifies an unknown man in the tapes (1, 7, 9) as Thami Mnyele.

30 Ibid; John Matshikiza, pers. comm. (Dec 2003).

31 Patrick Fitzgerald, interview (26 Dec 2001).

32 Moira Whyte, interview, (3 March 1993).

33 This postcard was kindly shown to me by Mrs Sarah Mnyele.

34 Cal Saloojee, interviewed by Howard Barrell (Harare, 5 Aug 1989), 928–30, Karis-Gerhart Collection, reel 3; Barrell, 'Conscripts to their age', 328–30. Barrell writes that the ANC did not like the term 'suicide squad' but accepted it as a rhetorical device because it signalled determination and created apprehension among defenders of the status quo.

35 Ernst Fischer, The Necessity of Art: A Marxist Approach (Baltimore: Penguin, 1963), 42, 196, 137, 295. Fischer had published the book in German in 1959 in an effort to evolve a new Marxist approach to art, one embedding art history in a study of social pressures; he was writing in the aftermath of, and in reaction to, Khrushchev's 1956 revelations of Stalin's misrule. Fischer was expelled from the Communist Party in 1969.

36 ANC Second Submission to the TRC, Appendix One, Section 5.

37 Barrell, 'Conscripts to their age', 328–30.

38 The UDF did not adopt the Freedom Charter until August 1987.

39 Saloojee, interview by Howard Barrell, Karis-Gerhart Collection, reel 3, 930; Mike Kahn, interview (5 Jan 2003).

40 Serote, autobiographical essay, 25.

41 Albio Gonzalez, interview (2000); Rhona Ogbugo, interview (20 Dec 2002); Judy Seidman, interview (6 Jan 2003).

42 Marion Sparg, Jenny Schreiner and Gwen Ansell (eds.), *Comrade Jack: The Political Lectures and Diary of Jack Simons, Novo Catengue* (Johannesburg: STE, 2001), 7; Rhona Ogbugo, interview (Dec 2003).

43 Sparg et al., *Comrade Jack*, 31.

44 Ibid, 96, 100.

45 Joe Slovo, writing in *African Communist*, 1981, quoted by Karis and Gerhart, *From Protest*, 37; Comrade Reggie Mpongo, quoted in Sparg et al., *Comrade Jack*, 31; Uriel Abrahamse, interview (Dec 2005).

46 Shubin, *ANC*, 401.

47 Shubin, interview (20 May 2005).

48 Commission of Inquiry into Recent Developments in the People's Republic of Angola (Stuart Commission Report) (14 March 1984), Lusaka.

49 Ibid.

50 Ibid, 7.

51 Judy Seidman, interview (6 Jan 2003).

52 Rhona Ogbugo, interview (Dec 2003); General Herman Stadler, interview with Howard Barrell (Pretoria, Oct 1990), Karis-Gerhart Collection, reel 3, 1049.

53 Pete Richer, interview (4 Jan 2006).

54 Jonas Gwangwa, interview (15 July 2001); Baleka Mbete, interview (26 July 2001); Chris van Wyk, interview (19 Dec 2002).

55 Known only as Mathloko, Dikgole and Thiba.

56 Interviews: Boitumelo 'Shimane' Molaolwa, Kraaipan, and Edward 'Tiger' Ramorwagadi, (Sept 2006).

57 Pulane Mabalane, Truth and Reconciliation Commission, Human Rights Violations, Mmabatho (8 July 1996).

58 Bill Ainslie, interview (14 July 1989); Serote, 'Liberated voices', 14–18.

59 T Magweza, 'Dawn breaks' (1984), 9.30 pm Thursday broadcast on Radio Freedom, Track 11, Rounder CD 4019 (1996); Mnyele to Teresa Devant (n.d.) postcard, Gonzalez Collection; SAIRR file of news clippings on the Gaborone Raid, Box 39.7, Cullen Library, Wits.

60 Shubin, ANC, 266.

61 Ibid, 237.

62 Daryl Glaser, *Politics and Society in South Africa* (London: Sage, 2001), 195, citing the work of Alex Callinicos, Karen Jochelson, Michael Morris and V Padayachee; Stephen Ellis and Tsepo Sechaba, *Comrades against Apartheid: The ANC and the South African Communist Party in Exile* (London: James Currey, 1992), 140; Martin Legassick, *Armed Struggle and Democracy: The Case of South Africa* (Uppsala: Nordiska Afrikainstitutet, 2002), 57.

63 Mnyele, 'Thoughts for Bongiwe and the role of revolutionary art', *Staffrider*, 7, 3&4 (1988), 297.

64 Wikus Johannes Loots, testimony, 10/5/1999, AM 4149, TRC.

65 Nat Serache, interview (Oct 2006).

66 Serote, autobiographical essay, 22.

67 *Sunday Star* (10 March 1985), 8.

68 Ibid.

69 Cal Saloojee, interviewed by Howard Barrell, Karis-Gerhart Collection, reel 3, 925, 933.

70 Shubin, ANC, 272.

71 Track 7 (n.d., 1984?), Radio Freedom, Rounder CD 4019 (1996).

72 Mnyele to Teresa Devant (n.d.), postcard, Gonzalez Collection.

73 Gordon Metz, 'Learning to live without the enemy', *African Arts* (winter 1996), 59.

74 Uriel Abrahamse, e-mail to author (2005); Bongiwe Dhlomo, interview (1989).

Chapter 7

Weapons of War

Thursday, 13 June 1985. It was early winter in Gaborone. The air was dry, dusty, and cold in the morning. Thami got up wearily and put on a warm, green-checked shirt. In his shirt pocket he placed Mint Imperials, so he could pop one in his mouth whenever fatigue overtook him, and lip ice to counteract the desic-cating air. He felt lonely. His son Sindi, now five, had visited with his uncle Alex the previous week, but the boy was now back with Rhona's mother and father in Tembisa, where he normally lived. A few days before, Thami had said goodbye to Rhona at the Gaborone station as she boarded a train north, carrying 'sensitive' documents. He planned to join her soon in Zambia, but hadn't yet packed. As she boarded the train, he assured her he wouldn't be sleeping at home.

Thami's name had been on a list of people the Botswana government was encouraging to leave for their own safety, but he was reluctant to lose the place where he was in closest touch with home. For a week he had been transferring his art supplies to Medu members. And he was saying his goodbyes. He phoned his father to say he was going to France or Scandinavia to study art. The day before he had told his comrade and fellow music lover Uriel Abrahamse, 'If I never see you again, please do not stop collecting music.'[1]

He walked out of the unplastered brick house they were renting in Tlokweng, the nondescript village that lies between Gaborone and the South African border. They were lucky to find someone willing to rent to them. Not all local landlords wanted the problems that came with housing South African exiles. Unknown persons typically visited refugees at odd hours. Who knew whether they were depositing guns and grenades on the premises? Searching for weapons, the police might come and dig up the yard, or worse. Perhaps Thami's mild manner, plus the presence of his wife and the visits of his child, convinced the landlord he presented no threat to the property. The house was more comfortable than Albio and Teresa's garage – it had bedrooms, a lounge, electricity, and there were burglar bars on the windows – but the lodging was, of course, temporary.

Although Tlokweng bears the name of a Tswana chiefdom, the more prominent part of the village looks like a commercial strip along any African highway. It displays none of the graces of an old Tswana capital with rounded islands of thatched homesteads. In 1985 drivers typically rushed past its rectangular, tin-roofed structures because they wanted to leave behind the tedium or danger of dealing with South African and Botswana border guards. Quitting Botswana, they wanted to get to the border before it closed at 8 pm. If they were late and the boom had been raised and lowered for the last time that day, they could always bed down in the Oasis Motel. Shouting and laughing beer-drinkers in the Oasis bar might keep them awake, though, and on the weekend the music from the Beat Street Disco played so loudly that the thudding racket reached Thami's house. Nevertheless, both Tlokweng and its signature hotel did function for some people as oases from the stress of being near the border at a time of 'unrest', as the South African newspapers called the current waves of political violence in the townships.

People seemed to be looking for Thami of late, and he wasn't always sure why. Two weeks earlier some South African art students had shown up, asking him for military training. Thami said he didn't want to be paranoid, but needed to be careful. The week before he and Riaz Saloojee had gone to the train station to meet a couple of men from home, but one of them behaved so suspiciously that the ANC detained the man for questioning. Even that morning at the museum a 'guy from home' had been asking for him with some urgency. When Gordon Metz replied that he hadn't seen Thami for months, another museum worker piped up, 'But I saw him in town today.' The South African, who said his name was Lebisi and that he came from Thami's home area, went away and said he would return later. He did not. Gordon was suspicious. Everyone was living in a state of nervous anticipation.[2]

Tim Williams dropped in at Thami's place and together they walked over to George Phahle's. The three men agreed they wouldn't be sleeping at home that night. Wally was spreading the same word among the comrades, taking care to state the imperative 'harshly' when he bumped into Thami, whose dreaminess he knew well. Wally also went in search of George Phahle, his old friend from Alex. The son of teachers, George was an extroverted entrepreneur and township music lover married to Lindi, a pretty social worker seriously committed to children's issues.

A relative of Lindi, Joseph Malaza, a former Hertz employee who had gone into the car rental business for himself, was staying with them. (One of his rented cars had broken down and he had come to fetch it, though he may also have been acting as an ANC courier.) George was doing well in his flamboyant way since arriving hurriedly from South Africa in 1976, accused of helping to bomb the Carlton Centre in downtown Johannesburg. He had started a transport company running between Gaborone and Lobatse and now owned at least one 75-seater bus. The South African Police now suspected him of transporting trained MK cadres to safe houses in nearby Mogoditshane and Lobatse, as well as channelling new refugees into the ANC. George had indeed trained in Angola and, along with Lindi, was active in MK. He generously gave MK units money for food and provided them with lodging. He assured Wally that he and Lindi were leaving for Harare that night.[3]

At around noon Dick Mtsweni's ten-year-old granddaughter, Busi, looked out of the window of their house in northern Gaborone. A pickup truck with tinted windows drove past. What drew her attention was the large camera lens protruding through a slightly opened window. Why would anyone be photographing our house? she wondered. She knew her grandfather ran errands for the ANC, delivering food supplies to the hundred or so refugees the movement supported. Sometimes he even picked up high-profile ANC people at the airport. For the most part, though, he busied himself with taking literacy classes and maintaining his own household. The old man had two wives and moved happily between their houses. He had relocated the family from South Africa in 1981, first to Dukwe. His sons were in exile, though he protected Busi by not revealing where they were, if he knew.

In Gaborone that day Thami also saw Willie Kgositsile, poet and lecturer at the university, and his wife Baleka, the new chairperson of Medu and lead singer in its jazz group, Shakawe. Thami saw the couple, sent by the ANC in 1983 as cultural workers, almost daily. Just over a month before, a local newspaper had interviewed Baleka about Medu's hopes and needs. While voicing thanks for Canadian and Scandinavian aid, she lamented the ensemble's lack of working space, which limited its publishing, recording, and photography ventures. She said Medu's 25 members wanted to launch an arts programme for small children.[4] She spoke so expansively that she seemed to believe the future was wide open. That Thursday afternoon she and her husband dropped Thami off at their house near the university, telling him to make himself at home while waiting for a reception at the museum to begin at 5 pm. 'Make some coffee,' she said. 'Don't sleep at home tonight,' Baleka repeated.

Mike Hamlyn also knew that sleeping at home was unwise, but that isn't why he had recently moved from a big house to its servants' quarters. As a university student without a full-time job, he simply couldn't continue to pay his share of the rent. For two and a half years he had lived with Uriel Abrahamse near the university in a full-size house nicknamed 'The Boys' Club'. The name fitted, partly because he and Uriel had a knack for playing with children. A couple of nights before, Mike had spent the evening playing Meccano with Mike and Carol Kahn's two children. The Kgositsiles' two children often stayed with the young men. Mike had just taken the final exam for his degree in physics. Everyone believed he would pass because the quiet redhead was known locally as someone who understood how things worked: he could fix computers, cars, and even motor scooters. Informally he had just learned that the university would award him its first-ever first-class pass in physics. To celebrate, he was going to the Capitol cinema on the mall that night to see Paul McCartney's *Goodbye to Broad Street*.

A couple had moved into the big house two weeks earlier and would share the rent with Mike. She, Roelie Geer, a young working-class woman from Holland, was due to give birth later in the year. He, Ahmed Geer, a computer programmer, originally from Somalia, had just found a job in Botswana after searching fruitlessly for a new home in Holland and Zimbabwe. After responding to Mike's ad in the local newspaper the couple finally stopped moving from servants' quarters to servants' quarters, as they had for the past six months, and acquired the components of a stable life, while Mike had a cheap place to stay as he awaited his exam results, playing the clarinet and working for Medu and MK on the side.

Duke Machobane, a refugee from the 1976 student revolt, had recently graduated from the University of Ibadan in Nigeria, where he had studied English literature, thrilled to be a student at Wole Soyinka's alma mater. (He had even travelled to Ife to interview the Nobel laureate.) While in Nigeria he had maintained his ties with home by poring over issues of *Staffrider* and belonging to organisations of student exiles, though their factionalism perturbed him. Duke joined the ANC only after arriving in Botswana. His MK speciality was mobilising young South Africans who visited him there.[5] Duke was now teaching at

Matlala Secondary School in Tlokweng. He had recently married Rose, a girl from Lesotho, whose small nephew was currently staying with them.

Tim Williams sent his wife Stella and his children away from their Broadhurst home. As night drew near, he sat up and waited. Wally drove to the village of Mochudi, carefully placing his pistol under his seat.

What gave rise to this widespread fear of imminent attack? Of late something dramatic had happened every month, reminding everyone that Botswana was a dangerous 'forward area'. The first incident had taken place in February, unbeknown to the exiles, when 20 highly placed South African policemen held a 'target development meeting' in a Security Branch safe house across the border in Ottoshoop. Sleeping over, they were joined the next day by Kat Liebenberg, head of Special Forces in the SADF. Based on the work of informers they determined that Nat Serache's house was an MK transit facility and so they conspired to murder him. Soon a bomb exploded in the Broadhurst home Nat shared with another refugee. Both men typically turned off the lights last in the front bedroom in order to make spies think they slept there. Their ruse worked. SADF agents placed a hollow charge bomb in that room and at ten minutes past midnight on 13 February it exploded with such force that it sliced the refrigerator in half. Though the blast covered Nat with rubble, he survived because he was sleeping in another room. Thabo Mbeki, then head of the ANC's international department, visited him in hospital and ordered him moved to Lusaka.[6]

Then in March a car bomb killed Vernon ('Rogers') Nkadimeng, a member of Sactu and the ANC, who had been working for a Canadian aid agency. The bomb was so powerful it lifted the car engine two storeys high, right through the roof of the man's flat, leading Uriel to reflect that 'it was a complete overkill'.[7]

The locus of these spectacular attacks on refugees had only recently shifted to Gaborone. In the early 1980s most South African raids into Botswana had taken place in the north because they were linked to its war in Namibia and Angola. Why was the Gaborone area becoming so vulnerable? In April a large arms cache, including mines, mortars, a bazooka rifle, pistols, and grenades, was found in a suburb of the city. When commissioner of police Simon Hirschfeldt was asked who had been storing the arsenal, he gestured over the weapons and ammunition laid out in neat rows and replied, 'Your guess is as good as mine.'[8] The Botswana government had to avoid giving the South Africans the impression it was willingly harbouring terrorists.

South African foreign minister Pik Botha dated the beginning of the threat from southern Botswana to August 1984, when a spate of MK attacks began. By the day in June when the Gaborone exiles were all warning each other not to sleep at home, South African intelligence had identified 36 violent acts as originating in Botswana. In addition, a hand grenade had just been lobbed in Cape Town at coloured member of Parliament Llewellyn Landers, then being promoted to deputy minister in the central government. If this attack were avenged, the government might give the impression that it was protecting coloured people, too. But why were these attacks linked to Botswana?

South African officials publicly claimed that Soviet influence was spreading through Southern Africa from the USSR's expanding embassy in Gaborone. The minister of defence General Magnus Malan told the Transvaal provincial National Party congress in October 1984 that the Soviets were becoming more active in Botswana. Afrikaans newspapers were even referring to their landlocked neighbour as 'our own Cuba'. In fact, the Russians delivered no arms to the ANC in Botswana. They had contact with the ANC only in Lusaka, perhaps because they feared jeopardising their diplomatic mission if they met in Gaborone.[9]

The South African press suggested that President Quett Masire had turned away from the 'moderate' policies of his predecessor, Sir Seretse Khama. And yet Khama and Masire used nearly identical language to explain their refusal to sign a non-aggression pact. They said there was no need for an accord because they opposed their country being used as a 'launching pad' (Masire) or 'springboard' (Khama) to attack their neighbour. They argued that to sign such a pact would amount to a loss of sovereignty. Masire feared that if South Africa stationed troops on the border it might use the pact as an excuse to invade. Members of Botswana's Parliament agreed. And so, the Botswana government refused to sign a draft military accord. It didn't even send an official representative to the Komatipoort ceremony when the Nkomati Accord was signed on 16 March 1984.[10]

The Botswana government had indeed permitted the ANC and the PAC to set up offices in Gaborone from which they could disseminate propaganda, like issues of *Sechaba*, and help refugees, as when Dick Mtsweni delivered food. Allowing Botswana soil to be a base for sabotage was another matter: it invited attack. Shortly after the discovery of the arms cache in April, the Botswana government asked a number of ANC members to leave the country for their own safety. Police commissioner Hirschfeldt probably convinced no one when he professed ignorance of the origins and purposes of the little arsenal. The big picture was not mysterious. South Africa was paying more attention to Botswana because the Nkomati Accord had shifted the origins of sabotage eastward. Botswana was assuming Mozambique's former role as a staging area for MK attacks on South Africa.

Meanwhile, ANC delegates were gathering in the Zambian town of Kabwe to elect its new National Executive Committee. This meeting, the first big ANC conference since 1969, was bound to be contentious. Members would debate whether there should be racial barriers to ANC membership. They would also have to consider the complaints of the cadres who had mutinied in Angolan camps. Some suspected the

South African military of wanting to 'escalate' its conflict with the ANC during the Kabwe conference.[11] If the SADF managed to provoke ANC retaliation, it could justify attacking the movement's leaders when they were concentrated in that small Copperbelt town.

In addition, the anniversary of the 1976 student uprising was approaching. In three days it would be nine years since Hector Pieterson had received the first mortal wound in that short-lived but catalytic revolt. If the ANC and its sympathisers planned a mass commemoration on that date, they could fill the streets with crowds. The precise logic of South Africa's security elite cannot be recaptured easily because the documents recording it have been destroyed or, at least, are inaccessible. But we do know how the elite was structured.

The intelligence elite consisted of tiers labelled with titles and tasks reflecting its military culture. There were roughly six levels of intelligence officers within the police force, that is, beneath the level of the commissioner of police (General Johann Coetzee), who oversaw all police functions. The security branch, charged specifically with gathering and acting on data concerning political activities, was headed by Johan van der Merwe, and his head of intelligence was Alfred Oosthuizen, under whom General Herman Stadler and Major Craig Williamson worked. (These men received information from other countries as well as South Africa; Williamson had a subordinate, John Louis McPherson, whose job title was 'chief of the Africa Desk', and who therefore dealt with Botswana.)

The top tiers of the Security Branch received reports from regional offices. The Western Transvaal Security Branch, based in Potchefstroom and commanded by General Johannes Steyn and Colonel Wikus Loots, in turn coordinated data from commanders of sub-branches in Zeerust (Captain Philip Crause) and Soweto (Brigadier Muller). These regional sub-branches placed agents and informers in Botswana in order to infiltrate MK special operations and military intelligence. Just over the border in Zeerust, for example, Captain Crause directed a staff of about a dozen people who collected information about all the refugees, and he himself handled informers. Subordinates – majors, lieutenants, and warrant officers – would read and type up informers' reports, and the commandant would then coordinate them so they could move upward in the Security Branch hierarchy. The informers themselves fell into two categories: police constables who were undercover agents and, at the lowest level, informers who worked for the police on contract.

If a raid were to take place, there were many likely targets. Chris Hani, deputy commander of MK, was known to visit. (Doreen Nteta, who had studied with him at Fort Hare in the 1960s when he was known as

Martin, would occasionally glimpse him in Gaborone.) But these high-profile leaders were hard to locate as they were constantly in unpredictable motion. Easier to find were the local ANC members whose daily patterns could be traced by informers and reported back to the intelligence units inside South Africa. Their profiles in the Security Branch's 'terrorist photo album' could be continuously updated by intelligence reports sent by the army as well as the police. (The SADF Special Forces had its own Directorate of Covert Intelligence, though some doubted how well it cooperated with the police.)[12] Thami's photo was in the album, according to Anton Pretorius, a lieutenant attached to the intelligence unit in the Security Branch's Soweto office.[13]

Four informers worked especially closely on the ANC exiles during the weeks leading up to 13 June. Two were police constables – Freddy Baloyi and Isaac Mazibuku. They earned the label 'deep cover agents' by infiltrating ANC structures so they could report on exactly what each exile was doing. Two were contract workers – Cecilia Maake and Manuel Olifant. They relayed logistical information, such as where certain cars were parked. Other informers managed to keep their identities a secret. McPherson, as head of Williamson's Africa Desk, visited two sources in Gaborone at least once a month to give them instructions and to debrief them. Pretorius thought all ANC members in Gaborone were involved in military work; they were responsible for the current 'onslaught' of hand grenade attacks in Soweto. He was particularly interested in Tim Williams, who worked in 'MK military intelligence', as well as Patrick Thomas Ricketts ('Comrade Blahz') and Riaz Saloojee ('Calvin Khan'). He considered Saloojee the 'father and the founder' of the hand grenade units operating in Soweto and on the Rand. These men, and Rhona, were said to have attacked targets with hand grenades and given 'crash courses' in throwing them, to have provided safe houses for people and arms caches in transit from Zambia, and to have recruited MK members and set them up in cells. Crause had pieced together enough data to believe that George Phahle received refugees and transported them to safe houses, that the Solidarity News Service disseminated propaganda inciting people to violence, and that weapons were hidden in the ANC head office.

General Steyn, co-commander of the Western Transvaal Security Branch, summed up the situation: 'According to a continuous flow of confirmed information and evidence, it has indisputably been established that terrorists of the African National Congress, Pan Africanist Congress and other terrorist organizations have since 1984 used Botswana soil as one of the main infiltration routes into the Republic of South Africa.'[14] One problem with this sweeping tone of certainty is, as a former soldier and military correspondent put it, 'intelligence operatives lie … The better liars they are, the better they are at their jobs.'[15]

The story of informer Manuel Olifant, African in appearance despite his name, suggests what might have led them to lie. It also reveals why they agreed to work for the police at all. In 1979, when Olifant was 18, his father urged him to cross the border from his native Mozambique and live with his 'grannies in Natal'. Frelimo had just won control of Mozambique and it seems that his family had backed the losing side, Renamo. Immediately upon crossing the border into South Africa at Komatipoort, he and his friends were picked up by the police and imprisoned for a week. Then they were sent to Vlakplaas, a farm later to become notorious as a place of torture, where black policemen or 'askaris' were trained and hidden. They spent a month at the farm before being recruited to fight Swapo in South West Africa as members of the counter-insurgency force called Koevoet. After Namibia became independent, Olifant was transferred to the Security Branch in Soweto where he worked under Pretorius and was paid from a secret fund to inform on ANC members.

Olifant had recently made two trips to Botswana. The first time he came with a police sergeant and they stayed at the President Hotel while pinpointing possible targets for a raid. The second time, in May, he entered alone on a false passport, and stayed for a week, spying on two vehicles and three houses: 'The Boys' Club', where Uriel and Mike lived; Tim Williams's house; and one where he was told Rhona stayed. He managed to spot Tim Williams once and felt excited, as if he were glimpsing a celebrity. By studying the 'terrorist album' and sitting in on interviews with informers, Olifant had gathered all he needed to know about 'MK soldiers' and 'the people who supplied weapons to the cadres'. As a junior in the police hierarchy, and a contractual one at that, he felt he had no right to ask questions. He knew that if he tried to leave the force, as his friends had done, the police would kill him. He also believed that if he had tried to join the ANC, disbelieving members of the movement would have 'slaughtered' him. All he wanted was promotion to a steady job as a warrant officer.[16]

Freddy Baloyi, known to his superiors as RS282, attended meetings with Thami and then reported what was said and done. He said that Thami's house was where Tim Williams and Christian 'MK Jeff' Pepane gave 'crash courses to recruits from South Africa' and where Lambert Moloi, chief of MK operations, stayed when he visited Botswana. Lieutenant Pretorius in Soweto collected the information on Thami, but considered Rhona a 'primary' target, while Thami was only 'secondary'. The reason for his distinction is difficult to trace. Despite all the money and effort spent tracking the exiles, their identities remained blurry in their hunters' eyes. Intelligence reports frequently referred to Thami as a musician rather than an artist. The man 'tasked with the coordinating of ANC activities in Botswana', Potchefstroom-based Colonel Wikus Loots, understood little about him: he thought Thami was involved in 'something about ensemble', adding 'It was either art works or music, but this was in the art direction. It was the physical drawing of paintings ... That he identified with the struggle, I do not doubt ...'[17]

In May about 20 high-ranking soldiers and policemen gathered at the Special Operations head office in Wachthuis, the police headquarters in Pretoria, in front of a very large map of Gaborone. The map was so detailed that it included the sites and numbers of every plot in the city. The meeting was chaired by the head of the army, General Constand Viljoen, and the head of the police, General Coetzee, as befitted a meeting of both forces. The military men predominated because military action was about to be taken. Two of the policemen, Steyn and Loots, presented evidence on 29 possible targets, based on material collected by the Western Transvaal police. Detailed aerial photographs of these houses were fastened to the perimeter of the map, as were photographs of individuals. Lines linked them to their precise location.

Commandants Charl Naudé and James Hills would monitor the invasion, though neither would be present.[18] Naudé was commandant of a secret unit within Special Forces. (In 1971 Special Forces had been founded to give South Africa small, highly trained fighting units, whose devastating and 'deniable' actions would 'sap an enemy's will to wage war'.)[19] His unit, named Barnacle, was manned by disgruntled white and black former Rhodesians, who were selling their combat skills to the South African army. Barnacle conducted operations involving 'eliminations' and 'ambushes against people of strategic importance', so it was well suited to planning the Gaborone Raid.[20] On the map Naudé pointed out the safe houses and transit facilities, where suspect vehicles were parked and their registration numbers. Each human target was identified and justified. Some, like Chris Hani, looked too hard to track down. 'We could not attach them to a specific target,' Loots said, so they were discarded. Other sites – like Mogoditshane and Francistown – were rejected as too dispersed. Meetings like this one were said to have whittled down the list of potential targets to around 19, and eventually to 10 or 11.[21] Pete Richer, then working for Solidarity News Service aboveground and MK intelligence underground, later learned that Oosthuizen and Van der Merwe had discussed his own death, initially including his name on the list of targets. They ultimately excised it because they feared alienating white South Africans by killing whites. They also eliminated the name of Barry Gilder, a trained MK cadre also working for Solidarity. Mike Hamlyn was never on the list.

On 4 June, after the number was decided, Special Forces head General Liebenberg flew to Cape Town with McPherson from the Africa Desk. Next to Parliament, inside the high-rise ministerial office block named after Hendrik Verwoerd, they set up an overhead projector and showed transparencies justifying the attack. Their audience was two powerful men: the minister of defence General Magnus Malan and the minister of police Louis le Grange.

The third and final phase of vetting an invasion also took place in Cape Town when the Coordinating Intelligence Committee – police commissioner Coetzee, SADF General Viljoen, and director-general of intelligence Niel Barnard – presented the final ten names to the State Security Council. The council was chaired by the state president and included his ministers for defence, law and order, justice, and foreign affairs. Pik Botha was at the time trying to persuade investors to keep their money flowing into South Africa. Because a raid was likely to jeopardise his efforts, he may have been conveniently absent from this meeting, though his approval was apparently obtained.[22] According to Peter Stiff's history of 'recce operations', the recent hand grenade attack on MP Llewellyn Landers was 'the proverbial last straw'.[23] The committee approved the names in one day.[24]

It is likely that the following argument was made about Thami. He lived in a house in which murders on a Swartruggens farm in March were possibly planned. That meant the house was used by the 'ANC Transvaal Rural Machinery'. No one knew exactly how many cadres slept in this safe house; the estimates ranged from 4 to 17.[25] Pete Richer thinks Thami was an intended target, probably because he was an important recruiter. He had a talent for building political, military, and intelligence networks because of his extensive contacts inside South Africa. And yet, Richer says, the government's intelligence, six months out of date, was clumsy. It targeted obvious aboveground ANC members and missed people, like Wally, who were actually in the MK command structure.

'Rehearsals' for the raid, to be called Operation Plexi, had begun at the beginning of April in Phala-borwa, and continued until the end of May. Special Forces soldiers were given a 'warning order' to be prepared, though they did not yet know what their target would be.[26] The next stage of the preparations took place over three to five days at a base outside Hammanskraal under the direction of Charl Naudé. During their training the men attacked mock targets made of poles and sacking.[27] Olifant was taught that 'you just break into a house and the next thing whoever you found there you will just shoot'. Shooting women was not forbidden, Olifant said. The instructions were simply to go into a house, kill the occu-pants, and then place a landmine to destroy the building.[28] Hans Louw, another raider, confirms this: 'We were given carte blanche to kill civilians. There was no prohibition.' Finally, the day before the raid, the operatives were given an intelligence briefing, complete with photographs and slides of the targeted houses and people. Louw distinctly remembers hearing Thami's and Rhona's names.

Barnacle operatives did not happily share the planning with the security police and a unit of SADF commandos called 5-Recce. (5-Recce, based at Phalaborwa, employed guerrilla tactics adopted from Rhodesia's Selous Scouts; its members were mainly black Southern Africans from war-torn countries under the command of white 'team leaders'.) Barnacle's 'Major Brian', a former Rhodesian policeman named Gary Branfield, told Peter Stiff that he and the 5-Recce planners disagreed about which targets to hit.[29] 'Brian' preferred to strike the highest echelons of local ANC members, while the Recce planners 'wanted to hit as many targets as possible, so ease of attack was their prime criterion'. Tactical reasons governed the number as well as the identity of the targets.[30] Does this mean that Thami was particularly vulnerable because he lived near the main road to the border?

By 13 June, 11 men had crossed the border into Botswana at different places and times. They settled into local hotels, seven of them at the Oasis. Some said they were on a hunting or fishing trip. One man gave his name as T Carlson when checking into the Gaborone Sun as an employee of Toy Town Clothes. Another, who had the brazen wit to call himself Tim Williams, gave his employer's address as Love Joy Motors.[31] Salesmen brought samples and fishermen carried rods. They drove sedans, Land Rovers and Toyota HiAce minibuses. Manuel Olifant took men pretending to be refugees or members of a police anti-stock theft team around Gaborone in groups of four or five and showed them the target houses. He had learned their location from touring the city with a female informer, as he himself had never penetrated any ANC structures.

Ten to twenty kilometres across the border lay a farm called Nietverdiendt ('undeserved' in Afrikaans). A tent was set up there to serve as the 'tactical operational room' or TAC HQ. Inside the tent Commandant James Hills communicated with the raiders via a radio, sending and receiving coded messages from Botswana. He strictly limited access to his own staff and highly placed policemen. Brigadier Serfontein was present as the representative of Special Forces chief Liebenberg. (According to Stiff, 'Brian' of Barnacle was unhappy with the behaviour of the senior police and military officers at Nietverdiendt: they were 'partying, drinking beer and braai-ing meat, as if celebrating a victory in advance', without caring about the welfare of their operatives.)[32] The army set up another large operational tent, about half the size of a church hall, in Speskop, Special Forces headquarters in Pretoria. Loudspeakers there would allow people to hear, forwarded from Nietverdiendt, coded feedback of the events about to take place in Botswana. Liebenberg and Craig Williamson, along with McPherson and some of his Africa Desk staff, were all at Speskop.

The operators were divided into 13 teams of varying sizes, each charged with a specific task. Near the four local bases of the Botswana Defence Force (BDF), two teams would scatter 'caltrops' (tyre-shredding, pyramid-shaped twists of wire that the operatives called 'stop nuisances'). After they had thereby immobilised the BDF, they would keep the Tlokweng road open so the raiders could easily return to South Africa. The precaution may have been theatrical; operatives believed the BDF had been forewarned and would present no problem. Other teams were allocated targets. They were told to 'clear the opposition, collect documents and blast the target houses with 5 kg "Hulk" charges made from PE 4 plastic explosive'.[33]

Like all the explosives used in the recent attacks on Botswana, their power was intentionally spectacular.

Sixty-three men – 53 of them black members of 5-Recce – climbed into a truck carrying all the equipment and arms, except for the two-way radios which the team leaders had hidden in their cars. Their arsenal included rifles that shone high-intensity beams when the trigger was pressed, 9 mm pistols, stun grenades, M 26-grenades, medical kits, gas masks, and water bottles. Then the truck was sealed. It drove past the helicopters, 50 to 60 tanks and armed vehicles standing by in case the BDF defended its country. (Manuel Olifant later observed that, if it had, 'Gaborone in particular would have gone into flames'.[34]) The truck crossed the border just before it closed at 8 pm and went to a deserted quarry where all the team members were to meet at 11.20. At the quarry the doors were finally opened, and the 63 men spilled out of the claustrophobic space; the steel container truck had no ventilation and no light. They spent the hour before the rendezvous lying on the ground, recovering, too, from the travel sickness that came from being tossed around in the lurching truck. Gaborone's streetlights were switched off at midnight, as usual. Concealing their helmets, bulletproof vests, and weapons, the motley invaders, dressed in jeans and T-shirts, piled into vehicles that would take them close to their targets. The team leaders gave them their final briefing in the cars as they sped to their destinations. At 1 am the teams heard TAC HQ give the code word to begin.

Thami had come home from the museum reception, despite all the warnings he had heard throughout the day. At 1.15 am he was still up and dressed. He hadn't even taken off his shoes. Perhaps he was packing. Wally later thought he must have been drawing, as his pens were uncapped. He couldn't see the vehicle approach because he had covered his windows with blankets as well as curtains. Because the team that came to Thami's home was the first to arrive 'on target', there were no sounds of gunfire to alert him. Six of the eight-man team emerged from the vehicle. Two stayed inside it, revving the motor. 'Nicholas' and 'Pierre' moved around to the back of the house, covering it with a 1000-round PKM machine gun in case a full contingent of guerrillas were sleeping there.

Thami may have heard the crunch of footsteps. Thinking, perhaps, that he was being joined by comrades, he may have moved toward the door. His hand would have gone to the light switch and then to the doorknob. Pulling the door toward him, he would have faced four heavily armed men and realised that the moment he had been dreading for five years had finally arrived. Slamming the door on his hunters, he ran through the kitchen and out of the back door, desperate to get over the fence and disappear into the night. Nicholas and Pierre opened fire. The bullets caught Thami as he started to scale the fence. Within seconds his body was hanging lifeless from the wire.[35]

Nearby, a thorn tree grew. Thami died next to the spiky branches he had often drawn to express the hard and bleak beauty of his world.

The raiders then sprayed the rooms – paintings, paints, furniture, easel – with shotgun fire. One of the raiders, named Sergeant Piet, was startled to discover that he had needlessly illuminated the rooms with the light mounted on his carbine, even though the electric lights were blazing. They spent 40 cartridge cases in the living room alone.[36]

The team captain proudly told Stiff that it took them only 55 seconds to kill Thami. In less than a minute they had shot open the unlocked front door, thrown stun grenades into every room, and 'riddled [Thami] at point-blank range'.[37] Then they photographed his corpse. For ten minutes they stuffed his papers, including some drawings, into canvas bags, before blasting the house to 'rubble with a "Hulk" charge'. The men decided not to set booby traps, as they didn't want to harm innocent bystanders who would no doubt pick through the wreckage.

Stiff's stories, virtually the only ones available to anyone attempting to reconstruct the event, come from informants eager to demonstrate their efficiency and their bravado. Several people doubt that Thami, a trained cadre, would have opened the door.[38] As photographs attest, the house was not, in fact, reduced to rubble, though it was riddled with bullets. Even clothes hanging in a closet, like a servant's khaki shirt with red trim that Thami had picked up at a used-clothing sale, were pockmarked with bullet holes. A bottle of India ink lay shattered on the floor. The doors, windows, water and electricity installations were badly damaged. So was the art that the raiders had not packed into their canvas bags. On a broken bureau lay copies of Thami's poster depicting a young boy shyly shaking hands with an armed guerrilla.

Withdrawing to the nearby Tlokweng Road, the raiders fired on the few passing vehicles, tossing a hand grenade into one that failed to stop. Its driver, Prince Mampane, flung himself into a ditch just before his car went up in flames.

Had the raiders targeted Thami's art because they loathed its values and feared its power? The suggestion is tempting, because it is, in some symbolic sense, true. And yet, Pete Richer cautions, raiders on a murderous mission tend to be too excited to act on such precise and abstract motives. They, too, are traumatised. Olifant, for example, couldn't find one of the three houses he was responsible for, the one where Rhona was believed to live. When he radioed this fact back to his commandant, he was told to abandon that target. Stiff writes that the raiders expected Thami to be at other ANC safe houses nearby, either Target One Bravo or Target One Alpha.[39] If this story is true, he was killed before anyone knew who he was. He died because the raiders encountered him when they were primed to kill. A raid, Richer says, is made up less of verifiable facts than of conflicting emotions and experiences. Hans Louw remembers concentrating on the task, as he had been trained to do, so that he would feel nothing and endure the 'chaos'.

Richer describes his own confused reaction to the raid. Living across from Mike Hamlyn's house on Pudulogo Close, he was awakened by the sound of shattering glass, followed by explosions. He packed his wife and two young children into the car and drove out, thinking they had heard fireworks. They passed the raiders' vehicles leaving in the opposite direction, then returned home and went to bed. Another comrade pulled a pin on a grenade and sat frozen in the bush, holding it in his hand, until his comrades discovered him. The same confusion was undoubtedly true of the attackers. In addition, most had served in Angola and hadn't been taught to discriminate between valuable and worthless booty. They shot at the SNS telephone and computer, and took away the telex machine. They even packed volumes of the South African *Government Gazette* into their canvas bag. Louw observes, 'We came back with a lot of trash.' They broke the body of Duke Machobane's small nephew in two by shooting him at close range after he was dead. When they returned to South Africa to drink and celebrate the success of their mission, they shouted snatches of what they had observed – someone screaming, someone dying – but no one could give a coherent account.[40]

The citizens of Gaborone were similarly confused. Upon first waking, some thought the BDF was engaged in shooting practice. As the mortars and grenade explosions joined the machine gun fire, they began to wonder if they were hearing the sounds of an attempted coup. After all, the president was touring the Kalahari and the vice-president was in China. Many people were too scared to investigate or even to switch on the lights. They lay in the dark and listened to the sounds boom across the flat land, amplified by the quiet night. They heard the heavy vehicles race back towards Tlokweng Gate. Some learned only the next morning from the BBC radio news what had happened. The few who stood outside the Beat Street Disco to see the raiders withdraw swore they were grinning as they waved goodbye.

Mike Hamlyn, having returned from the cinema only two hours earlier, was gunned down in his underwear as he crouched at the foot of his bed in the servants' quarters. In the main house Ahmed Geer was shot dead as he opened the front door in response to a command in English. His wife was wounded as she hid in a closet. Dick Mtsweni was shot in his bed, and his granddaughter was wounded as she tried to escape through her bedroom window. George and Lindi Phahle pushed a piano against their bedroom door, but it was shoved aside, and they were both gunned down, while Joseph Malaza died when shotgun bullets penetrated the closet where he was hiding. Duke Machobane was killed in his bed, and his six-year-old nephew died as he ran crying from his room.

Only Tim Williams escaped. When he heard the vehicles arrive, he looked through the curtains and saw the raiders. Running out of the back door, he scaled a fence and jumped into the next yard. Hiding under an automobile, he heard the attackers destroy his home, and spent the rest of the night running from house to house. A neighbour, Basi Zondi, also a South African, was killed when he went to his door to investigate the noise. As the attackers were leaving, they commanded an ambulance driver rushing to aid the wounded in Tlokweng to abandon his vehicle and walk back to town.[41] He did. Only one of the raiders, the pseudonymous 'Tim Williams', was wounded, accidentally shot in the leg by one of his own men.

In all, 12 people died, only seven of whom were associated with the ANC. Two of the victims were Tswana women, still in their teens, who had recently arrived in Gaborone to find jobs – one as a typist, the other as a domestic – and had the misfortune to find lodging in servants' quarters alongside two South African women who were indeed ANC members. The young Tswana women were both Seventh Day Adventists, feeling that God alone would bring a righteous government one day. Their faith made them apolitical. (Stiff's account, published in 1999, persists, however, in calling the two women 'Cuban and Soviet-trained intelligence operators'.)[42]

Some people in Gaborone grew fearful of refugees, shunning them in public and refusing to rent property to them. One old man, seeing them as competitors, told a local reporter, 'Refugees should all go to Dukwe. Why are we still so backward in Botswana that we have to employ people from outside?'[43] His point of view, if not his reasoning, was endorsed by nearly all the hundred delegates at a Botswana Democratic Party meeting the following weekend: they voted to remove all refugees to Dukwe.[44] Others worried that the BDF had colluded with the invaders. How else were they to explain the absence of Major-General Mompati Merafhe and Brigadier Ian Khama, and the ease with which the caltrops had stopped any defensive action by the BDF? Merafhe, the commander of the BDF, denied that the army had been forewarned and intimidated by 'night-raiders, murderers and common criminals', but cautioned that engaging the invaders in street combat would have resulted in a much bloodier scene.[45] At some sites the police showed up an hour after the raid ended. A week later Botswana security policemen escorted Tim Williams to Gaborone airport and put him on a flight to Lusaka 'for his own security … [and] for other security reasons'. South African agents involved in the raid were said to be disappointed that 'one of the big fish' had got away.[46] Freddy Baloyi and one other undercover agent also went to Lusaka, convinced that their identities were still unknown. They were wrong: after interrogation, the ANC had Baloyi killed.[47]

Perhaps to compensate for Williams's escape, the agents made Dick Ntsweni, the old man struggling with illiteracy, into a 'big fish' who ran the ANC's finances in Botswana. They suggested that Ahmed Geer was in touch with the Palestine Liberation Organisation. They said grenades had been found in the quarters of the two dead Tswana women and that one of them was Rhona. Their lies raise the question of how successful the raid really was in its own terms. The job of portly Craig Williamson was to manufacture the illusion of a glowing success. Dressed in a three-piece suit, he did so one week later, after even President Masire had expressed consternation at the failure to display any captured weapons. His image was broadcast on television and in the newspapers as he held up Thami's drawings of strong and angry masses with their fists in the air, calling the pictures 'weapons of war'. He also put on display Russian weaponry – one pistol, two grenades, an RPG 7 night-sight, a Dragonov sniper's night-sight rifle, and a RPD machine gun – which he claimed justified the raid. He had borrowed the guns from security policeman Eugene de Kock, who now says that all of them had been captured in Ovamboland, Namibia.[48] Hans Louw confirms that no weapons at all were captured in the Gaborone Raid.[49] Laudatory articles appeared in magazines like the army's own *Paratus,* making full capital out of the borrowed arms' Russian origins. 'The Soviet-backed African National Congress was dealt a body blow,' it crowed. The first South African newspapers to appear after the raid celebrated its success in cinematic terms. 'The guns of Gaborone' headlined the *Sunday Times,* whose reporting was based on stories supplied by the police. 'That's what they feed us,' one of its reporters admitted frankly.[50]

They've got as much drive as their Toyotas. KILLARNEY TOYOTA 646-8416

THE CITIZEN

INCORPORATING THE FINANCIAL GAZETTE Johannesburg, Friday 21 June 1985

27 CENTS Plus 3 cents GST

drive our Toyotas, you drive a hard bargain. RIVONIA TOYOTA Tel 803-1049.

GABORONE RAID: ANC INFO SEIZED

SPY CHIEF: HERE'S THE PROOF

Maj CRAIG WILLIAMSON of the Security Police with an AK 47 assault rifle fitted with a special silencer which he said was normally only issued to a specialised Russian force.

By TONY STIRLING

A "TREASURE trove" of intelligence including details of eight years of African National Congress bank accounts, was captured in the SA Defence Force raid on ANC targets in Gaborone, Botswana, last Friday.

This was revealed at a special Press conference in Pretoria yesterday by South African master spy and member of the Security Police, Major Craig Williamson.

Maj Williamson said that the veil of secrecy relating to the raid was being slightly lifted to give the South African and international Press an opportunity to learn the nature of the information captured and the reasons behind the raid.

Included in the haul, apart from tens of thousands of ANC propaganda documents, were detailed telephone account statements giving num-

bers dialled — many of them in South Africa — which are being followed up by the Security Police.

According to Maj Williamson no arrests have yet been made in South Africa as a result of the information received, but police action and arrests could be expected to follow.

Maj Williamson said that eight of the 12 people named as killed in Botswana have been identified from Security Police records as active members of the ANC.

According to the information disclosed by Maj Williamson, one ANC big fish was killed in the operation which was con-

ducted by units of the SA Defence Force.

He was Dick Motsweni, known to the ANC's military command as Mkhulu (the big one) who was in control of the ANC's finances and logistics in Botswana.

George Phahle, a transport operator, and his wife, Lindiwe, also killed

TO PAGE 2

Hijack: Swiss offer to mediate

BERNE. — Switzerland yesterday offered to mediate in the American hostage crisis and called on Lebanese Justice Minister Mr Nabih Berri to free some 40 people seized by Shi'ite gunmen, a Swiss foreign Ministry spokesman said.

"Switzerland has of-

fered its good offices to Mr Berri to help in any way we can to resolve this crisis," Foreign Ministry spokesman Mr Georges Martin told reporters.

The offer was made by the Foreign Minister, Mr Pierre Aubert, through the charge d'affaires in Lebanon, Mr Fermo Gerosa, who delivered the message personally.

He declined to comment on the response from Mr Berri, who is negotiating on behalf of the Shi'ite gunmen holding the hostages, mainly Americans. They have demanded that more than 700 Shi'ite prisoners be released by Israel.

But Mr Berri was

TO PAGE 2

OFS TAB bets scandal

By TONY STIRLING

A SCANDAL has erupted over the running of the Free State Totalisator Agency Board (TAB). "Bet now, pay later" punters have taken the TAB for a ride — leaving them with a bill of almost R800 000 in un-

on credit totalling about R400 000.

After he failed to pay, the punter — a very well-known gambler, from the Reef who a few years ago made a betting 'killing' of

ery of the outstanding amount.

According to The Citizen's information, a number of prominent personalities are among those who were given credit

Jo'burg rates' rise cut

By Janine Stein

A RECORD R1 014 million budget was passed by the Johannesburg City Council last night after agreement was reached to cut the increase in assessment rates.

Since the start of the budget debate on Wednesday, a cloud of uncertainty has existed over the first budget to exceed R1-billion as the ruling National Party Independent Ratepayers Association coalition in the council lacked one vital vote to see it through.

In terms of a special regulation surrounding the passing of financial increases, a special majority of 24 was needed in the 47-strong council in order for the budget to be passed.

The ruling coalition could not gather enough votes as the NP Whip, Mr Johan Fick, is presently in America.

Coupled with the Progressive Federal Party's firm opposition to the budget as proposed by the chairman of the management committee, Mr Francois Oberholzer, it seemed as if the proposals would not be passed.

Yesterday, Mr Oberholzer agreed to drop the increase in assessment rates from a proposed 2,88 cents in the rand to 2,80 cents.

This, in effect, means the average householder with a property value of

Police Major Craig Williamson on the front page of *The Citizen*, 21 June 1985, holding the weapons 'captured' during the raid on Gaborone one week earlier.

In the world of power, the timing of the raid undermined South Africa's efforts to resist international calls for divestment. The leader of the Progressive Freedom Party, Frederik van Zyl Slabbert, warned that the 'guns of Gaborone' might backfire on South Africa by escalating the violence and damaging South Africa's reputation internationally.[51] The apparent innocence of the targets and the brutality of the raid made it hard to defend doing business with South Africa. The British foreign secretary called the raid 'indefensible'.[52] The United States withdrew its ambassador for several months. That protest was as far as Ronald Reagan's administration could go without jeopardising its policy of 'constructive engagement', that is, using diplomatic pressure and negotiation to persuade the country to dismantle apartheid. (Reagan noted weakly that while the raid was 'not something we heartily approve of', he questioned whether 'South Africa was striking back at the people who were guilty [of violent acts], or just in a general direction …')[53] The United Nations secretary general called the attack a violation of the UN Charter, and the Security Council held an emergency meeting five days later.[54]

The raiders gave the raid their own peculiar meaning. Their tales conform to a pattern, as if to say 'Look how chaotic things were, I made mistakes, but then I sorted things out; isn't it funny?' They reveal a subculture of thinly camouflaged bravado. Sergeant Piet's stories go as follows, 'I was so excited that I used the lamp mounted on my carbine, though the light wasn't necessary …We got lost on our way back to the border, but eventually found our way … In a Rustenburg Wimpy bar we heard news of the raid on the radio, but lied to the other diners that we weren't involved, and then left.'[55] The tales have the incongruous air of boyish close scrapes, as if the reader or listener is being asked to empathise with, but mainly to admire, the ingenuity of the killer. Louw denies that the sedans got lost on their way back to South Africa; their path had been 'properly secured' north of the Tlokweng border post where there was no fence. And, he adds, no operatives drove back casually via Rustenburg in their cars.

Violence was bleeding throughout the region. Many of the fighters had learned their skills defending white Rhodesia and South West Africa. One had fled the collapse of Portuguese Mozambique. Some would become mercenaries; one (Gary Branfield) dying in Iraq, another (Hans Louw) ending up in a Pretoria prison after 'assassinating' a Greek mafia 'drug lord'. The end of white supremacy had bred a generation of men who gauged their worth by their capacity to hunt people and to recount their successes with an air of false humility. Mike Hamlyn's father, by all accounts an apolitical man, recognised with horror, 'They killed our son in our name.'[56]

Among white South Africans the Gaborone Raid evoked feelings of horror and shame similar to those of Mr Hamlyn. Some credit the attack with undermining white moral confidence, a necessary prelude if

3/86

rixaka

Cultural Journal of the African National Congress

THAMI MNYELE 1948 — 1985
'The madmen are frightened and sleepless. Thami lives amongst us.'

INSIDE | INTERVIEW WITH KINGFORCE SILOE | THOUGHTS FOR BONGIWE DLOMO | 'APARTHEID MUST BE ISOLATED'

Cover of the 1986 commemorative issue of *Rixaka*. (Original photograph taken at Culture and Resistance festival, 1982, by Michael Kahn)

a negotiated settlement was to end apartheid. Most news reports of the time painted the victims as innocents. One Canadian who witnessed the wreckage in Gaborone exclaimed in a fit of hyperbole that it was as if a monastery had been bombed. But of course, most of the victims had been trained soldiers. They would surely have preferred to be remembered as having, like Thami's figures, 'an upright posture, an elevated head, a firm neck, and a tight muscle', not the meek attitude of someone in spiritual retreat.

People who defended the raid would point to the subsequent decline in incidents of sabotage. Even the survivors agreed that they were now unable to inflict much damage across the border. As Shimane, Thami's grenade pupil, confirmed, 'The raid broke almost everything.' (Botswana now seemed so dangerous a place to Shimane that he didn't dare visit it again and went into exile via Mozambique.) MK cadre Barry Gilder observed that subversive acts emanating from Botswana were disrupted for almost two years.[57]

While the raid's carnage brought death, shame, and a brief respite from sabotage, it may also have planted seeds of empathy. One Christian intelligence officer believed, like many others, that ANC members were 'the devil incarnate and armed to the teeth'. Then he began to analyse the papers captured during the raid. Among them was a Bible taken from the home of one of the victims. Opening it gingerly, he found underlined the same passages as he had marked in his own Bible. 'What are we doing?' he began to ask himself.[58] While charming, this story has the air of a set piece. It is possible to find other versions of the same story being told by battle-hardened criminals. Eugene de Kock, for example, reports beginning to wonder who was right and who was wrong after finding a well-thumbed Bible in the rucksack of a guerrilla he had captured.[59] The template for this story may originate deep in the psyches of veterans trying to build empathetic bridges to former enemies now in power. Perhaps it also helps them to make sense of their own lives, holding on to one object of faith (the church) while another one (the state) crumbled in ignominy.

In 2006, from the vantage point of a prison cell within a democratic South Africa, Eugene de Kock observed that the incursion into Botswana achieved nothing. At the time, though, the raid portended a wider and meaner conflagration. Two weeks after Thami died, De Kock would take command of

Vlakplaas and make its counter-insurgency work more brutal than ever before, in the end to no avail. Within a decade he would call himself 'a veteran of lost ideologies', punished for acts secretly decreed and then denied by politicians and generals.[60] Thami Mnyele sacrificed his potential as an artist and lost his life when, in the cauldron of the 1980s, a dying regime flailed out with murderous force, defending itself and a colonial world-view whose time was long gone.

NOTES

1   Baleka Mbete, interview (26 July 2001); Uriel Abrahamse, e-mail (26 Jan 2005).
2   Uriel Abrahamse, interview (Dec 2005); Mbete interview (26 July 2001).
3   Serote, *Hyenas*, 101.
4   'Mmegi meets Medu's chairlady', *Mmegi wa Dikgang*, 2, 16 (4 May 1985), 3.
5   Mbulelo V Mzamane, *The Children of the Diaspora and Other Stories of Exile* (Florida Hills: Vivlia, 1996), 123–34.
6   Serache interview (Oct 2006); Amnesty signed by Judge R Pillay, 31 May 2001, AC/2001/228, case E.
7   Uriel Abrahamse, TRC (21 Nov 2000).
8   'Press shown mystery war materials', *Daily News* (Gaborone) (29 April 1985), 1. The following weapons had been found: 3 Chinese-made anti tank non-detectable mines, 156 x 200 grams of TNT slabs, 87 magnetic bar mines, one mortar, one bazooka rifle, 20 mm pistols, four commercial bar mines and free flare mines, 57 dynamite sticks, 32 slabs plastics explosives, 115 RGD hand grenades, 39 commercial shaped charge mines, three bar mines, 9340 7.62 mm ammunition round, 667 rounds of pistol ammunition, 25 detonator tins, one military type two-way radio.
9   Interviews with Peter Richer, Uriel Abrahamse, Vladimir Shubin.
10 Patrick Laurence, 'Sympathy, but no aid for the ANC', *Rand Daily Mail* (Dec 1982); Richard Dale, 'Not always so placid a place: Botswana under attack', *African Affairs*, 86, 342 (Jan 1987), 74-8; 'South African attack on Botswana', IDAF Briefing Paper no 18 (Sept 1985).
11 Advocate Malan expressed sympathy with this idea but doubted that it characterised military thinking generally, TRC (21 Nov 2000).
12 Pete Richer, interview (4 Jan 2006). Eugene de Kock observed that professional jealousy preoccupied higher ranking police and military officers, but did not significantly hinder the work of lower level operatives (interview, 26 Nov 2006). Hans Louw notes that intelligence could be outdated because units did not always share it efficiently (interview, 4 Feb 2007).
13 TRC (4 Oct 2000), 16.
14 TRC (3 October 2000), Amnesty hearing of Johannes Albertus Steyn, 2, quote from 248 of written evidence submitted by Brig Loots.
15 Hilton Hamann, *Days of the Generals: The Untold Story of South Africa's Apartheid-era Military Generals* (Cape Town: Zebra, 2001), 158.
16 Manuel Olifant, TRC evidence (20 Nov 2000).
17 Wikus Loots, TRC evidence (2 Oct 2000), 38–9.
18 Ibid.
19 Peter Stiff, *The Silent War: South African Recce Operations, 1969–1994* (Johannesburg: Galago, 1999), 21.
20 Hamann, *Days of the Generals*, 140-1.
21 Gen Herman Stadler, interview with Howard Barrell (Oct 1990), Karis-Gerhart Collection, reel 3, 1056.
22 Hamann, *Days of the Generals*, 134.
23 Stiff, *Silent War*, 472.
24 The archives of Military Intelligence have been scrubbed clean of interest and revelations: a letter about cross-border operations dated 30 April 1985, refers to 'Strategic guidelines re Botswana' but the document is missing. Because it was sent by the head of the army (Viljoen) to the minister of defence, it seems to be a routine request for authorisation ('machtiging') from a higher echelon. After the raid, MI documented domestic (e.g. the Catholic Bishops' Conference) and international reactions; the sole reference to the ANC appears in this document, in the context of expecting the ANC to use the raid to exploit public outrage. In July and September Botswana's foreign minister, Gladys Chiepe, seems to have gone to Pretoria to present her government's grievances, on the second occasion to her counterpart, Pik Botha. No documents explaining, justifying, or planning the raid survive. One letter, written apparently to brief Malan when he was facing a commission of inquiry in 1988, mentioned that Verster and Liebenberg asked name-blacked-out to draft a plan quickly to take about eight troops to Botswana and destroy ANC houses in 1985. Verster may be Colonel Johan 'Joe' Verster, who became, in 1988, the first head of the Civil Co-operation Bureau (CCB), whose members had been required to resign from the SADF and then were secretly rehired with pension and medical benefits (Hamann, *Days of the Generals*, 142–3). What is telling about this document is that it emphasises houses, not occupants.

25 Steyn, TRC evidence (3 Oct 2000), 13.

26 Hans Louw, interview (4 Feb 2007).

27 Stiff, *Silent War*, 473

28 Olifant, TRC evidence (20 Nov 2000).

29 According to Dr Alexander von Paleske, Gaborone, (Letter to editor, *Mmegi*, 23, 91 (20 June 2006)), confirmed by Eugene de Kock and Peter Stiff, 'Brian' was the code name of an ex-Rhodesian army man named Gary Branfield, who was killed as a mercenary in Iraq in 2004. Von Paleske writes that Branfield had been a member of the Recce murder squad that had killed Joe Gqabi in Harare.

30 Stiff, *Silent War*, 472.

31 'Were these men involved in Gaborone Raid?' *The Reporter* (Serowe), 2, 30 (10 August 1985).

32 Stiff, *Silent War*, 476. Eugene de Kock says these 'deniable' units were based on British and Israeli models.

33 Stiff, *Silent War*, 473–4.

34 Olifant, TRC (20 Nov 2000).

35 Stiff, *Silent War*, 480–1.

36 'Hell in the morning', *Botswana Guardian Midweek* (19 June 1985), 2.

37 Stiff, *Silent War*, 489.

38 Wally, in particular, resents the story, recorded by Stiff after interviewing Sgt Piet and one other killer two years later, saying that Thami would never have been so naïve. Hans Louw agrees.

39 Ibid.

40 Olifant, TRC evidence (20 Nov 2000); Louw, interview (4 Feb 2007).

41 'Terror attack victims named', *Botswana Daily News* (Gaborone) (17 June 1985), 2.

42 Stiff, *Silent War*, 480.

43 Maphalela Mukuka, interviewed by *Botswana Guardian Midweek* (19 June 1985), 2.

44 'Ninety-eight of the 100 delegates at the BDP meeting of the South Eastern Region voted in favour of removing refugees to Dukwe.' See 'Remove refugees call', *Business Gazette*, Gaborone (19 June 1985), 7.

45 Mxolisi Mgxashe, 'Merafhe briefs press', *Botswana Guardian* (21 June 1985), 2.

46 Stephen Terblanche, 'Key ANC "terro" escaped the net', *Sunday Times* (Johannesburg) (end June 1985).

47 Anton Pretorius, AM 4389/96, TRC (4 Oct 2000). Pretorius indicated that other captured informers were imprisoned in the MK prison Quatro.

48 Stiff, *Silent War*, 474; Hamann, *Days of the Generals*, 134 quoting *TRC Report* (Cape Town: TRC), vol. 2, 152–3; Eugene de Kock, interview (26 Nov 2006).

49 Louw notes that Special Forces used only Eastern Bloc weaponry , so it was not difficult to find arms that could be used as incriminating evidence of the Communist 'onslaught'.

50 'Van Rensburg demands "Sunday Times" apology', *Mmegi wa Dikgang*, 2, 24 (29 June 1985), 6.

51 Tos Wentzel, '"Guns of Gaborone" may backfire on us – warns Slabbert', *The Star* (n.d.).

52 Alex Brummer, Patrick Laurence, Michael Simmons, 'US recalls SA envoy in protest at Botswana raid', *The Guardian* (London) (15 June 1985), 1.

53 'We won't break off relations – Reagan', *The Star* (19 June 1985).

54 'World shocked', *Botswana Guardian Midweek* (19 June 1985), 8.

55 Stiff's footnotes 10 and 36 in chapter 28 of *Silent War* credit Sgt Piet as the source of these stories.

56 *New Internationalist*, 159 (May 1986).

57 Gilder in Hilda Bernstein (ed.), *The Rift: The Exile Experience of South Africans* (London: Jonathan Cape, 1994), 196.

58 Richer, interview (4 Jan 2006).

59 Jacques Pauw, *Into the Heart of Darkness: Confessions of Apartheid's Assassins* (Johannesburg: Jonathan Ball, 1997), 41. De Kock was referring to Swapo guerrillas he had encountered in Namibia in the 1970s.

60 Pumla Gobodo-Madikizela, *A Human Being Died That Night: A South African Story of Forgiveness* (Boston: Houghton Mifflin, 2003), 77.

Chapter 8

Where is home?

Thami's remains returned to South Africa 19 years after he died and a decade after South Africa's first democratic elections. Everyone involved in the four-day ceremony reintroducing him to South African soil had a particular reason for being there. A few believed ardently that a beloved figure must come home. Soil and bones and a monument would connect them to the dead man. They were served by energetic people who hadn't known Thami, but revered what they knew of his life. Some seemed eager to impress party officials with their devotion and their ability to get jobs done. One minister appeared to use the funeral service to win recruits for his church. Others wanted to dance in the streets and sing freedom songs on a public holiday. Still others were swept up in this combination of the heartfelt and the expedient and came simply to see what they could see.

If a ceremony can bring back the dead, whom did this event resurrect? One wonders if Thami, witnessing the public ritual making sense of his life, would have been astonished at what he had become.

That the event was taking place at all was a tribute to Sarah Mnyele's formidable energy, even at the age of 84. She won the support of a prosperous Tembisa mortician who donated a coffin. She lobbied the Ekurhuleni Metropolitan Council, responsible for Tembisa, so relentlessly that it contributed R95 000 towards the reburial. The council even promised to help erect a monument in Thami's honour above the new grave in Tembisa. Perhaps it would also establish an education fund in his name.

Mayor Duma Nkosi appointed a round-faced and sunny young man from Venda, Bethuel Munyai, to work closely with the exhumation and reburial committee overseeing the grant. Armed with a cellphone, Bethuel laboured for months to set up structures and establish contacts that would allow the event to take place. Some family members initially resisted Bethuel's frequent phonecalls. They found them unremitting, even pestering, but eventually gave in to his undeniable good will.

...o where is the sea now,
o where is home?

Now a shrill bird in the air asks of the sun
the world shrinks around us
sickness increases, and
...keep living here

Thami Mnyele, untitled, 1979, Phillip Segola Collection. (Photograph by Mark Henningsen)

It took two years for the pieces to fall into place. A plan to exhume Thami in June 2004 had failed because all the necessary permits hadn't been obtained. Burying him in a special site in Tembisa rather than in a normal graveyard would require special permission from the city council. By early September the preparations were near enough to completion for the Ekurhuleni mayor to announce them to more than 50 people at a formal luncheon in Germiston's mayoral parlour. Exultant that his hard work was paying off, Bethuel's tongue slipped over two facts as he welcomed Thami's family and friends. He amused Nomathamsanqa by proclaiming, 'I'm exhuming your daddy on 21 September', as if he were the gravedigger, and he said the ANC had donated the R95 000, whereas the money actually came from the Ekurhuleni Metropolitan Council. Rather than endorse this elision of the party and the council, ANC staff members working in the party's Luthuli House headquarters were adamant: the party would bear no financial responsibility for the event.

Why was the money allocated at all? Some guessed that certain council members were hoping to rise in the party lists by using the commemoration to make themselves better known. Some even thought that politically ambitious people who had been 'on the other side' during the apartheid years were publicly supporting the exhumation in order to cleanse their names of any collaborationist stain. There was no escaping the basic fact, though, that the exhumation was happening because Sarah wanted it.

When Sarah spoke to a reporter from the Johannesburg *Star*, she gave full rein to her talent for invention. She told of warning Thami in 1978 that he was on a police hit list. She had learned this news in a dream, she said, and it made him flee into exile. Sarah went on to say that she visited Thami in Botswana the following year when he was critically injured in an automobile accident. Because she did not have a passport, her neighbours 'put me in the boot of the car and we drove past the police without any problems'. Upon her return, she said, she was tortured and then jailed in Johannesburg's notorious Fort prison for two years because she refused to reveal her son's location. Her stories enthralled the *Star*'s reporter. Unwilling to stop weaving her fabulist's spell, she added that she had also evaded the police in order to bury her son in 1985.[1]

In January the Truth and Reconciliation Commission's reparations committee had paid Sarah and her sole surviving son R30 000 as compensation for Thami's death, so her motive in telling these tales was probably not venal. She may even have believed her own stories because they bore some emotional semblance to the actual events. In these tales she becomes a cause of action, rather than a pawn. When she suffers, she does so heroically. Her stories place her at centre stage in her son's death.

In the early hours of 21 September 2004 I joined, at Nomathamsanqa's invitation, ten people gathered in the departure lounge of Johannesburg International Airport to start their journey across the border to Gaborone. Two old ladies – Mrs Mnyele and Mrs Msimang – waited in wheelchairs, their impassive faces masking any possible fear at the prospect of flying. Mrs Mnyele, the frailest member of the party, wore a new yellow crêpe dress and matching coat. Her failing eyesight required her friends to alert her when her slip was showing. Three younger members of their retinue moved around them, taking various degrees of care. Stout Mpho, dressed in a red blazer, buoyed them with her air of confidence, as did Bethuel, his hands full of tickets and passports, serving as point person with airport staff. Mrs Mnyele's 50-year-old son Happy stood by.

The arrival of two younger women galvanised the waiting group. Thami's 27-year-old daughter, Nomathamsanqa, strolled down the corridor, neatly dressed in khaki slacks and a white shirt. Surveying her grandmother's new clothes she worried that she had underdressed. Mrs Mnyele had only recently relented and allowed her to attend, after arguing that there wasn't enough money in the trust to pay her way and that she should stay in Tembisa and prepare food for the mourners. Nomathamsanqa softly gave her grandmother and friends one all-inclusive greeting. Immediately one of the older guardians of traditional manners chided her for not greeting each person with a handshake and by name.

As the child of her father's first wife, Nomathamsanqa had inherited paternal ties that were often a mystery to her. Certainly she had never benefited from them. She braced herself. She knew she was about to learn a lot about those bonds and the rifts that had fractured them. Rhona, Thami's second wife, swept up to the group, covering her own uneasiness with a large smile. It is perhaps fortunate that Mrs Mnyele, who had never hesitated to criticise the propriety of Rhona's dress, couldn't see clearly her pink linen jacket and white skirt, with its modest, ruffled slit up the side. Rhona's father, Mr Segale, stood nearby in a sober brown suit, giving her ballast.

Airport staff ushered the little group through passport control to a waiting area near a glittering shop selling watches, where no one was curious to browse, and eventually on to the South African Express plane. Above the Kalahari grasslands the morning winds slammed into the small aircraft, making the ride unusually bumpy for those accustomed to flying. Those unused to being airborne accepted the buffeting without complaint. Perhaps they thought the turbulence was normal or even appropriate to the task at hand.

A grey, cool morning greeted us in Gaborone, as if a sombre lid had been placed over the usually sunny city. The spring rains had not yet begun to fall, so the wind whipped red dust across the tarmac. The smell of Kalahari soil mixed oddly with the sweet scent of frangipani blossoms, bringing a vague sense of promise to an otherwise gloomy day. The nearly bare trees were beginning, incongruously, to sprout blossoms.

Staff from the South African High Commission whisked the party into a half-dozen utility vehicles. The lead car, in which Mrs Mnyele sat with her friends, bore on its hood the new South African flag, whose multi-coloured Y-design Thami could never have imagined. Arriving in the centre of town, they entered a brand-new building facing the downtown mall. Its glass doors reflected the corporate headquarters of the diamond parastatal, Debswana. This six-storey structure had passed for a skyscraper in Thami's day, though now its lustre has been dimmed by the flashy architecture in Gaborone's many new, outlying malls. Gaborone had once looked like an alternative to a South African city; now it seemed indistinguishable from one.

Ushered into a meeting room to the right of the High Commission's main entrance, the group was served refreshments and invited to sit around a conference table. There they were addressed by the local reburial committee, formed in response to the Johannesburg initiatives. Motsei Madisa, a trim woman of middle age, spoke in deliberate tones. Her precision suggested the skills she would bring to local government if she won an upcoming electoral campaign, advertised by a poster taped to the door of her pick-up truck parked outside. A Motswana who had known Thami in the 1980s when she volunteered her services to the struggle, she spoke about the logistics of the burial.

Trying to scotch any potential grievances, she asserted her points in a no-nonsense manner: the family could not renege on the purchase of a Botswana coffin just because a Tembisa mortician had offered to donate one for free; she asserted local control of the ceremony by noting that time constraints obliged Bethuel to speak only at the reception and not at the grave site.

Other members of the High Commission staff and local reburial committee adopted the same firm tone. Noting that not everyone around the table was fluent in Setswana, Neliswa, a chic official dressed in black and white, brought the language back to English when it strayed into the vernacular. Johan Oberholster, another official, kept modestly to the sidelines, undoubtedly appreciating this effort not to marginalise him. (Mrs Mnyele spurned his handshake, but perhaps she didn't see him hold out his hand.) Phillip Segola, a South African émigré and old friend of Thami, appreciated Johan's modesty. 'The only thing wrong with him', he joked later, 'is that he's an Afrikaner.' Phillip, a graphic artist sporting a shaved head and a loose linen jacket, added an air of stylish gravitas to the proceedings. All signs pointed to a major, though unspoken, commitment to propriety. No feuds or personal agendas would be allowed to disrupt the honourable exhumation of Thami Mnyele.

When Rhona left the meeting to choose the Botswana coffin, determined to find a cheap one, Nomathamsanqa and I walked down the Gaborone mall. The Botswana Book Centre, the only bookshop in town in her father's day, still existed, but its quality was now far surpassed by the local branch of a South African chain, located in one of the new malls. The shop seemed to carry mainly textbooks, and there was no sign of a hot political broadsheet like the *Medu Newsletter*.

Following Phillip's advice, we stopped at the National Museum and Art Gallery to see an exhibition of Chinese embroidery. In silk thread the artists had drawn pictures of gardens and portraits so life-like that it was hard to believe they were not actually photographs. Standing in the centre of the octagonal gallery, Nomathamsanqa spun around and tried to imagine the walls covered with her father's probing drawings rather than silk tigers and bouquets. In late 1980, when Thami had mounted his one-man show in that room, she had been three years old, and he had just abandoned her and her mother. She now felt polite interest in what he had been up to in exile.

The High Commission staff drove the ten-person South African party to lunch in the hotel Thami had known as the Holiday Inn. In the early 1980s it had provided Gaborone with what passed for luxury: a swimming pool, a bar and restaurant, and basic international hotel décor. Now owned by hotel and casino magnate Sol Kerzner, it had acquired more than a new name, the Gaborone Sun. Its interior was bursting with images of flowers, inserted in latticework along the walls, depicted on chintz upholstery and in reproductions of Impressionist paintings. The dining room presented a similar picture of profusion. Along one wall stood half-a-dozen chefs, carving joints of meat, stir-frying woks, dishing up curries. They faced a buffet bearing a multitude of salads and desserts. There seemed to be no end to the abundance: elsewhere on the same floor, Kerzner had built a casino; and each hotel room boasted a mini-bar. The little party served itself and settled down to lunch in foursomes, while the few, like Rhona, who knew Gaborone well, received local well-wishers. They all needed to fortify themselves for what came next.

A convoy of suburban utility vehicles transported the party to a cemetery known unsentimentally as 'Extension 14'. The ANC had recently repainted the black wrought-iron fence around the graves of seven victims of the 1985 raid. It had also cleared the ground of the weeds and aged bouquets that had given the site a neglected air. The placard bearing, under the heading 'Victims of the 1985 South African Commando Raid on Gaborone', the names of the dead, had weathered the 19 years without damage. Thami's name lay fifth. In years past, Rhona and Mrs Mnyele had placed flowers at the site, but Nomathamsanqa was making her first visit. She asked me to photograph the grave while it still bore her father's remains. The sun had burned off the gloomy cloud cover of the morning. The weather – a brilliant blue sky accompanied by cool breezes – now embodied hope, the sort of mood Thami had tried to capture when he entitled his one-man show 'Statements in Spring'.

The schedule stated that after Phillip Segola had said a few commemorative words, the gravediggers would begin cutting into the dry brown soil at 2.30 pm. They would stop digging at a decent distance from the remains, resuming their work at 3 am in order to finish the job by dawn when the final ceremony began. Where exactly did Thami lie? Mrs Mnyele pointed to the end grave. So did Rhona and her father. That was where they had been leaving flowers for the past 19 years. No, others said, he must have been buried in the middle because that was where his name was located on the placard. The order laid down by the schedule fell apart.

What did others who had been present on that terrible day in June 1985 remember? People whipped out their cellphones. Uriel Abrahamse was phoned at the ANC headquarters. Wally Serote was reached in Johannesburg and asked for his advice. When Wally suggested consulting the graveyard register, Mrs Mnyele, who had by then withdrawn with her friends to the flagged car, snapped, 'You weren't there, Wally. How could you know?' She was adamant. The last grave belonged to her son. Rhona approached the car to mollify her. Phillip consulted with the gravediggers. Someone phoned the police and asked them to bring a photocopy of the relevant page from the cemetery register. More than two hours later the mourners were still scattered around the grave in attitudes of enquiry or consternation, cellphones aloft, hands pressed to lips, heads bowed.

Privately, a few people murmured that it didn't really matter which grave was exhumed. After all, Phillip said, the purpose was not to commemorate only a particular set of bones, but the spirit of the sacrifice. Nomathamsanqa agreed. Some people reasoned that the double grave at the far end must belong to George and Lindi Phahle. The slight depression in the second-to-the-last grave at the near end must have belonged to Mike Hamlyn. His parents had already exhumed his body, without ceremony, and taken it back to Durban. These two clues suggested that the placard was right, so the middle grave must belong to Thami. Rhona struggled to put a brave face on the confusion, joking that she must have been leaving flowers on Duke Machobane's grave all these years, even though she had never known him. Then, hit by a wave of sorrow, she covered her face with her hands, pressing her fingertips to her eyelids. Nomathamsanqa felt moved for the first time that day.

An entirely different attitude toward the remains inspired Mrs Mnyele. She wanted to wrap the bones in a special cloth, according to Xhosa tradition, she said. She wanted her life to be changed by the way she cared for them. She wanted to keep a talisman in the form of soil and a couple of small bones from the grave that she would place in a plastic shopping bag. She wanted to rebury the bones in her Tembisa yard in order to show the ancestors (*baholo*) that their son had returned. Thami was restless, she said, because he had been buried far from home. His roaming spirit was making her sleepless and robbing her of sight. His bones and only his bones could set her at peace. Never one to brook disagreement lightly, she knew where they lay: in the farthest grave.

When the blue-uniformed policemen arrived carrying photocopied sheets from the graveyard register, they put the drama to rest. The pages themselves did not necessarily offer unambiguous proof, the plot numbers had been written over too many times to be reliable. Perhaps their uniforms gave the reassuring stamp of authority to the document in their hands. Perhaps Mrs Mnyele was too tired to continue resisting. She agreed to approach the grave.

Rhona Segale Mnyele Ogbugo, Sarah Mamanyena Mnyele and Phillip Segola at the exhumation of Thami Mnyele, Extension 14 cemetery, Gaborone, Botswana, 22 September 2004. (Photograph by author)

As the mourners reassembled within and outside the wrought-iron fence, Phillip thanked Mrs Mnyele for acquiescing. Led into the enclosure by Rhona, the old lady spoke to Thami's spirit. She described what the *amaburu* (Afrikaners) had done to her son and praised former Botswana president Quett Masire for having given him a proper burial. She told her son that she was bringing him home, that there was more freedom (*inkululeko*) now, but the struggle still wasn't finished, though he had died to make life better. There was still HIV/AIDS to be combated, she said, and Thami would somehow help the cure to be found. Once he was at home she would rest in peace. Perhaps she would even regain her eyesight. She added with pride, for the audience's benefit, that she had been a member of the African National Congress since 1936. She patted the air gently with her right hand as if stroking her son's head. Rhona maintained her composure by pressing her lips with her forefinger, though her darkening eyes told of her renewed grief. An old mad woman wandered up and stood solemnly to one side, wearing a threadbare cast-off white coat, embroidered with the image of Mickey Mouse. As the small crowd dispersed and sunset rapidly approached, two men finally began dropping their picks into the middle grave.

Early the next morning when we rose from our plush rooms in the Gaborone Sun, it became clear that Happy had spent the night drinking the entire mini-bar in the room he shared with Bethuel. He executed a few smart dance steps in front of the hotel, before being firmly ushered into one of the cars waiting to transport the party back to the cemetery.

Shortly after 7 am we arrived at Extension 14 to take our seats under a canopy and listen to the five scheduled speakers. Behind us sat several rows of local and diplomatic dignitaries. All had chosen clothing to honour the occasion. Men wore dark business suits, while women put on a colourful and dramatic display: Rhona, in an orange coat and dress with rhinestone sandals; Nomathamsanqa, in a long pink outfit with flowing pastel scarf; Eunice Komane, the South African high commissioner, in a turban of ANC colours plus a matching Kente-style stole; Thandi Modise, a former MK cadre, in a violet West African *bubu*. Happy wandered into the proceedings from time to time, only to be ushered out firmly and politely when his mutterings and shouts – 'I'm never coming back to Botswana! Harry Boy!' – threatened to distract the mourners. How can he feel no shame? Nomathamsanqa wondered.

Like the ladies' dress, the ceremony was an eclectic and, in the end, harmonious blend. The Anglican priest, Trevor Mwamba, spoke of 'life everlasting'. The most popular song, judging by its repetition and the verve with which it was sung, seemed to be the American gospel hymn 'We are coming home'. People launched with ease into struggle songs like 'Hamba kahle, Umkhonto' (Go well, comrade), which had been sung at Thami's first funeral. They still shot their fists into the air in response to cries like 'Viva the Tripartite Alliance' and 'Viva the South African Communist Party'. Mrs Msimang crossed back and forth easily between Christian and struggle idioms. When initially asked to lead a prayer, she demurred, 'I only know the struggle,' before going on to address God in practised tones.

The speeches conjured up an image of Thami that sometimes strayed from the facts. His age and the date of his arrival in Botswana had already been cited incorrectly in the press and in brochures; he had died at the age of 36, not 29, and he had moved to Botswana in 1979, not 1978 as *The Star* reported. Mrs Komane said that he had been legally sentenced to death in South Africa, but he had, in fact, chosen exile freely. His mother had not been imprisoned without trial for two years, as she claimed. Nomathamsanqa wondered if her father had actually had two Xhosa clan names – Miya, Zizi – as his mother alleged; she thought they were mutually exclusive. Of Ndebele and Tswana heritage herself, Mrs Mnyele was making up her own custom and calling it 'Xhosa'.

A person who dies a violent death risks being remembered primarily for the manner of his passing. Few mentioned Thami's art, though the SABC afternoon news noted that he and the current speaker of the South African Parliament, Baleka Mbete (formerly Kgositsile), had been 'instrumental in popularising the present ANC logo'.[2] Even in death Thami's personal life was being sacrificed for the movement.

The ceremony achieved a reconciliation so wondrous and personal that Thami's heart would have been gladdened. Mrs Komane ended her talk by quoting lines from a poem Thami had written on a drawing he had given Phillip the year after he crossed into Botswana. The drawing consisted of five leaves impressed in the centre of a sheet of paper. To the left he had drawn three figures gesturing, their arms and legs splayed. Above their heads Thami had written words announcing that the signs of spring were beginning to appear on flowers and that generations kept being born. But, he went on, 'bitterness increases / and the world shrinks around us / now a shrill bird in the air asks of the sun / o where is the sea now, o where is home?'

Between the initial tone of hope and this concluding note of despair, he expressed the following words of love that reached across a quarter-century and embraced Nomathamsanqa: 'now what will happen now, / the house I built has fallen and / has wounded my daughter'. She had never heard him express regret at having lost and possibly imperilled her. 'I had always had this idea that my father never cared about me. My view was that when he died, I was old and smart enough to have remembered him, had he made some effort to keep in touch with me,' she said. Now, at the age of 27, hearing his lament, she was struck with deep sadness at what she had lost.

Then the digging resumed. The mourners gathered around and within the fence, while cameramen recorded the events for newspapers and television. Men wearing khaki overalls, face masks and gloves, carefully lifted shovelfuls of dirt out of the grave until the plastic handles of the original coffin were revealed. They were placed to one side as the digging continued with even greater care. Mrs Mnyele keened, occasionally brushing away Happy as he leaned over her shoulder voicing his own concerns. Soon a skull emerged. A white sheet, on which Mrs Mnyele had sprinkled snuff, was slid gently under the rest of the bones, bundled up and placed beside the deep pit. The bones were carried to the waiting coffin, which, after the benediction, was placed in the white hearse. The handles were returned to the grave.

The procession of vehicles snaked out of Extension 14 and back to the High Commission where tea, small sandwiches, and cakes lay waiting. Two tubs of clean water were leaned against the outer walls so that people fresh from the cemetery could rinse their hands.

At the airport the High Commission staff made it clear that their support had been exclusively logistical. They could pay none of the extra expenses, such as the hotel accommodation, and certainly not the P400 for Happy's mini-bar adventure. Bethuel had not been aware of this arrangement, but graciously paid the party's bills out of the Ekurhuleni council grant. On the plane Happy asked Rhona to buy him a brandy, and she demurred with a rueful smile.

Nomathamsanqa made the three old ladies happy by dutifully filling out their customs and immigration forms on both sides of the border. Under the heading 'Purpose of Visit' she thought for a moment before writing the word 'Exhumation'. We emerged into the international arrivals lobby in Johannesburg and gathered in a tired little knot, not quite sure what direction to take next. The coffin had arrived at the cargo terminal and needed to be transported to Tembisa, but there was no sign how this was to be done.

Soon we heard joyful singing in the distance. It grew louder and louder. A dancing gaggle of black-T-shirted ANC supporters moved toward us carrying yellow posters. The posters read 'Reburial of revolutionary cadre' and bore Thami's photo plus the date and place of the ceremony to be held in the Tembisa stadium two days later. They also carried Thami's words, 'For me as a craftsman, the act of creating art should compliment [sic] the act of creating shelter for my family or liberating the country for my people, this is culture.' The words hearkened back to the community idealism of the 1980s and may have seemed antique to those who now took liberation for granted. For Nomathamsanqa they resonated with the words her father had written in 1980 when he lamented that the house he had built had fallen and injured her. Each of his intentions – to create art, to liberate his country, to shelter his family – had been embattled by his times. Among the flagrant losses, there had been gains. One of them was her recent discovery of his concern for her.

The group encircled the family, then danced down the corridor into the domestic arrivals area, effectively spreading their good news of homecoming through the entire airport. As the crowd moved on, a man wearing a crisp white shirt and the white beaded necklace of a sangoma appeared among the family.

Wally had accompanied the Tembisa celebrants to the airport and, as he recalls, met Nomathamsanqa for the first time as an adult. His eyes sparkled as he was struck by the beauty of his old comrade's child. 'Do you remember me?' he asked. 'No,' she replied. Wally stood with one arm around Happy, who nestled into the implied acceptance of the strong man's embrace. To gain relief from the brewing intensity of the homecoming by moving to more familiar ground, Nomathamsanqa and I picked up her car and drove to the side of the highway to Tembisa. There we waited to join the convoy after it left the cargo terminal with the hearse.

Two hours passed in the hot sun. Nomathamsanqa mused whether the exhumation was really necessary. More pressingly, she wondered if the convoy would be easy to spot in the Wednesday afternoon traffic. Then a long line of speeding cars accompanied by the police drove up the hill towards us, all with their headlights on. Inside the bakkies the passengers were pressing posters to all available windows. Nomathamsanqa inserted her vehicle among them. In a tour de force of vehicular choreography the cars sped without stopping into Tembisa. At every intersection where other traffic might have intersected the convoy, a police car sat flashing its lights. Sometimes sirens blared. The cortège swept in one continuous movement through the township streets. When it halted briefly and some local people asked Nomathamsanqa for a lift, a marshal quickly advised her to accept no one, as he wanted to keep any possible trouble at bay. Soon they reached Mr Modiba's mortuary.

The MK marshal, a stony-faced woman wearing camouflage fatigues, marched down the street swinging her arms high, as she led the coffin from the hearse to its temporary resting place in the funeral parlour. Around her swarmed a jubilant crowd, waving ANC banners and South African flags, carrying posters, singing tunes accompanied by a couple of drummers and tuba players. Their black T-shirts bore Thabo Mbeki's face on the front and the slogan 'A people's contract to create work and fight poverty' on the back. Though in the background a billboard proclaimed 'Gauteng is now a better place for all', along the route taken by the cortège it seemed that nothing much had changed despite the hopes and efforts of Thami and his cohorts – brand-new shanties were being constructed out of corrugated-iron sheets, sometimes just across the street from what looked, by contrast, to be exceedingly comfortable bungalows. Bystanders cried 'Amandla!' and shot their fists into the air, just as they had in the 1980s, days that Thami had missed at home. Many of the celebrants were too young to have known the man they were celebrating, but the music, the colours, and the openness of it all were intoxicating.

Panyaza Lesufi, an up-and-coming spokesperson for the provincial government, accompanied the coffin as it was carried up the back steps of the mortuary into a large hall. The crowd crammed itself around the coffin and onto the mezzanine balcony. Lesufi introduced the family seated behind him on a low dais, apologising with a laugh for addressing the crowd in a colonial language like English. Mrs Mnyele stood and thrust her fist into the air. The crowd applauded, but she was too weary to speak. The past 24 hours had contained so many new experiences that even she, who loved crowds and performance, was silenced by fatigue. The crowd dispersed, leaving the bones to spend the night alone in the funeral parlour where they would remain until a guard of honour and a motorcade fetched them the next afternoon, bringing them to spend one last night in Mrs Mnyele's house at 533 Endulweni.

Thursday was a day of rest until 6 pm when the Memorial Lecture Programme began in Tembisa's Multi-Purpose Centre. It proved to be the occasion for some good-natured grousing: that the programme was 'poorly organised' because it began an hour late; that Wally, the scheduled keynote speaker, was missing because he had chosen instead to speak at Friday's funeral; that the introductions omitted mention of Naniwe, Thami's first wife, who was present. ('[Ignoring the first wife] is not the African way,' complained the wife of one of Thami's old friends.) Local people filled only half the seats in the hall. Thami's posters were on display, but few bothered to look at them; their size was reduced by the expanse of the walls, and so was their impact. The fact that the speeches were delivered only in English made some of the audience restless. Lesufi, acting as master of ceremonies, allowed the crowd to sing and dance between speeches, partly in order to spice up the proceedings.

Introducing Duma Nkosi, executive mayor of Ekurhuleni and a veteran of the struggle, Lesufi thanked him for supporting the exhumation; Nkosi's navy-blue track suit projected the sartorial style of martyred MK commander Chris Hani. The crowd listened respectfully to Nkosi's address in English, but laughed at his joke – that his own father claimed to be descended from Jesus – only when he repeated it in Zulu. Since he hadn't known Thami, he was obliged to make generic remarks – Thami had not died in vain; the ancestors are important to us – and he knew no better than to repeat Mrs Mnyele's claim to have been detained for two years. He simply wasn't able to conjure up Thami's spirit.

Pat Twala read the obituary, which had been written by Mandla Langa. A burly man of gentle demeanour, Pat had known Thami, but he wasn't free to convey the warmth of his memories. Like Nkosi, Pat had risen to high office within the new order. He had become chief executive manager of the East Rand Water Care Company, the only regionalised waste-water management company in the country. The work was a far cry from the underground activities carried out by Pat and Thami in Botswana, when parastatals were legitimate targets for attack.

Jaki Seroke, then and now a PAC member, took the podium to describe an encounter Thami had once had with a white hobo. Spotting the wasted man in a Johannesburg park Thami had remarked to Jaki, 'Look, there's a man who's affected by apartheid and doesn't know it.' Thami proceeded to ask the man in Afrikaans, 'How's it going, baas?' The poor-white man, sensing that his fallen status was being mocked, had reacted with anger. Jaki went on to mention interesting conversations he had had with Thami while reading *The Necessity of Art*, but his story had inserted into the evening a vestige of still simmering anger at white privilege. It is possible to imagine that Thami's gift for compassion was somehow mixed up in the tale, though Jaki failed to note it.

The last speaker, Comrade Blahz, cast aspersions on some people who were successful in the new order, though he did not name them. Presumably he excluded Nkosi, Lesufi, and Pat when he charged,

'Some people are selfishly taking advantage of our people who fought and died.' His remark was greeted with the warmest applause of the evening, even though he, too, spoke in English. After the ceremony he elaborated on his hope that MK's military achievements would be celebrated. Currently without a full-time job, he dreamt of constructing a 'freedom trail', starting at Cuito Cuanavale in southern Angola, where South Africa lost a crucial battle against Cubans and Angolans in 1987. It would trace the route MK cadres took on their way back to South Africa, thus further embedding in popular consciousness the idea that 'freedom wasn't free'.

Bethuel brought the evening to a close by announcing the concluding events on the Friday and proclaiming in ringing tones, 'Our task is to mobilise so there's no one in Tembisa who doesn't know Thami Mnyele.' Those who had indeed known Thami, their bodies now thickened with middle age, clustered in one corner of the hall before dispersing for the night, trading stories of the 1970s and the lively conversations they had enjoyed with Thami then. One wife continued to fume over the failure of anyone to mention Naniwe. Rhona, wearing a chic and eclectic version of Nguni dress, crossed over to where Naniwe sat and the two wives met for the first time. Naniwe told Rhona that she could not have survived the reburial and praised her fortitude.

The events in Tembisa's Mehlareng Stadium on the Friday morning had such a festive air that it would be quite wrong to call them funereal. The date itself was a public holiday, Heritage Day, decreed to celebrate the pasts of all South Africans. The MK honour guard carried the coffin down a path bordered by flower-bedecked plinths with blossoms strewn between them. Mrs Mnyele wore a new blue suit with polka-dot trim and a wide-brimmed white organza hat. Later she would turn a few delighted dance steps on the stage and wave her bouquet of flowers at the crowd. She was, however, so tired that her words were read for her: 'At long last, my son, you are back. My dreams have been realised. Go well, my son, all is now well.'

Someone distributed Freedom Park baseball hats and T-shirts bearing the slogan 'Freedom wasn't free'. Technicians operating a console in front of the coffin played music recorded by the appropriately named group Brothers in Arms.

The stadium held a crowd of modest size, their position advertising their rank. The podium, donated by the South African Post Office, held the family and most of the dignitaries, whose names were announced as they arrived. Other honoured guests were seated on white plastic chairs to the left of the coffin exposed to the fierce sun, while those without close connections sat sheltered in the stands. At the top of the stands youth sang and danced when bored, prompting speakers to chide them occasionally for

for their 'indiscipline'. None of these 'young lions' could possibly have known Thami. Ideally they would carry forward the promise of his life.

Because the gathering was a state occasion it is not surprising that Thami's spirit seemed to have vanished. He was absorbed into a larger celebratory project and made to point the way to what remained to be done. It didn't seem to matter how factually accurate the statements were. Duma Nkosi set the tone at the beginning of the service by saying that Mrs Mnyele's 'two-year detention' would now be written into history. Bethuel urged ANC branches to respond to social challenges by drawing people in and solving their problems. As an example, he noted that initially he had had to tell Mrs Mnyele that there were no resources, but ANC leadership at all levels had turned the situation around because they had the courage to care for society. He concluded by paraphrasing Fidel Castro: 'do whatever you do for the revolution, as we did it for you'.

The mix of myth and inattention continued when Rhoda Sekgororoane gave the view from Botswana and Joyce Moloi spoke for the SACP. Rhoda noted that Batswana were proud of Thami's presence and displayed his work in the museum. Both well-intentioned statements are debatable: Thami's art wasn't hanging in the museum's small exhibition space, and, not long before, Jonas Gwangwa had berated a Gaborone audience for forgetting the sacrifice of South African lives in that city. Joyce had to shout 'Amandla!' and 'Viva!' over the noise of the young lions in the stands. Before they could erupt again, she rushed to assert that her comrades had not become involved in the struggle to benefit themselves. 'We need to use those spears [of the nation] in a correct way – selflessly – while most people are still poor and there is AIDS.' Perhaps inevitably the speakers revealed more about themselves and the present, than about the dead, whom they hadn't known.

The youth grew notably silent only when the speakers stopped using English. Baleka Mbete had them in the palm of her hand, and not only for linguistic reasons. Dressed in a jacket bearing a beaded Asante child figure on the back and crowned by a quasi-Zulu hat (an *isicholo* decorated with beads in ANC colours), she began her presentation by singing 'Ke a rona' (I am yours) with Thandi Modise and another comrade. Then, without notes, she regaled the crowd with memories of their days in Medu: Thami was a true African in the spirit of *ubuntu*; he could never have become a commercial artist because he was a passionate person who felt deeply about what was happening around him; his story must be told in schoolbooks so we know where we have come from and where we are going. She concluded by noting that it was Heritage Day, the brand-new holiday meant to instruct South Africans in their common heritage.

Baleka's former husband, the poet Keorapetse Kgositsile, spoke entirely in English. Sent to represent Pallo Jordan, the new minister of arts and culture, he sketched the last day of Thami's life, lamenting that the comrades in his unit couldn't bury him because they feared another attack. He read one of his poems, 'Red song', which Thami had liked. The poem contained lines like 'the night keeps winking' and 'a tough tale', which had also appealed to Wally and which Thami had illustrated for him. The high-spirited stands produced a fair amount of inattentive commotion during his talk.

Wally shrewdly embraced the stands by speaking first in the vernacular and then in English. He also strategically connected Thami's life with his current project – developing Freedom Park. He began by casting his mind back to when the two had first met in the early 1970s, at a time when they were trying to make sense of their country. Their communities, and especially their mothers, had helped them, because they understood that young people need to be guided by history and tradition. Thami had shown his art to Wally's grandmother, who was 'the first critic of our creativity', but she had been mystified, asking Thami, 'Why did you distort the face and shoulder, legs and hands of that man? Why is that person in such pain?' After he had explained, she responded, 'That pain must never make you bitter.'

Wally used his grandmother's wise words as a bridge between Thami's life and the future. Freedom Park, he said, would avoid generating bitterness by paying homage to all South Africans who had suffered, ranging from the first Khoisan labourers through the soldiers fighting in the two world wars to the victims of the struggle. Many 'knowledge systems' would build the park, one of them being, no doubt, the supernatural knowledge possessed by sangomas, whose ranks Wally had recently joined.

The obituary, written and read by Mandla Langa, a former comrade who was now chairperson of the country's Independent Communications Authority, repeated Wally's theme. Mandla began by quoting lines from Martinique poet Aimé Césaire's 'Return to my native land':

but at the execution let my heart preserve me from all hate
do not make of me that man of hate for whom I have only hate

Césaire wrote that he was an advocate for his own race, not because he hated any other but because he wanted 'to prescribe at last this unique race free' to produce 'the succulence of fruit'. These sentiments, Mandla said, could have been written by Thami.

Would Thami have enjoyed the performances at his funeral? What would he have thought of the tur-baned torch singer in an evening gown and elbow-length gold gloves who commanded the stage, singing a long tribute, with only Mrs Mnyele appearing to move in time to the music? Her sound did not resemble the jazz that had inspired artists like Dumile and Thami. How would he have felt about a troupe clad in Zulu-style skins and head rings who danced beneath the stage and later back in the Multi-Purpose Centre where lunch was served? The flamboyant minister who concluded the service with booming words 'God sees individuals, not groups' might have made Thami wince. He would surely have shuddered at the humour of a drunk standing by the side of the Tembisa road, holding his beer bottle aloft, shouting 'Amandla', and grinning as the cortège passed by.

At the burial itself Lindi and Michael, Thami's two surviving siblings by his father's second marriage, joined the family under the canopy. They brought with them a letter Thami had written to his father shortly after going into exile, as evidence that he had not forsaken that side of his family. Since they had learned of the exhumation and reburial from the news, they felt the need to assert publicly that Thami had never been estranged from them. They bore their own recent sorrows to the funeral. Both their parents and two of their siblings had died within the past year. The Rev. Mnyele had died of a broken heart, Lindi said, a few months after his wife, Dorothy, had succumbed to cancer. Then their brother Sipho had died of a heart condition, followed by another brother, Johannes, who had died of AIDS.

The pattern of inviting and not inviting, informing and not informing, including and excluding continued: Sarah held a cleansing ceremony ten days after the reburial, but invited neither Rhona nor Nomathamsanqa. The accretion of myth around Thami continued, too: Pallo Jordan mentioned him in a ceremony that evening when he accepted for the South African government the video archive of the Dutch Anti-Apartheid Movement. Jordan said, 'In the video we [just] screened, you may have noticed the presence of Thami Mnyele in one scene of a rally in the Netherlands.' The quality of the nearly quarter-century-old film may have prevented the audience from realising that the figure was, in fact, not Thami at all.

One of Thami Mnyele's notable traits was keen sensitivity to disrespect. He might have found strange the respect paid to him during the four commemorative days: the stress on his martyrdom more than his art, the myth-making, his ascendancy to iconic status in contradiction of his collective ideals. Perhaps he would have smiled, aware that state occasions create myths the state needs.

Thami would surely have been 'humbled', a word he used frequently, by the grief his memory still evoked, as when Rhona wept at his Gaborone graveside, or my eyes filled with tears upon glimpsing the lights of the funeral cortège bound for Tembisa. He would probably also have been humbled when his friend Mpe brought along to the Multi-Purpose Centre a book of Michelangelo's sketches. Pointing to a drawing of the man who served as the model for the Libyan sibyl, he asked me, 'Don't you think he looks like Thami?' He was unaware that I had once talked with Thami about another part of the Sistine ceiling, the one where the artist drew himself as a sack of flesh.

Mpe's simple gesture toward Michelangelo's drawing cast a net over time and place. By conjuring up Thami's beauty and his dreams, he drew the dead artist and his friends closer to one another. Similar small episodes of casting and retrieving were doubtless occurring among other mourners, hidden from public view. In this way, the reburial succeeded in forging deeper links between the dead and the living, as well as among the living, than anyone watching the public display could possibly have guessed.

Thami would surely have derived joy from the fact that his reburial allowed his daughter to open her heart to him. Upon hearing his 1980 poem of lament at having harmed her, she felt for the first time that he wanted her to understand his situation. She began to understand 'how difficult his life was then'. She thought it was as if he had asked God to 'find a way of making my daughter understand that I really cared about her, so that she can be free of all these feelings she's harbouring against me'. And, she imagined, God might have replied that once she heard the poem 'she'll understand'. She did. In this one case, the personal was victorious over the collective. The 'inside' won out over the 'outside'. Thami would have been pleased. He would have delighted, too, in her bearing: she has the dignity of a citizen. In his daughter's demeanour of unselfconscious self-respect, the intended fruits of his sacrifice can be seen.

NOTES

1   Baldwin Ndaba, 'Struggle hero's remains coming home', *The Star* (15 Sept 2004).
2   'SA activist's remains exhumed in Botswana', SABC News (22 Sept 2004).

Epilogue

The War of Values

I glance at my fingertips as I sit waiting to meet one of the four men who stood, I have reason to believe, on Thami's doorstep 21 years earlier. My hands are surprisingly still. Good, I think. If I concentrate on making a simple business enquiry, I will be able to carry off this encounter.

What can I hope to learn from someone who will doubtless deny everything if asked a direct question? I want simply to read his face. And yet, by the time our conversation ends, I discover more about his world than I had ever hoped to know. His face, his words, his pictures, and even his office décor open a door on the war of values that raged in South Africa in the 1980s.

Two recent newspaper articles have brought me to this office. They both allege that its occupant participated in the raid on Thami's house. They say the businessman is probably the 'Sergeant Piet' named in Peter Stiff's recently published history of South Africa's late-apartheid covert wars. The man has done nothing to refute the accusations.

P, as I shall call him, is tall, fit, and straight, but the first impression I gain of him is that he is glaringly bright. He wears a yellow shirt and cream-coloured trousers; his hair, moustache, and the hair on his arms are golden. His eyes are very blue. I feel the need to squint when I look at him, though I may simply be bracing myself to study the face that I mean to read and remember. I note that his nose is broad and snubbed. On closer examination, I see his clothes are soiled. He explains he has been working underneath his car. With little encouragement he goes on to tell the story of his life: how he grew up on a farm, went to boarding school in the Orange Free State, and then served in the military for a year. He explains, defensively, that the alternative would have been a year in prison. And yet, he observes, being in the army does make a man of you. He jokes that the army taught him the importance of making his own bed.

Today he sells insurance. He has returned to the very city where he may have killed in order to sell policies to people wanting protection against loss. He has stacked piles of documents neatly on his desk and he blusters that people should enter his office with their chequebooks open. It is clear, however, that he cares very little about the work. When asked what sets his firm apart from any other, his face melts into indifference and he replies weakly, 'Not much.' Turning to his computer, he starts to open files of photographs, revealing what does matter to him.

The first pictures show him cradling a gun in his arms, his face bearded and radiant as he squats beside a felled elephant, its tusks pointing upwards. Soon those tusks will belong to the rich foreigner – a Korean, an American – who paid tens of thousands of dollars for the joy of hunting in what the safari company calls 'Authentic Africa'. P sells his extensive experience as a hunter to a firm advertising its shooting tours of Botswana game reserves as 'adrenalin-rushed days' in 'pristine' Africa. 'We all hunt,' he says with quiet pride, referring to his white colleagues, fellow Afrikaners who have pitched up on these 'unspoiled' shores of the Kalahari within the past dozen years. We look at photographs of dead male kudu, their horns spiralling majestically. The straight-horned gemsbok look like relatives of unicorns. Pointing to a leopard, dead, with its eyes open, P notes that its spots are properly called 'rosettes'. We seem to have entered a timeless, even fantastical, world: before men had to seek refuge from the tedium of office work, when animals wore badges, before things got 'spoiled'.

P opens another file of pictures. They show the house he built for his family – his wife and two sons in their early teens – to which they moved less than seven months ago. The home sits on a hilltop with, he points out, '360 degree views'. From there you can see the South African border where it is marked by the Notwane River. In the distance you can spot the hill at the base of which his office sits, though the precise site appears, appropriately enough, as an insignificant dot in the photo. There is an outdoor shower so you can sustain the illusion of camping even while living in luxury. And the house is indeed luxurious. It is built on an open plan with few interior walls and no ceilings. P calls his new home a 'farm' but when I ask if he has any cattle, he replies that he has too little land, only four hectares. That land is sufficient, though, to allow the family to live in splendid isolation. No neighbours are visible.

The sense of unbounded space is important to P. He later comments that one problem with the United States is that its land is divided up into private property. You would find it hard to pull over to the side of the road and camp there, he says, as you can freely here.

When I ask P if he misses South Africa, he replies with a single word, 'No'. He doesn't elaborate, but the fact that he left in 1994, when the first democratic elections were held, suggests why he might not have wanted to stay. He has been careful not to mention race. In front of me, he shows rather elaborate courtesy toward the African people in his office, even startling one young daydreamer in the reception area by asking if he can help him.

P's less guarded colleague suggests one reason why they all left. He refers unapologetically to 'shit human rights', by which he means laws requiring employers to pay pensions and welfare benefits and making it hard for them to dismiss workers.   This colleague calls himself both a 'boer' and a 'Motswana', though he has lived in Botswana for only three years. Some of his ideas about South Africa seem frozen in the apartheid era, as when he refers to the Transkei and Bophuthatswana as if the homelands still existed.

The walls of the office display a kind of art, none of it, of course, like the work P probably shot at in Thami's home 21 years earlier. The carvings, baskets, and prints represent a stereotyped and timeless vision of Africa: it is a continent of wild animals and tribal black peoples. The wooden busts depict a dignified but generic black man and woman. The Tswana baskets are hung with their bowls toward the wall so their intended design is hidden. The animal prints display the greatest flamboyance: a lioness lapping water with her two cubs has been drawn in purple and orange pastels. Because all this art was purchased at a nearby shop it reflects the tastes of the insurance brokers less dramatically than the one item they supplied: the mounted head of a buffalo, shot by P. Its horns nearly span the stairwell.

In this space I enter a world that assigns certain kinds of romantic values to what it means to be a man (he hunts and shelters his family), a citizen (he is above the law), and an African (he lives in isolation without regard for national boundaries). Because these ideals have all been achieved, it seems as if it is indeed possible to turn back time and live free of legal constraint. P seems to have been fighting for an Arcadian paradise. He displays a distaste for private property, albeit a selective distaste. He wants the freedom to build and hunt and sleep in un-owned nature. Innocent enough on their own, perhaps, and hardly uncommon, these pre-capitalist values, in the particular time and place of late-20th-century South Africa, helped give rise to a murderous rage.

A month later I enter Pretoria Central Prison to meet another of the Gaborone raiders. His name is Hans Louw and he has recently been transferred to the medium security section of the prison. 'Why are you here?' I ask him. 'Because I killed a drug lord,' he replies.

Louw, like P, presents a striking figure. Dressed in the regulation orange jumpsuit, he seems fit: wiry and lithe. His hair and beard are neatly trimmed. He looks people unwaveringly in the eye when he speaks to them. It is hard to reconcile this dignified man with the stories he has to tell about his '15 $\frac{1}{2}$ years in the forces and 9 $\frac{1}{2}$ years in nine prisons', a period longer than his entire adulthood. To put it another way, he has spent two-thirds of his life in an all-male world.

In snatches during the visiting hour, Louw tells me a brief version of his story. He was born 44 years ago in the northern Cape but soon moved with his family across the border to South West Africa and grew up there. Louw's complexion is brown, but, throughout our first conversation, he never refers to national or ethnic identity; only once does he use a word that connotes belonging, when he says he has become Muslim. He seems equally at ease in English and Afrikaans. In 1979, at the age of 16, he began training with the Special Forces in South West Africa and 'grew up' among them. He 'relished' the rigorous training and still says, 'I am proud they gave me the best training there was.' By the age of 20, he had been 'selected' to become a member, the first coloured South African to be chosen. His prison fitness makes me think he still exercises according to the tough standards set by Special Forces. His direct and calm manner suggests that he learned to exert iron self-discipline over the outward show of his feelings.

When he was 23, he participated in the Gaborone Raid as part of the team that attacked Duke Machobane's house. His commander was formerly in 5-Recce, so he and his men meshed easily with the parts of that unit being deployed in Gaborone. It was not unusual, he said, for men from different parts of Southern Africa to be used on cross-border raids.

During his entire career, before and after the raid on Gaborone, he says he gave '1000 per cent' of himself to Special Forces – 'I had to work twice as hard to prove myself' – but his rank never rose higher than staff sergeant. Honoured to be named a team leader, a task rarely given to non-whites, he led an operation that killed seven young comrades in a Lulekani, Phalaborwa, bar in March 1986. Eight months later the plane of Mozambican president Samora Machel was made to crash, he says, because its pilot followed false beacons directed by South African military intelligence. Louw was part of a 'clean-up' team whose job was to go to the site of the plane crash and kill any survivors, but there were none.[1] In 1989 Louw was rewarded for his '1000 per cent' commitment with a certificate praising his skill as a team leader.

Upon the release of Mandela, he says, 'we did everything in our power to derail the elections' by supplying guns to self-defence units on the East Rand; the goal was to ignite a civil war among black people. When he 'resigned' after democratic elections were successfully held in 1994, he was paid only R15 000 for his 14 years of 'loyal service'; he received no pension because he was not registered or paid as part of regular military staff. He then signed up with a firm of mercenaries called Executive Outcomes and served for two years in Sierra Leone, fighting for the man, Ahmad Kabbah, who would become president in 1996. Wounded there, he came back to South Africa.

A trained killer living in peacetime, his life began to unravel. He abused drugs and alcohol. Two white brothers paid him to murder the drug lord. His marriage fell apart. Today his parents and siblings will have nothing to do with him. He relates this tale of disintegration with a firm voice. He may have used the same tone when he told a few fellow prisoners, MK and APLA veterans who were harassing him, that he and they had to learn to get along with one another. He grows slightly more intense when he says, referring to people who would judge him, 'They must find the cause why I was killing people for money.' He comes closest to identifying those causes when he says simply 'I looked up to white people' and 'We lived in a pack, we hunted in a pack'.

Today Louw understands that he was once deluded by the 'gaudy rhetoric' of people like General Magnus Malan, who made him believe that 'defeat in Namibia would compel us to retreat to the streets of Pretoria and spark a global wave of communist triumphs'. Now he sees that this threat masked 'a grim common thing', the deliberate execution of black civilians and, more broadly, a war 'against blacks' throughout the region. He appreciates the commitment of people like Thami, who were so intensely nationalistic that they were willing to 'give their lives for their cause'. Their faith made them as resilient as green branches: 'they could be bent, but not broken'. And so, the war against them was unwinnable. Louw credits Eugene de Kock, 'fellow casualty' of the dirty wars to maintain white supremacy, with having helped him to face painful questions about war, murder, memory, and guilt. (Like De Kock, Louw feels bitter that the decision-makers have gone unpunished.) The Truth and Reconciliation Commission also inspired him to 'confess the atrocities that I have committed'.[2] So did a period in solitary confinement in 2001 when he reflected on what he had done. In the 1980s, he says, 'we believed what we done was right. We believed that every black man who is not with us is against us.' Now that he sees through the sham of that faith, he writes with a ferocity based on painful knowledge, whose truth should resonate far beyond South Africa: 'A nation has no business sending its young men into battle without lasting moral justification, not only because it is hard to die for your country but because it is equally hard to kill for your country.'

Thami Mnyele was one victim of P's and Hans Louw's skills and the regime that exploited them. Born the same year as apartheid, Thami grew to oppose its values 'from the bottom of [his] heart'. His creative and committed spirit grew in a rough environment. He came to sacrifice his personal life for his vision of the public good. He would have been moved by the question that plagues Hans Louw: why was he killing for money? For him, manhood did not mean hunting or dominating the landscape. He idealised the future South Africa as a place where communal harmony and equality could flourish. (We must remember that, shortly before he died, he told a friend that when the revolution succeeded, he would be at the airport, trying to persuade Afrikaners, people like P, not to leave.) Citizenship was, for him, about community and not about isolation. Perhaps the one trait he and P shared was a romantic opposition to capitalist competition. With Hans Louw, he shared a capacity to devote himself wholeheartedly to a cause. The fact that Thami's short life ended not in a dream home but in a rented house under machine-gun fire raises a troubling question: who won the war of values, and why?

NOTES

1   'Ex-CCB man claims SA lured leader to his death', *The Herald Online* News (13 Jan 2003). Four years later, Louw says that no one has disproved his statement.
2   Hans Louw, letter to author (Feb 2007).

Art and Revolution

Thami Mnyele's struggle ended in an early grave. One of his alleged killers now lives in the splendour of an isolated hilltop home. What do these fates, so terrible in their disparity, tell us? What might Thami's sacrifice mean?

In the heat of the struggle, Thami and his fellow activists believed they were fighting to give birth to a new culture. They genuinely regarded the 'late bourgeois world' as morally decrepit or, to use Wally Serote's phrase, 'sick with wealth'. Their task was to deliver the deathblow. They didn't talk about seizing power for its own sake, preferring to allude to the better world they would shape. They saw themselves as cultural revolutionaries.

When he first went into exile, Thami approached the word 'revolution' gingerly. He would quote someone else who had used it, as if the word were too hot for him to handle. He pondered the implications of Guinean president Sékou Touré's words, 'It is not enough to write a revolutionary song. You must fashion the revolution with the people.' What did that mean practically? Thami turned to activist lawyer and art lover Albie Sachs, and warmly approved his definition of revolution as a 'conscious act'.[1] Sachs seemed to be describing the heightened awareness and commitment that grew slowly in Thami as he struggled with his desire to lead an ordinary life and to become a great painter. But what should those 'conscious acts' be?

Thami grew bolder the longer he was in exile. He freed 'revolution' from its inverted commas. His use of the word was still gestural, though, and its meaning somewhat opaque. As mass demonstrations boiled up in South African streets, he was able to extol the ideal cultural worker as someone with 'clear political insight, a skilled hand and firm revolutionary morality'. Artists were now making angry and yet optimistic work that was, he wrote, repeating Sachs's word, 'soaked in the conscious language of revolution'. Their 'banners and posters and graphics' represented nothing less than 'the birth of a new culture'.²

These 'cultural workers' found it pointless to define the content of that new culture. It could not be dictated, because it would come only from the 'process of the struggle', as Wally put it. It had to grow out of the will of the people. Wally wrote that South Africa would one day have 'a culture which will destroy exploitation, and create a new man and a new country'. He predicted, in the sweeping and euphoric language of the moment, that 'freedom, peace and progress' would come into being and be 'cherished and protected by every single man and woman'. Referring obliquely to the devastating disdain accorded African culture by white society, Wally swore that 'traditional [African] art' would be included in 'their search for new forms to express their new consciousness'.

Who would do the searching and the incorporating? The answer seemed to be: the state. It would control education and mass media and 'even … create new institutions that can directly encourage the development of culture'.³ Wally's language bears the mark of his SACP membership, as well as the scars of generations of disrespect.

Security police chief General Herman Stadler, who read closely all issues of the ANC magazine *Sechaba*, where Wally published these thoughts, dismissed the goals as 'utopian'. Stadler was not wrong. Until the battle was won, the cultural workers could merely hope that their dreams would come true: that a cultural revolution would produce a South Africa that included the culture of all its peoples; that there would be communal ownership and collective responsibility; that the people's will would shape decisions. Stadler was, of course, contributing to the circumstances that kept the goals 'utopian'. As long as the comrades remained vulnerable to attacks by the security police and the army, they would never have enough security to plot the future.

These activists had adopted the rhetoric of social justice, which the Enlightenment had attached to the concept of revolution. They were assuming, more specifically, the 19th-century belief propagated by Marx and Engels that once the masses were mobilised, they could change the forces that made society and, therefore, human nature. This faith made the word 'new' ring like a bell throughout their messages. Because the Cold War had not yet ended, the ideas of the socialist anthem, the 'Internationale', still had inspirational force: 'We shall build a new world, our world / He who was naught shall be all.' And so, Thami and his fellow committed artists worked in the hope that their art was not simply opening a window on a different reality, but actually helping to produce one inspired by communal ideals.

What happened?

Today the visual needs of the South African public seem to be fed by shopping malls, television, and advertising. Commerce has appropriated the icons of the struggle. A six-metre-high bronze statue of Nelson Mandela, caught in mid-jive, stands beaming at shoppers in the centre of Johannesburg's biggest and most glittering mall. In the same complex, a man-made waterfall, lit to appear gold, cascades down several stories as if to celebrate the historical wellspring of all that wealth. Global consumer fashion shapes popular taste, just as Nadine Gordimer predicted in 1982. At the Culture and Resistance festival she had warned that the people might one day want things other than what freedom fighters thought they should have. Those days have come to pass. People joke that they often evaluate each other by the car they drive. 'You know her,' they will say, 'she drives a BMW.'

Twenty-first-century South Africa boasts a lively gallery scene. It is internationally connected and globally appealing. Advertisements on facing pages of a late-2004 issue of *Art South Africa*, a stylish new quarterly, encapsulate the sea change in the art world. On the left, bold letters announce a Dumile Feni retrospective exhibition at the Johannesburg Art Gallery. The ad includes Dumile's 1966 sketch of a man, chin upturned, struggling to grasp something above his head. The right-hand page announces a show by Moshekwa Langa at the Goodman Gallery. It features a mixed media piece: photographs show off models and celebrities around whom he has written graffiti like 'Google', 'Zimbabwe', and 'I love my Pashmina'. One wonders whether Dumile, Serote, and Mnyele would think this art travesties or fulfils the revolution they were trying to achieve.

The revolutionaries dreamt of and fought for a particular kind of cultural revolution – collectivist, communist, non-materialist. Why did it not come to pass? Part of the answer emerges from comparison with what happened in Russia, the country whose story held such inspirational power for Thami and his comrades in the 1980s.

The social conditions in Russia were ripe for revolution in 1905 and 1917, as they were not in South Africa at the end of the 20th century. Russia under the Tsars was more autocratic and centralised than South Africa. The Tsarist state had absolute power over its citizens, and there were no individual liberties. The Russian bourgeoisie was timid. The peasantry was largely illiterate and, until relatively recently, enslaved. The proletariat in the few large factories and cities was the most militant and revolutionary in Europe.

Russian artists and other members of the avant-garde intelligentsia were casting about for ideas about what should follow the autocratic system when it was destroyed. They had no model for a materialist culture and, in any case, not all of them were Marxists. Some even tended toward anarchism, preferring that communities should govern themselves and be linked by a vague spirit of cooperation. While their solutions varied, 'all of them', as critic John Berger puts it, 'were aware of the strange dynamic of the Russian situation: their backwardness had become the very condition for their seizing a future, far in advance of the rest of Europe'.[4] Some artists embraced that 'backwardness' by rediscovering ancient Russian art. They were busy trying to discover new ways of expressing what it meant to be Russian, including by capturing peasant life from the inside. Kazimir Malevich, for example, frankly confessed that he modelled his highly abstract paintings – a simple black square, for example – on the Russian Orthodox holy icon. He hung the painting as if it were an icon representing the universe in a peasant hut.

At the same time as the Russian avant-garde looked to the past, they searched for 'the most advanced, the most modern means of expression', and the black square was surely that.[5] Predating similar abstract experiments in oil by several decades, the painting was revolutionary. These artists were also exhilarated by mechanical advances that modern times had put at their disposal, and they expressed this new thrill in their work. (Vladimir Tatlin's architectural designs, for example, were so futuristic that some of them couldn't even be built.) Intoxicated by the thrill of the new, they loathed the idea that culture could be evaluated in the marketplace. They believed, rather, that art should be uncontaminated by the profit motive. After the revolution, they founded an art school, albeit short-lived, that aimed to give birth to art that was cheap, modern, and available to everyone. The artists who produced this 'art of 5 kopeks' would not be ranked on a hierarchical ladder.[6] They would all be, in the words of the 1980s, 'cultural workers'.

Scholars still debate the impact and meaning of this intellectual ferment. Historian Frederick Starr casts the avant-garde's ideals in a pernicious light. He sums up Bolshevism as the destruction of the middle class and the peasantry by urban intellectuals in the name of the worker. In Starr's view, then, utopian ideals were responsible for the most terrible social damage.[7] Other scholars link Starr's indictment to the art world by noting that the utopianism of the avant-garde led to the pictorially conservative school of socialist realism, used so effectively by Stalin to glorify his own dictatorship. The art of both the modernists and the socialist realists represented a dangerously simplistic vision of how things should be and look; the artists were anti-democratic in the sense that they presumed that a new world – albeit more just, economically stable, and beautiful – could be imposed upon the people, whether they wanted it or not. They were making a totalitarian demand that radical change should be forced on society.[8] Still other scholars have drawn attention to the avant-garde's deep roots in Russian culture. What appears to be new – the desire to restructure human beings, for example – actually had its origins in the country's ancient religious culture.[9]

The Russian Revolution, in other words, played out in a peculiarly Russian way, in both art and politics. The new turned out to be not so new, or free, after all. These critiques of Russian revolutionary art suggest, at the very least, the dangers of presuming that models and stated values drawn from a specific historical experience can usefully be applied elsewhere.

The Russian scenario was radically different from that in South Africa, where democratic values were widely disseminated among all races, even if they were grievously belied by state policy. The class structure was different, too. During the apartheid era, the South African peasantry was dying as a class; unlike in early 20th-century Russia, 'peasant agriculture [had] all but disappeared'.[10] In fact, neither rural nor urban Africans were as revolutionary as their Russian counterparts. Rebellions in the reserves occurred occasionally, at times influenced by communists, but they were local, and many chiefs and peasants had values more patriarchal than democratic. Neither were migrant workers necessarily radical: they battled sometimes against employers and sometimes against people they considered upstart youth, as in 1976. The African proletariat was more militant in demanding higher wages than in fighting for public ownership or self-management. Workers felt relieved to have jobs when wage employment was precious and shrinking. Joining forces with community organisations in the mid-1980s, many hoped to use workplace democracy as the basis for creating a national democracy, rather than a dictatorship of the proletariat.[11] And so, there was little chance of a cultural revolution in either its Chinese (peasant) or Russian (worker) guise being imposed on South Africa.

South Africa in the 1980s was not an economically backward country. It had long been embedded in international capitalist networks. Unlike pre-capitalist Russian peasants, people tended to regard the market less with suspicion than with a desire to buy commodities. They were growing more and more entranced by the international world of mass media. As we have seen, the South African revolutionaries railed against these facts. Most of them were not aware of the deep social structures – serfdom, the church, the limited industrial revolution, to name three powerful examples – that had shaped pre-revolutionary Russian culture. This ignorance led many to adopt Soviet cultural rhetoric uncritically and, in the end, fruitlessly.

What were the expressive consequences of this struggle for a socialist cultural revolution in a world which was, as it turned out, not ripe for one?

Perhaps a wooden folk sculpture, coincidentally a Russian one, can help us answer this question. A bear sits on one side of a sliding bar and a woodcutter sits on the other. When the bar is moved, first the bear strikes the wood, then the man. Locked in place, they can be made to hit the wood over and over again alternately, as if they were imitating each other. I imagine the woodcutter to be like the revolutionaries in South Africa in the 1980s and the bear to stand for their enemies. The two adversaries were certainly not moral equivalents, but they were locked in a relationship that constrained them both. Their actions stemmed, of course, from their strategic needs – the imperatives of combat – and the result was an embrace of deadly reciprocity. One side made an assertion; the other contradicted it. One side attacked; the other counterattacked. Thami indicated his awareness of the consequences of this situation when he wrote, 'There can never be artistic freedom or freedom of expression from a people in captivity.'[12]

Many of his images, especially the later ones, when he was in MK, were created 'in captivity', in the sense that he drew them to refute the state's version of reality. A reactive, rather than a revolutionary, perspective may be seen if we look at the way he and his comrades treated four subjects in their graphic design: African folk art, men, the Soviet Union, and individuals.

None of Thami's imagery came from indigenous art forms, despite Wally's contention that traditional art should be used to express the 'new' consciousness. Why was that? To have drawn inspiration from rural art would have risked confirming the government's definition of African culture as essentially tribal. He disregarded the designs on headrests, canes, pipes, shields. In principle, he revered African art because it was functional and fashioned by the people, but he never specified precisely what appealed to him about it or used its symbols and forms in his work. All his imagery came from life in modern industrial societies: AK-47s, saxophones, blackboards, wrenches, and hammers. Some of the poster designs even have the air of advertising, a reflection of his stint at J Walter Thompson, where he served the economy's growing need for black consumers. By ignoring rural art, he was asserting his own and the movement's modernity and urbanity.

By the same token, in response to white supremacy's denial of African manhood, posters depicted guns and fists. The cadres' psychological need to behave like Che Guevara may have felt as great as their practical need. They wanted to assert their virility by riding tanks victoriously into South African cities, even though, as Nelson Mandela acknowledged, 'we [the ANC] cannot stand up to you on the battlefield'.[13] They were driven to overturn an image of themselves as eight years old, even when fully grown. And so, Radio Freedom broadcasts always began by referring to earlier generations of African warriors. The movement's literature used the word 'revolutionary' to refer almost exclusively to men.[14] Thami's own definition of culture reflects a masculine point of view: culture means providing shelter for one's family. (By implication, women raise children.) The bear's hammer blow said 'boy', the woodcutter's strike answered 'man'.

While the South African establishment swore that the Soviet Union was the biggest threat to the region, the cadres celebrated that country and its creed as their saviours. Becoming combatants blinded the comrades to the conditions that set late-20th-century South Africa apart from Russia in 1905 and 1917. (The Angolan camps taught Russian history for inspirational rather than critical purposes.) They could not perceive the inexorable growth of an advanced consumer society or plan how to deal with it. It took them by surprise.

The slogans on their posters had been generated by revolutionary movements elsewhere and in another era: 'Forward to unity and commitment', 'Workers' unity will crush exploitation', 'Women arise! Unite for people's power'. These sentiments – expressed in archaic speech – informed their artistic production. The 'cultural workers' found them comforting and uplifting because they contradicted the official story that 'non-whites' were happy with the government's reforms.

Partly because the government was trying to fracture African nationalism by granting privileges to selected urban insiders, the revolutionaries responded by disparaging individualism and exalting the collective. Thami drew generic, undefeated men and women because a woman shooting her fist in the air might inspire someone else to thrust up her arm. Workers seated at a table discussing shop-floor issues might encourage others to do the same. To depict 'the masses', it wasn't necessary to distinguish them from one another. After drawing a dejected Tim Williams in 1980, he never again produced a probing portrait of an individual. He did draw posters of historical figures like jailed activist Dorothy Nyembe, but these posters, based on photographs, display pictorially what their rhetoric decrees: Nyembe was shown, not as a woman with a personal history, but as a 'symbol of the courage and resilience of our women' (see p. 180).

When the government denied that the movement had any hope of success, the cadres had to answer with glowing optimism. It must have cost them a good deal of effort to maintain this positive attitude to the future. They had to lunge toward optimism whenever they heard the tales of depravity and treachery coming from within the enemy's forces, and even from within their own ranks. Thami had to endorse 'the masses' in his pictures, though he knew they contained dangerous people. In this regard he was treating them the same way as did Soviet artist Boris Kustodiev in 1920 when he painted 'Bolshevik', in which a bearded colossus stands waving an impossibly long red banner above crowds flooding through the streets of Moscow. Kustodiev's painting, and the ecstatic spirit behind it, contrasts starkly with that of another colossus, painted by Goya c. 1810. That giant is a naked hulk striding across a dark landscape populated by streams of refugees. The two pictures epitomise diametrically opposed views of human nature and, therefore, attitudes toward the future. In the midst of battle, Thami and his comrades were bound to express the optimism in Kustodiev's work, even if in their hearts they knew that Goya's disquieting vision was true.

Goya's political stance presents a telling contrast to the one that Thami chose to adopt. The Spanish painter made no secret of the fact that his sympathies lay with the *ilustrados* (men and women of the Spanish Enlightenment). He painted their sober clothes and thoughtful faces as a form of homage to their democratic ideals. They are the kind of people Immanuel Kant would have called true revolutionaries because they stood for the life of the mind in contrast to the defence of inherited privilege. And yet, Goya was also a court painter. He did not give the Spanish king and queen false beauty, and he did not hide their love of privilege. Their faces radiate satisfaction with their glittering fashions and jewels. Within their ranks, though, one can find a royal child not yet captive to those values, his face lit up with his own playful concerns. Goya was a revolutionary artist because he set himself outside political affiliation. His task was to record his observations of humanity.

As the turmoil of the 1980s bore down on him, Thami chose to try to create a new reality through, not in, his art. John Berger notes that this pragmatic urge tends to produce work that has only an immediate and short-term effect. To have enduring power, art must be complex and embrace contradictions. (Berger observes that Lenin's wife, Krupskaya, and perhaps even Lenin himself, knew this, but that Stalin did not.) 'Fine art', or 'long-term art', needs to allow for ambiguity and to express the totality within which it exists. In this way it increases self-consciousness and is not 'an immediate and limited guide to direct action'.[15] Goya's refugees are caught in a cataclysm, but they aren't necessarily virtuous. The Moscow crowd beneath the waving red banner is different. It looks toward the future with optimism. Its revolutionary faith has saved it from the dark side of human nature. In order to 'guide direct action', Thami had to fight his tendency to pay meticulous attention to detail and to plumb a range of emotions that included despair. Only after purging himself of these habits was he able to produce didactic pictures of valiant workers with their fists in the air. The longer he was in exile and the hotter the conflict grew, the less ambiguous and detailed his images became.

Though art produced by pro-ANC activists was said to have emboldened people, it was not revolutionary in the sense of breaking new visual or conceptual ground. It was engaged too closely in combat with the regime and too intent on refuting what the regime stood for. None of the posters packs the innovative graphic power of, for example, El Lissitzky's 'Red wedge, beat Whites'. In this poster, dating from the Russian civil war in 1920, the four words are part of the design. They drive home unambiguously, but creatively, that the red revolutionary forces had pierced to the heart of the white reactionary circle. The words amplify the force already possessed by the geometrical shapes.

Combat demanded that cadres took rigid oppositional stances. They were captives of the logic of sacrifice. Facing the possibility of death, they had to have faith in the correctness of their actions. They had to obey their movement. A reverential tone entered people's voices when they murmured about what the 'structures' would and would not allow them to do. All these forces acted on their artistic imaginations in quite conservative ways, as they rocked back and forth, locked in a dangerous dialogue with the enemy.

Another explanation of the relatively conventional visual production of the 1980s may lie in the simple fact that revolutionary art moves in a different cycle from political revolution. Bill Ainslie was fond of pointing this out, and many other artists have voiced the same thought. Early 20th-century Russian painters were, not surprisingly, eloquent on this issue, though they hardly spoke with one voice.

Wassily Kandinsky, for example, emphatically sided with Ainslie when he swore in 1914, 'I do not want to show the future its true path.' His vision was resolutely spiritual and opposed to materialism. He believed that he lived in a time of liberation, but he defined that new freedom as marked by 'the loosening, the revaluation of the petrified, bound, firmly ordered forms which only yesterday were infallible'. Pure artists, in their role as 'the slaves of humanity', were creating new values.[16] This 'new' world was quite unlike the material one envisaged by some members of the Russian avant-garde. Kandinsky revered colour with a spiritual intensity. Because he was following his own private vision, his pioneering canvases swim with amoeba-like shapes and explode with swirling colours. They defy connection to the world we ordinarily see and to the world that had hitherto been seen in paint. But they were not linked to the world of politics.

Malevich saw a much closer relationship between artistic and political revolution than did Ainslie or Kandinsky. He explained, with reference to Cubism and Futurism, that those moments were 'the revolutionary forms of art, *foreshadowing* the revolution in political and economic life in 1917'.[17] When Malevich painted his famous undifferentiated black square in 1913, he was opening new conceptual ground that would have repercussions on non-artistic fronts. He was taking away the mystery of painting by reducing it to its basic properties: a canvas and paint. He was dissociating art from the religious and political authorities it ordinarily served. In a more popularly accessible way, Malevich made a similar statement the following year when he collaborated with artist and poet Vladimir Mayakovsky on a pair of political cartoons:

a peasant woman in a red dress stabs soldiers with a pitchfork, and a red-shirted peasant man cuts them down with a scythe. The images were soon followed by the acts themselves. 'Foreshadowing' happens because new images come out of a new way of thinking, and so do revolutions. They bubble out of the same intellectual wellspring.

There was no equivalent artistic revolution in South Africa. The world of 'he who was naught shall be all' did not win. The cultural revolution that actually occurred in South Africa after 1990 resulted in the wider acceptance of cultural mixture or *métissage*. Soap operas on television began to mix languages and races in all sorts of formerly unthinkable situations. African restaurants, serving 'fusion' food, proliferated. Musical styles mixed, too. The South African revolutionaries achieved inclusion in the capitalist world they knew – not, despite their rhetoric, in a new one.

The first blow in that direction within the art world was struck under the aegis of business. Perhaps the style of Thami's first poster, the one that Wally criticised for looking like an advertisement, 'foreshadowed' – to use Malevich's word – the post-apartheid world better than he could have imagined, or would have wanted.

One cruel South African irony is that the 'late bourgeois world' began dispensing with artistic segregation the same year Thami died. A show called *Tributaries*, sponsored by an icon of the bourgeoisie, the German car manufacturer BMW, opened galleries and tastes to African art. The curator, Ricky Burnett, wanted to hold a mirror up to 'South Africanness' so that, without erasing distinction or cultural difference, the exhibit treated everyone's work equally, just as Thami and the artists of '5 kopeks' had wanted to do. When the 111 pieces went on view in a Johannesburg warehouse prior to travelling to Germany in 1985, rural art was hung beside urban; those with formal training displayed their work alongside those without; traditional and modern craft was given as much respect as high art. (An Ndebele doll was placed next to a bronze sculpture of a character from Günter Grass's novel *The Tin Drum* because they resembled one another.) For these reasons, the show went down in South African art history as 'pivotal' and a 'watershed'.

At the time, Burnett chided the narrow concept of political art that guided artists like those in Medu. All who 'resolutely seek some sense of truth', he stressed, have political worth and should not be marginalised by ideological prejudices. Change – the subject matter then preoccupying black artists – would come from 'those who allot to the power of the imagination a supreme position in the hierarchy of being, and [from] those who insist on the freedom to pursue the imaginative life'. Burnett doubted real change would come from the barrel of a gun or from conformity to a political line.[18] He was effectively endorsing Kant's belief that 'A revolution can never bring about the true reform of a way of thinking'. (Burnett would undoubtedly have defined the wellspring of real change as the imagination, rather than Kant's preferred faculty of reason.)

Burnett's show broke the lingering stranglehold of colonial attitudes on the South African art world, where, he noted, there had always been 'the danger of a self-congratulatory parochialism developing'. No major exhibit of South African art would ever again be exclusively white. The BMW show opened the way for more African artists to leave behind their 'transitional' status by bringing them to the attention of critics and patrons.[19] In time, Thami's name would be associated with this development.

The Thami Mnyele Foundation was set up in Amsterdam in 1990. Funded in part by the city itself and in part by the Dutch Department of Cultural Affairs, the foundation offers young South African artists residential scholarships and studios so they can, while producing their own art, 'become acquainted with European culture and … exhibit their works of art in cultural institutions'. Thus the name of Thami Mnyele, a Black Consciousness adherent who was never able to study overseas, has come to symbolise the breaking down of old continental boundaries.

We are left to wonder what would have happened to Thami's art if he had lived into the 1990s, free of the constraints that impinged on him when he chose to be a combatant. What would he have drawn if he were no longer obliged to take rigid oppositional stances against the apartheid regime? He might have followed the path of revolutionary artists who engaged in a form of cultural *métissage*. The first half of the 20th century provides a number of models: painters who sought to turn their skills to the service of a political ideal in a time of peace. He could, for example, have found inspiration in Malevich and the others who used Russian folk art – carvings as well as icons – as the basis for their bold departures from the academic art that had supported the hierarchical values of the old regime.

Or he could have turned to Latin American revolutionary artists like Diego Rivera, who painted murals that gave moral and historical instruction to the largely illiterate masses. In the 1930s Rivera confronted a professional challenge similar to the one that plagued South Africa's 'cultural workers' in the 1980s. On the one hand, he was not at all shy about considering himself a 'propagandist'; on the other, he believed that the artist translated and condensed the aspirations of the multitudes of his age. (The bigger the multitude, he wrote, the greater the artist.)

But when did the masses have the right to assert that the artist had translated its hopes incorrectly? Rivera fobbed this question onto the future. Some day proletarians, he wrote, would take possession of art and use it against the bourgeoisie. Until then, Rivera was happy to use 'my art as a weapon' in the class struggle leading to the creation of a classless society. In its aftermath, all art would be communist.

Like Russia, Mexico differed crucially from South Africa in a way that complicated the applicability of its lessons. Mexican peasants were already used to turning to Catholic devotional art for moral guidance. Rivera took religious narratives and turned them to the service of Marxist values. In the process he taught onlookers a new way of thinking about the relationship between the conquistadores and the Indians, as well as between capital and labour.[20]

These Mexican and Russian artists were producing pictures hard on the heels of revolutions and civil wars, rather than of negotiated settlements. If we turn to a country that gained its independence with very little bloodshed and had been kicking over the traces of its colonial heritage for over a century, a less didactic picture emerges.

Thami might have turned to a less explicitly political model of *métissage* in the work of Brazilian painter Tarsila do Amaral, who was creating a new hybrid style, one that acknowledged the indigenous and Western roots of Brazilian identity. She painted large-limbed, clay-like figures that were reminiscent of those, so lacking in muscle, drawn by Thami in the early 1970s. But their emotional impact is different. Instead of conveying powerlessness, do Amaral's naked bodies express tropical languor and a playful transformation of the European tradition of depicting the nude. Unlike Thami, do Amaral was part of a movement that was able to use humour in its search for a new, mixed, national identity.

Members of this broader movement, called the 'Antropofagists', were challenging the idea that they had to choose between aesthetic values that appeared to be polar opposites: modern as opposed to primitive, original as opposed to derivative. Their major spokesperson, Oswald de Andrade, wrote in 1928 the 'Manifesto Antropofago' (Cannibalist Manifesto). He used humour to express his adherents' refusal to become enmeshed in the kind of oppositional statements that Thami had to make. It is worth quoting a few lines of his manifesto in order to capture this radically different way of making political statements about identity and freedom:

> We want the Carib Revolution. Greater than the French Revolution. The unification of all productive revolts for the progress of humanity. Without us, Europe wouldn't even have its meager declaration of the rights of man. The Golden Age heralded by America. The Golden Age. And all the *girls*.[21]

Saying they had the right to 'eat' the work of all cultures and to produce something new, de Andrade was urging his artistic followers in Brazil to cannibalise world culture rather than to reject it. In contrast,

Thami's circumstances in the early 1980s led him to assert that distortion and the mystical must be rejected in art. None of these revolutionary Brazilian artists had been obliged by the heat of war to make such a puritanical statement.

Seen within the wide temporal context of the late 20th century, Thami Mnyele's misfortunes were many. He lived at a time when he had to invent what an influential curator of contemporary African art, Okwui Enwezor, has called a 'counter-imaginary' world: his art had to oppose colonial power, because he was in active combat against what he experienced as a late-colonial regime.[22] And so his imagination was not free. He did not have the liberty to 'eat' playfully the images of the West, as Tarsila do Amaral had done in Brazil a century after its colonial period ended.

Further, Thami was caught in a situation where he needed to draw inspirational pictures, and yet the rest of the world was moving away from faith in the moral power of painted images. Critic Robert Hughes has called Picasso's 1937 masterpiece, 'Guernica', 'the last great history painting', in the sense that it was meant to change the way large numbers of people thought and felt about power. Photographs and films subsequently took over that role. 'Mass media', Hughes observes, 'took away the political speech of art.' Television robbed painters of political impact, just as war photography took away the work of the war artist.[23] Perhaps the most influential picture of Thami's time was not a painting, but the photograph taken of schoolboy Hector Pieterson as he was carried, dying, by a grimacing fellow student in 1976.

Another cruel irony was the inexorable growth of advanced consumer society at the same time as Thami was championing collectivism. Business was winning the war of values. Thami was railing against the capitalist valuation of art at the same time as paintings were becoming banks for investment capital, yielding higher returns than ever before. He died five years before a Sotheby's auction broke a world record by selling paintings worth $435 million. The new rich in Russia would soon enter this market. It is difficult to say whether the revolutionaries should have foreseen these developments. It is, in any case, doubtful whether this awareness would have made any difference to their strategies.

The idea of self-sacrifice has fallen on hard times.[24] It probably even puzzles people, especially those engaged most energetically in market transactions and consumption. Revolutionaries who not long ago had iconic status have become logos. Che Guevara's ideological clout, for example, has been reduced to formulaic swatches of light and shadow, based on a photograph, signifying 'dead beautiful young idealist'. He has become a celebrity.

Opposition to capitalism still persists, of course, but it tends to take different forms from the heroic stances adopted by Che and by Thami Mnyele. We have seen one of its current faces in the Arcadian dreams of P, one of Thami's alleged murderers. In a terrible twist of fate, he has been able to shelter his family by investing in spectacular real estate. His anti-capitalism is self-contradictory: while he values the lonely battle of man against nature, free of modern constraints, he wants the material life of a 21st-century suburban entrepreneur. For the time being, P seems to have achieved it all: pride in his virtue and manliness because he shelters his family, owns valuable property, and hunts. No one would call him a hero, certainly not in the sense of being a great man who meant to achieve something larger than his own self-interest.

What might Thami's sacrifice mean? Thami's life tells the story of someone who became a captive of the logic of sacrifice: accepting constraints on imagination, submerging personal need in the collective ideal, acting without knowing how time would warp his sacrifice. Wanting to inspire a socialist cultural revolution in a world that was not ripe for it, he was locked into refuting the dominant culture, without the means to create a new one. It proved dangerous and, in the end, futile to draw political and artistic models from elsewhere, especially when advanced consumer society was grinding its way across the cultural landscape as inexorably as a tank. His life story brings to mind Kant's aphorism, restated as follows: reform in ways of thinking – as when Thami began to think of himself as someone with the power to change the dominant order – can lead to revolutionary activity; and yet, revolutions themselves can't bring about reforms in a way of thinking, because they are more about feeling and ultimately based on faith.

Time called Thami Mnyele. He left, and he asked to be remembered. What should we remember him for? When time called him, he served its needs, or, as he would have said quite sincerely, the needs of 'the people'. 'What matters are the needs which art answers,' John Berger writes. Thami and his comrades needed to bring the apartheid regime to the negotiating table, and they believed they could do so by making South Africa's military forces and its citizens vulnerable to unprecedented attack. Unlike Goya, Thami accepted that an artist should not just record reality, but also try to create it. Turning away from what he called 'the warmth of fine art', the prospect of fame or renown, the comfort of family life, and the pride in being a man who sheltered his family, he acted, without fanfare, upon his love for humble people. In an age of celebrity, his integrity evokes respect, and even awe.

NOTES

1   Mnyele, 'Art can never be neutral'; Mnyele, Review of *Images of a Revolution* by Albie Sachs (1983?), Seidman Collection.

2   Mnyele, 'Thoughts for Bongiwe', *Rixaka*, 3 (1986), 30.

3   Serote, 'The politics of culture'. Serote gave this paper on behalf of the Medu Editorial Board at the Foundation for Education with Production 'Cultural Studies' workshop in Gaborone.

4   John Berger, *Art and Revolution: Ernst Neizvestny and the Role of the Artist in the USSR* (New York: Pantheon, 1969), 30.

5   Ibid.

6   Katerina Clark, *Petersburg: Crucible of Cultural Revolution* (Cambridge, Mass.: Harvard University Press 1995); Robert Hughes, *The Shock of the New* (New York: Knopf, 2002), 87.

7   Frederick Starr in Yevgenia Petrova (ed.), *The Origins of the Russian Avant-Garde* (St Petersburg: State Russian Museum in assoc with the Walters Art Gallery, Baltimore, 2003).

8   Boris Groys, 'The other gaze: Russian unofficial art's view of the Soviet world' in Ales Erjavec (ed.), *Postmodernism and the Postsocialist Condition: Politicized Art under Late Socialism* (Berkeley: University of California Press 2003), 59. See also Groys, 'The birth of socialist realism from the spirit of the Russian avant-garde' in Hans Gunther (ed.), *The Culture of the Stalin Period* (London: Palgrave Macmillan, 1990) and *The Total Art of Stalinism: Avant-Garde, Aesthetic Dictatorship, and Beyond* (Princeton: Princeton University Press, 1992).

9   See John E Bowlt and Olga Matich (eds.), *The Laboratory of Dreams: The Russian Avant-Garde and Cultural Experiment* (Stanford: Stanford University Press, 1999).

10 Nicoli Nattrass and Jeremy Seekings, *Class, Race and Inequality in South Africa* (New Haven: Yale University Press, 2005), chapter 3.

11 See Glaser, *Politics and Society*, chapter 7.

12 Mnyele, 'Thoughts for Bongiwe', 30.

13 Allister Sparks, *Tomorrow Is Another Country: The Inside Story of South Africa's Road to Change* (Chicago: University of Chicago Press, 1996), 204.

14 Raymond Suttner, 'Masculinities in the African National Congress-led liberation movement: The underground period', *Kleio*, 37 (2005), 71–106.

15 Berger, *Art and Revolution*, 55.

16 Wassily Kandinsky, 'The Cologne lecture' in C Harrison and P Wood (eds.), *Art in Theory, 1900–1990: An Anthology of Changing Ideas* (Oxford: Blackwell, 1992), 94; Kandinsky, 'On the artist' in K C Lindsay and P Vergo (eds.), *Kandinsky: Complete Writings on Art,* vol. 1 (Boston: G K Hall, 1982), 409–18.

17 Berger (*Art and Revolution*, 31) argues that Cubism 'marked in its own field the end of precisely that era – the era of capitalism, bourgeois individuality, utilitarianism – which Russia, it seemed, was about to transcend without ever having entered'. See also Berger, 'The moment of Cubism', *New Left Review*, 42 (1967). The emphasis on 'foreshadowing' is mine.

18 Ricky Burnett (ed.), *Tributaries: A View of Contemporary South African Art* (Johannesburg: Communication Dept BMW South Africa, 1985).

19 Sidney Kasfir, *Contemporary African Art* (New York: Thames and Hudson, 1999), 44.

20 David Craven, *Art and Revolution in Latin America, 1910–1990* (New Haven: Yale University Press, 2002); Hughes, *Shock of the New*, 108; Diego Rivera, 'The revolutionary spirit in modern art', *Art in Theory*, 404–7.

21 Oswald de Andrade, 'Cannibal Manifesto'. I am grateful to Horacio Costa for this reference.

22 Okwui Enwezor, *Snap Judgments: New Positions in Contemporary African Photography* (New York: International Center for Photography, and Steidl, 2006), 41, 29.

23 Hughes, *Shock of the New*, 111.

24 The notorious contemporary exception to this pattern is, of course, the suicide bomber, though it might be argued that his act stems, in part, from a revulsion against consumer values and a longing for spiritual reward as well as personal renown.

SOURCES AND ACKNOWLEDGMENTS

People who helped me in my research are all named below in the section headed Interviews. Many of them have enriched my life with their friendship. Additional acts of generosity include: Nomathamsanqa Mnyele driving me to Makapanstad and to talk with her grandmother, whom I first met thanks to Montshiwa Moroke; Patrick Ricketts introducing me to Vryburg, Mafikeng, and Pretoria Central Prison; Albio Gonzalez, Philippa Hobbs, and Judy Seidman generously sharing their personal archives, which, in Albio's case, included wonderful photographs that he sent to me electronically; Rayda Becker hospitably introducing me to people in the Johannesburg art world; Christina Nyathi Jikelo and Reggie Letsatsi helping me to see art at Fort Hare, as did Jo Burger at the Johannesburg Art Gallery; Bokwe Mafuna introducing me to key people in Alexandra Township; Andy Taylor and Phil Sandick accompanying me around Gaborone; Eric Miller, Wayne Oosthuizen, and Melita Moloney working valiantly on the photographs; Inus Daneel translating a document from Afrikaans; Rhona and Emeka Ogbugo welcoming me into a home that includes Omamma and Kelly. The Marion and Jasper Whiting Foundation gave me a research grant in the summer of 2001. I am deeply indebted, too, to Dean Jeffrey Henderson for helping me financially at a vulnerable moment.

I am grateful to friends and colleagues who read and criticised draft chapters: Megan Adams, Fredrick Barth, Sue Cook, Brenda Danilowitz, Peter Hawkins, Jeannette Hopkins, Tom Karis, Chabani Manganyi, Patty Rosenblatt, and my skilled and gracious editor Pat Tucker. At Jacana, Russell Clarke, Russell Martin, and Jenny Young were responsible for producing the book. I also thank individuals who read, and usually corrected, particular chapters in which they figured: Molefe Pheto (chapters 3 and 4), Rhona Ogbugo (chapters 1, 2, 5, 6, 7), Tim Williams (chapters 5 and 6), Albio Gonzalez and Teresa Devant (chapters 1, 5, 6), Nomathamsanqa Mnyele-Kaunda (chapter 8), Hans Louw (chapter 7 and epilogue), and Ricky Burnett (Afterword). This list of valued critics must include participants in seminars or lectures at the following places: Boston University (the Luce Foundation, the College of Fine Arts, and the Humanities Foundation), Yale University (African Studies), and Harvard University (Adams House).

The following generous people let me write in their homes: Irene Staehelin (Chatham), Patty and Mike Rosenblatt (Newton), Adele and Norman Taylor (Woodbury); and Liz Delmont provided a fine, recurrent base in Johannesburg. The Bogliasco Foundation in Genoa, Italy, gave me a fellowship in 2006 that allowed me to rewrite the final chapter or 'Afterword'; while at the foundation, I especially benefited from conversations with Professor Justin Stagl. I was able, thanks to Professor Johan Bergh and Thariza von Rensburg, to put the finishing touches to the manuscript while a research associate in the department of historical and heritage studies at the University of Pretoria.

INTERVIEWS

Abrahams, Lionel, Johannesburg, 16 December 2003.

Abrahamse, Uriel, Johannesburg, 23 December 2005.

Adler, David, Johannesburg, 25 May 1989; 22 January 2000; with Josie Adler, 4 July 2001.

Ainslie, Bill, Johannesburg Art Foundation, 14 July 1989.

Andersson, Muff, Johannesburg, 27 December 2001.

Andersson, Neil, Johannesburg, December 2002.

Arnold, Ben, The Bag Factory, Johannesburg, 7 July 2001.

Binca, Lindi Mnyele, Johannesburg, 5 January 2005.

Callinicos, Luli, Johannesburg, 20 December 2003.

Cornell, Carohn, Cape Town, 17 January 2000.

Cuzzolin, Piero, Johannesburg, 13 July 2001.

De Kock, Eugene, Pretoria Central Prison, 26 November 2006.

Dhlomo, Bongiwe, Johannesburg Art Foundation, 14 July 1989.

Dundas, Neil, Goodman Gallery, Johannesburg, 14 July 2001.

Dyer, Steve, Pretoria, 13 January 2005.

Figlan, Mpikayipeli, Johannesburg, 11 July 2001; 19 December 2001; 19 September 2004; 6 January 2005.

Fitzgerald, Patrick, Johannesburg, 26 December 2001.

Gonzalez, Albio and Teresa Devant, Barcelona, Spain, 2000.

Gwangwa, Jonas, Johannesburg, 15 July 2001.

Hobbs, Philippa, Johannesburg, 10 July 2001 and 22 December 2001.

Hubbard, Michael, Birmingham, June 2003.

Jolobe, Kgomotso 'Jackie', Pretoria, 6 Feb 2007.

Jones, Basil, Kalk Bay, 8 January 2002.

Kahn, Carol, Cape Town, 30 December 2005.

Kahn, Michael, Cape Town, 7 January 2002; 5 January 2003.

Kgositsile, Keorapetse Willie, New Haven, Conn., 27 March 1992.

Kohler, Adrian, Kalk Bay, 8 January 2002.

Koloane, David, Johannesburg, July 2001.

Langa, Mandla, Johannesburg, 3 July 2001.

Louw, Hans, Pretoria Central Prison, 26 November 2006; 4,18 February 2007.

Mabandla, Brigitte, Johannesburg, 30 December 2001.

Mafuna, James Bokwe, New Haven, Conn., April 1991; Johannesburg, 19 July 2001.

Magadlela, Fikile, Market Theatre, Johannesburg, 22 May 1989.

Martins, Dikobe Ben, Cape Town, 31 December 2005.

Matshikiza, John, Johannesburg, 20 December 2003.

Matsile, Jerry, Mafikeng, 28–29 September 2006.

Mbatha, Gordon, Rorke's Drift, 11 June 1989.

Mbete, Baleka, Cape Town, 26 July 2001.

Metz, Gordon, Cape Town, 30 July 2001.

Mnyele, David Freddy Harry, Vosloorus, 15 July and 23 December 2001.

Mnyele, Sarah, Tembisa, 15 July 1989; 21 December 2002.

Molaolwa, Boitumelo Edwin 'Shimane', Kraaipan, 28 September 2006.

Moroke, Montshiwa, Johannesburg, 15 July 1989; 13 July 2001.

Motana, Nape a, Johannesburg, 7 January 2005.

Nteta, Doreen, Boston, Mass., 3 June 2006.

Ogbugo, Rhona Segale Mnyele, Johannesburg, 20 December 2002; 23 December 2003; 2004–6.

Orkin, Andrew, Toronto, Ontario, 1 June 2002.

Ozynski, Joyce, Johannesburg, 14 July 1989.

Pheto, Molefe, Vlaksdrif, 12 July 2001.

Pogrund, Anne Sassoon, Boston, 15 April 2000.

Radley, Masindi, Alexandra, 27 December 2001.

Ramano, Victor, Alexandra, 10 June 1989.

Ramorwagadi, Edward 'Tiger', Vryburg, 27 September 2006.

Ramothibe, Ike and Dorcas, Alexandra, 18 July 1989.

Ramatsui, Naniwe, Pretoria, 8 January 2003.

Richer, Peter, Johannesburg, 4 January 2006.

Ricketts, Patrick, Pretoria, January and September 2006.

Röhr-Rouendaal, Petra, Birmingham, England, June 2003.

Segale, Alex, Johannesburg, 25 September 2004.

Segola, Phillip, Gaborone, July 2001.

Seidman, Judy, Johannesburg, 6 January 2003; Boston, 23 April 2004.

Serache, Nat, Gaborone, 12 October 2006.

Serote, Mongane Wally, London, 1990; Cape Town, 2000.

Setloboko, Joe, Market Theatre, Johannesburg, 22 May 1989.

Shubin, Vladimir, Moscow, 20 May 2005.

Sibisi, Paul, Durban, 8 July 1989.

Sithole, Noel and Khehla, Alexandra Township, 10 June 1989.

Smuts, Colin, Johannesburg, 16 July 2001.

Stopforth, Paul, Boston, Mass., 2005.

Thamane, Pauline Malebo, 4 January 2005.

Tladi, Lefifi, Mabopane, 17 July 2001.

Twala, Simon 'Jika', Alexandra, 27 December 2001.

Van Wyk, Chris, Johannesburg, 16 and 22 May 1989; 14 July 2001; 19 December 2002.

Whyte, Moira, Cape Town, 3 March 1993.

Williams, Tim, Pretoria, January 2006.

CORRESPONDENCE AND TELEPHONE CALLS

Abrahamse, Uriel, e-mail, 25 January 2005.

Burnett, Ricky, e-mail, 1 September 2001.

Buti, Sam, phone, 10 January 2005.

Callinicos, Janet Ewing, e-mail, 14 January 2004.

Deilkaas, Ellen Tveter, e-mail, December 2005.

Derkx, Theo, e-mail, 10 September 2001.

Desmond, Snoeks, Durban, mail, 2001.

Freemantle, Barbara, e-mail, May 2002.

Glennie, Jenny, phone, 6 July 2001.

Haenggi, Fernand, e-mails, 3, 8 September 2001.

Maritz, Nicolaas G, Pretoria, mail, 2 September 2004.

Pheto, Molefe, mail, 26 August 2005.

Pogrund, Anne Sassoon, e-mail, 3 December 1999.

ARCHIVES

Boston University, Africana Library, Karis-Gerhart Collection: South African Political Materials, 1964–90 (microfilm).

Gonzalez-Devant archive of Medu material, Barcelona.

Hobbs, Philippa, personal archive.

Johannesburg Art Gallery: Annual Reports, Steven Sack notes.

Michaelis Library, University of Cape Town: Culture and Resistance (Gaborone, July 1982), programme; *State of Art in South Africa* (Cape Town July 1979), programme.

Seidman, Judy, personal archive.

South African Archives Depot (SAA), Pretoria: Native Divorce Court, Central Division Case #110, 1952; KHK 2/2/159 N 12/3/3 (1/1) Tribal Schools in the Makapanstad Area; BAO 107/4/29 Politieke en ander Organisasies African National Congress.

South African National Gallery, Cape Town: exhibition scrapbooks.

Truth and Reconciliation Commission: testimony re Gaborone Raid October, November 2000; Amnesty signed by Judge R Pillay, 31 May 2001 (AC/2001/228); Amnesty Application 4149, 10 May 1999.

University of the Western Cape, Mayibuye Centre: Serote autobiographical essay (1995); Novib film.

Van Heerden Collection [of old South African textbooks], former Transvaal Department of Education, Pretoria.

William Cullen Africana Library, University of the Witwatersrand: Karis-Gerhart Collection; SAIRR Archives; SAHA, Julie Frederickse interviews.

BOOKS, ARTICLES AND THESES

Abrahams, Lionel, *The White Life of Felix Greenspan* (Johannesburg: M&G Books, 2002)

Ainslie, Bill, 'The African identity' in Clementine Deliss (ed.), *Seven Stories about Modern Art in Africa* (London: Whitechapel, 1995)

Ainslie, Bill, 'The living eye, a letter to Ngatane, Motjuoadi, Maqhubela and Sithole', *The Classic*, 1, 4 (1965)

Anti-Apartheid Beweging Nederland, 'The doors of culture shall be opened', photographic report of the Amsterdam Conference 13–18 December 1982

'Artistic announcement', *Bantu* (July 1972), 16–19

Barnes, A V S, *The Southern Cross Reader VI* (n.d.); *A Practical Guide for Bantu Teachers* (1950); *Bantu Schools of Tomorrow* (1950)

Barrell, Howard, 'Conscripts to their age: African National Congress operational strategy, 1976–86' (DPhil thesis, University of Oxford, 1993)

Berger, John, 'The moment of Cubism', *New Left Review*, 42 (1967)

Berger, John, *Art and Revolution: Ernst Neizvestny and the Role of the Artist in the USSR* (New York: Pantheon, 1969)

Berger, John, *The Shape of a Pocket* (New York: Vintage, 2003)

Berman, Esmé, *Art and Artists of South Africa: An Illustrated Biographical Dictionary and Historical Survey of Painters, Sculptors and Graphics Artists since 1875* (Cape Town: Balkema, 1983)

Bernstein, Hilda (ed.), *The Rift: The Exile Experience of South Africans* (London: Jonathan Cape, 1994)

Bernstein, Rusty, *Memory against Forgetting* (London: Viking, 1999)

Biko, Steve, *Black Consciousness in South Africa*, ed. Millard Arnold (New York: Vintage, 1979)

Black Review (Durban: Black Community Programmes, 1973, 1974/5)

Böeseken, A J, J J Oberholster, M C E van Schoor, N J Olivier, *History for the Senior Certificate* (Cape Town: Nasionale Boekhandel, 1957)

Bowlt, John E and Olga Matich (eds.), *The Laboratory of Dreams: The Russian Avant-Garde and Cultural Experiment* (Stanford: Stanford University Press, 1999)

Bradford, Helen, *A Taste of Freedom: The ICU in Rural South Africa, 1924–30* (New Haven: Yale University Press, 1988)

Breutz, P-L, *A History of the Batswana and the Origin of Bophuthatswana* (Natal: Ramsgate: P-L Breutz, 1989)

Burnett, Ricky (ed.), *Tributaries: A View of Contemporary South African Art* (Johannesburg: Communication Dept BMW South Africa, January 1985)

Callinicos, Luli, *Oliver Tambo: Beyond the Engeli Mountains* (Cape Town: David Philip, 2004)

Campbell, James, *Songs of Zion: The African Methodist Episcopal Church in the United States and South Africa* (New York: Oxford, 1995)

Campbell, James, 'Our fathers, our children: The African Methodist Episcopal Church in the United States and South Africa' (PhD thesis, Stanford University, 1989)

Campschreur, Willem and Joost Divendal (eds.), *Culture in Another South Africa* (London: Zed, 1989)

Carman, Jillian, 'Acquisition policy of the Johannesburg Art Gallery with regard to the South African Collection, 1909–87', *South African Journal of Cultural and Art History*, 2, 3 (July 1988), 203–13

Clark, Katerina, *Petersburg: Crucible of Cultural Revolution* (Cambridge, Mass.: Harvard University Press, 1995)

The Classic (Johannesburg, 1963–8).

Coleman, Gareth, 'A history of the South African Committee for Higher Education (SACHED), 1959–1987' (MA dissertation, University of Natal, Durban, 1989)

Craven, David, *Art and Revolution in Latin America, 1910–1990* (New Haven: Yale University Press, 2002)

Cuthbertson, Greg, 'African Christianity, missionaries and colonial warfare in South Africa at the turn of the 20th century', *Missionalia*, 28, 2/3 (Aug/Nov 2000), 143–64

Dale, Richard, 'Not always so placid a place: Botswana under attack', *African Affairs*, 86, 342 (January 1987), 73–91.

De Andrade, Oswald, 'Cannibal Manifesto'

De Jager, E J, 'Five South African artists', *African Arts*, 11, 2 (Jan 1978), 50–5

De Jager, E J, *Images of Man: Contemporary South African Black Art and Artists. A Pictorial Guide to the Collection of the University of Fort Hare Housed in the De Beers Centenary Art Gallery* (Alice: Fort Hare University Press, 1992)

Dodd, A D, W A Cordingley, W E Trengrove, *Discovering the World, Standard IV* (Cape Town: Juta, n.d.)

Drum, 'Thami and free beer' (22 May 1973), 46–7

Ellis, Stephen and Tsepo Sechaba, *Comrades against Apartheid: The ANC and the South African Communist Party in Exile* (London: James Currey, 1992)

Enwezor, Okwui, *Snap Judgments: New Positions in Contemporary African Photography* (New York: International Center for Photography and Steidl, 2006)

Erjavec, Ales, *Postmodernism and the Postsocialist Condition: Politicized Art under Late Socialism* (Berkeley: University of California Press, 2003)

Feinberg, Barry (ed.), *Poets to the People* (London: Heinemann, 1980)

Fischer, Ernst, *The Necessity of Art: A Marxist Approach* (Baltimore: Penguin, 1963)

Frankel, Glenn, *Rivonia's Children: Three Families and the Cost of Conscience in White South Africa* (New York: Farrar, Straus, Giroux, 1999)

Friedman, Graeme and Roy Blumenthal (eds.), *A Writer in Stone: South African Writers Celebrate the Seventieth Birthday of Lionel Abrahams* (Cape Town: David Philip, 1998)

Glaser, Daryl, *Politics and Society in South Africa: A Critical Introduction* (London: Sage, 2001)

Gobodo-Madikizela, Pumla, *A Human Being Died That Night: A South African Story of Forgiveness* (Boston: Houghton Mifflin, 2003)

Gron, Elizabeth, 'South African cultural exiles in Botswana: Medu Art Ensemble, 1976–85' (MA dissertation, University of Botswana, 1997)

Gunther, Hans (ed.), *The Culture of the Stalin Period* (London: Palgrave Macmillan, 1990)

Gunther, Hans (ed.), *The Total Art of Stalinism: Avant-Garde, Aesthetic Dictatorship, and Beyond* (Princeton: Princeton University Press, 1992)

Hamann, Hilton, *Days of the Generals: The Untold Story of South Africa's Apartheid-era Military Generals* (Cape Town: Zebra, 2001)

Harrison, C and P Wood (eds.), *Art in Theory, 1900–90: An Anthology of Changing Ideas* (Oxford: Blackwell, 1992)

Hayter, Stovin, 'Murder in our name', *New Internationalist*, 159 (May 1986)

Herreman, Frank (ed.), *Liberated Voices: Contemporary Art from South Africa* (New York: Museum for Modern Art; and Munich: Prestel, 1999)

Hobbs, Philippa, 'Shifting paradigms in printmaking practice at the Evangelical Lutheran Church Art and Craft Centre, Rorke's Drift, 1962–1976' (MA dissertation, University of the Witwatersrand, 2003)

Hobbs, Philippa and Elizabeth Rankin, *Rorke's Drift: Empowering Prints* (Cape Town: Double Storey, 2003)

Hughes, Robert, *The Shock of the New* (New York: Knopf, 2002)

Jones, Basil, 'Meaning in Mnyele's skies', *Statements in Spring* catalogue (1980).

Kandinsky, Wassily, 'The Cologne lecture' in C Harrison and P Wood (eds.), *Art in Theory, 1900–1990: An Anthology of Changing Ideas* (Oxford: Blackwell, 1992)

Kandinsky, Wassily, 'On the artist' in K C Lindsay and P Vergo (eds.), *Kandinsky: Complete Writings on Art,* vol. 1 (Boston: G K Hall, 1982)

Karis, Thomas G and Gail M Gerhart, *From Protest to Challenge: A Documentary History of African Politics in South Africa, 1882–1990,* vol. 5: *Nadir and Resurgence, 1964–79* (Bloomington: Indiana University Press, 1997)

Kasfir, Sidney, *Contemporary African Art* (New York: Thames and Hudson, 1999)

Kasrils, Ronnie, *'Armed and Dangerous': My Undercover Struggle against Apartheid* (Oxford: Heinemann, 1993)

Khumalo, Vusisizwe ka, 'Culture and resistance', *Pace* (Sept 1982), 9.

Koloane, David, 'Africus: The Johannesburg Biennale, a perspective', *African Arts* (winter 1996), 50–6

Langhan, Donve, *The Unfolding Man: The Life and Art of Dan Rakgoathe* (Cape Town: David Philip, 2000)

Legassick, Martin, *Armed Struggle and Democracy: The Case of South Africa* (Uppsala: Nordiska Afrikainstitutet, 2002)

Lodge, Tom, *Black Politics in South Africa since 1945* (Johannesburg: Ravan, 1983)

Makeba, Miriam (with James Hall), *Makeba: My Story* (Johannesburg: Skotaville, 1988)

Manaka, Matsemela, *Echoes of African Art* (Braamfontein: Skotaville, 1987)

Mandela, Nelson, *Long Walk to Freedom* (Boston: Little, Brown, 1994)

Marschall, Sabine, 'Strategies of accommodation: Toward an inclusive canon of South African art', *Art Journal* (spring 2001), 51–9

Masekela, Hugh and D Michael Cheers, *Still Grazing: The Musical Journey of Hugh Masekela* (New York: Crown Publishers, 2004)

Metz, Gordon, 'Learning to live without the enemy', *African Arts* (winter 1996), 57–9

Miles, Elza Botha, *Land and Lives: A Story of Early Black Artists* (Cape Town: Human and Rousseau, 1997)

Mosimane, Maleho, 'Bullets in the night', *Pace* (Aug 1985), 22–5

Mzamane, Mbulelo V, 'Black Consciousness poets in South Africa, 1967–80, with special reference to Mongane Serote and Sipho Sepamla' (PhD thesis, University of Sheffield, 1983)

Mzamane, Mbulelo V, *The Children of the Diaspora and Other Stories of Exile* (Florida Hills: Vivlia, 1996)

Neruda, Pablo, 'Death alone', *Selected Poems* (Boston: Houghton Mifflin, 1990)

Ngakane, Lionel, 'Dumile: A profile', *African Arts*, 3, 2 (winter 1970), 10–13

Ozynski, Joyce, 'Black art and black lives', *Sunday Express* (16 Oct 1977)

Ozynski, Joyce, 'Peanuts for the gallery', *Snarl*, 1, 2 (Nov 1974), 10–11

Pauw, Jacques, *Into the Heart of Darkness: Confessions of Apartheid's Assassins* (Johannesburg: Jonathan Ball, 1979)

Peffer, John, 'The struggle for art at the end of apartheid' (PhD thesis, Columbia University, 2002)

Peterson, Bheki, 'Culture, resistance and representation' in South African Democracy Education Trust, *The Road to Democracy in South Africa*, vol. 2 (1970–1980) (Pretoria: Unisa Press, 2006)

Petrova, Yevgenia (ed.), *The Origins of the Russian Avant-Garde* (St Petersburg: State Russian Museum in association with Walters Art Gallery, Baltimore, 2003)

Pheto, Molefe, *And Night Fell: Memoirs of a Political Prisoner in South Africa* (London: Allison and Bushby, 1983)

Posterbook Collective, *Images of Defiance: South African Resistance Posters of the 1980s* (Johannesburg: STE, 2004)

Pullinger, B and P Hart, *Disa Reader Standard I* (Bloemfontein: Nasionale Pers, 1947)

Purple Renoster (Johannesburg, 1956–72)

Ramphele, Mamphela, *Across Boundaries: The Journey of a South African Woman Leader* (New York: The Feminist Press, 1996)

Roskill, Mark (ed.), *The Letters of Vincent van Gogh* (New York: Athenaeum, 1985)

Sachs, Albie, *Images of a Revolution: Mural Art in Mozambique* (Harare: Zimbabwe Publishing House, 1983)

Sack, Steven, *The Neglected Tradition: Towards a New History of South African Art (1930–1988)* (Johannesburg Art Gallery, 1988)

Saltzman, Cynthia, *Portrait of Dr. Gachet. The Story of a Van Gogh: Masterpiece, Money, Politics, Collectors, Greed, and Loss* (New York: Penguin, 1998)

SASO Newsletter (1971–6)

Saul, Scott, *Freedom Is, Freedom Ain't: Jazz and the Making of the Sixties* (Cambridge, Mass.: Harvard University Press, 2003)

Schneider, Betty, 'Malangatana of Mozambique', *African Arts*, 5 (winter 1972), 40–5

Seekings, Jeremy and Nicoli Nattrass, *Class, Race, and Inequality in South Africa* (New Haven: Yale University Press, 2005)

Sello, Sekola, 'Blood in the sand', *Drum* (Aug 1985), 4–6

Sellstrom, Tor, *Sweden and National Liberation in Southern Africa*, vol. 2: *Solidarity and Assistance (1970–1994)* (Uppsala: Nordiska Afrikainstitutet, 1999)

Seroke, Jaki, 'Poet in exile: An interview with Mongane Serote', *Staffrider* (April/May 1981)

Serote, Mongane Wally, 'When Rebecca fell', *The Classic*, 3, 4 (1971), 5–7

Serote, Mongane Wally, *Yakhal' Inkomo* (Johannesburg: Ad Donker, 1972)

Serote, Mongane Wally, *Tsetlo* (Johannesburg: Ad Donker, 1974)

Serote, Mongane Wally, *No Baby Must Weep* (Johannesburg: Ad Donker, 1975)

Serote, Mongane Wally, *Behold Mama, Flowers* (Johannesburg: Ad Donker, 1978)

Serote, Mongane Wally, 'Introduction', *Statements in Spring* catalogue (1980)

Serote, Mongane Wally, *The Night Keeps Winking* (Gaborone: Medu, 1982)

Serote, Mongane Wally, *Selected Poems*, ed. Mbulelo Mzamane (Johannesburg: Ad Donker, 1982)

Serote, Mongane Wally, 'The politics of culture', *Sechaba* (March 1984), 26–31

Serote, Mongane Wally, 'Thami Mnyele: A portrait', *Rixaka*, 3 (1986)

Serote, Mongane Wally, *A Tough Tale* (London: Kliptown Books, 1987)

Serote, Mongane Wally, *On the Horizon* (Fordsburg: COSAW, 1990)

Serote, Mongane Wally, *Longer Poems: Third World Express, Come Hope with Me* (Bellville: Mayibuye Books, 1997)

Serote, Mongane Wally, *Freedom Lament and Song* (Cape Town: David Philip, 1997)

Serote, Mongane Wally, *Gods of our Time* (Randburg: Ravan, 1999)

Serote, Mongane Wally, 'Liberated voices', in *Liberated Voices: Contemporary Art from South Africa* (New York: Museum for African Art, 1999)

Serote, Mongane Wally, *Hyenas* (Florida Hills: Vivlia, 2000)

Shubin, Vladimir, *ANC: A View from Moscow* (Bellville: Mayibuye Books, 1999)

Simon, Barney, 'Dumile', *The Classic* (1968), 40–3

Southall, Roger, 'Botswana as a host country for refugees', *Journal of Commonwealth and Comparative Politics*, 22, 2 (July 1984), 151–79

Sparg, Marion, Jenny Schreiner, Gwen Ansell (eds.), *Comrade Jack: The Political Lectures and Diary of Jack Simons, Novo Catengue* (Johannesburg: STE, 2001)

Sparks, Allister, *Tomorrow Is Another Country: The Inside Story of South Africa's Road to Change* (Chicago: University of Chicago Press, 1996)

'Staffrider profile: Fikile', *Staffrider* (June 1980)

Stiff, Peter, *The Silent War: South African Recce Operations, 1969–1994* (Johannesburg: Galago, 1999)

Stuart Commission, Report of Inquiry into Recent Developments in the People's Republic of Angola (Lusaka, 14 March 1984)

Suttner, Raymond, 'Culture(s) of the African National Congress of South Africa: Imprint of exile experiences', *Journal of Contemporary African Studies*, 21, 2 (May 2003), 303–20

Suttner, Raymond, 'The character and formation of intellectuals within the ANC-led South African liberation movement', Paper presented to CODESRIA's 30th anniversary conference (Dakar, 8–11 December 2003)

Suttner, Raymond, 'Masculinities in the African National Congress-led liberation movement: The underground period', *Kleio*, 37 (2005), 71–106

Themba, Can, *The Will to Die* (London: Heinemann, 1972)

Tyson, Harvey, *Editors under Fire* (New York: Random House, 1993)

Van Jaarsveld, F A, Dorothea Behr, J J van der Walt, *Illustrated History Standard VI* (Johannesburg: Voortrekkerpers, 1958, rev. 1962)

Van Robbroeck, Lize, 'The ideology and practice of community arts in South Africa, with particular reference to Katlehong and Alexandra Arts Centres' (MA dissertation, University of the Witwatersrand, 1991)

Van Robbroeck, Lize, 'Writing white on black: Modernism as discursive paradigm in South African writing on modern black art' (PhD thesis, University of Stellenbosch, 2006).

Verwoerd, Hendrik, 'Bantu Education policy for the future', pamphlet (1954)

Von den Steinen, Lynda K, 'Soldiers in the struggle: Aspects of the experience of Umkhonto we Sizwe's rank and file soldiers. The Soweto generation and after' (MA dissertation, University of Cape Town, September 1999)

Walker, Cherryl, *Women and Resistance in South Africa* (London: Onyx Press, 1982)

Williams, Pat, 'Last paintings of Bill Ainslie, 1934–1989' (Wolfson College, Oxford, 1990)

Williamson, Sue, *Resistance Art in South Africa* (Cape Town: David Philip, 1989)

Younge, Gavin, *Art of the South African Townships* (London: Thames and Hudson, 1988)

Zetterqvist, Jenny, Refugees in Botswana in the Light of International Law (Uppsala: Scandinavian Institute of African Studies, 1990)

WRITINGS BY THAMSANQA HARRY MNYELE

'A new day', *Staffrider* (Sept/Oct 1980), 42

'Art classes', *The Zebra's Voice, Lentswe la Pitse ya Naga*, 1 (1981), 22

'Art can never be neutral' (23 September 1981), Seidman Collection

'Observations on the state of the contemporary visual arts in South Africa' (n.d., 1982?)

Review of *Images of a Revolution* by Albie Sachs (1983?), co-written with Judy Seidman, published in *Rixaka*, 3 (1986) under the initials L A

'Thoughts for Bongiwe', *Rixaka* 3 (1986), 28; reprinted with the title 'Thoughts for Bongiwe and the role of revolutionary art' in *Staffrider*, 7, 3&4 (1988), 297–302

INDEX